Citizen First, Banker Second

By A. Pat Daniels

History of a Texas Community Bank
and Stories About Its Politically Liberal Leader,
Walter G. Hall

A. Pat Daniels
P. O. Box 694
Houston, TX 77001

Manufactured in the United States of America
Typography and Printing by
D. Armstrong Co., Inc.
Houston, Texas

Library of Congress Catalog Card Number: 95-69947
International Standard Book No.: 0-9614885-3-0

Published by
Peninsula Press of Texas
P. O. Box 694
Houston, Texas 77001

WALTER GARDNER HALL

"I have been regarded by the 'establishment' . . . as something of a liberal when they were kind, a radical when they were irritated, and a communist when they were mad as hell, none of which bothered me in the least."

"I have been called a liberal and I suppose by some measure I am. This is because I know that change is inevitable, and orderly change is the most desirable kind."

Walter Hall has a quick explanation for his mixture of conservative banking and liberal politics, and his statement has been quoted often in newspaper and magazine stories:

"I am a citizen first and a banker second."

(Photograph by *J. Pamela Photography, Inc.)*

Table of Contents

Introduction

"Citizen First, Banker Second."

This is a phrase adopted many years ago by Galveston County banker and community leader Walter G. Hall. He uses it to define his position when he deviates from the path of the "traditional banker" to discharge what he considers his responsibilities as a citizen.

Banker Walter Hall, to me, is much more than a citizen of Galveston County. I consider him a true giant of Texas and a remarkable citizen of the world.

To many residents of Galveston County, "Walter G. Hall" and "Citizens State Bank" are interchangeable words and conjure up an image of a man and his financial organization enjoying a friendly partnership with his community.

This image is precisely one that all banks and all bankers seek to promote among their communities and their customers. But few have been able to complete the community picture with the success that Hall and his Citizens State Bank of Dickinson have realized.

Hall, 88 years old, goes to his bank office daily. He is not afraid of an eight-hour day or forty-hour week. He has a firm and active hand in the management and direction of the three banks and other business organizations he heads, and still finds time for many other activities. He is believed to be the oldest practicing banker in Texas and certainly one of the oldest in the nation.

This story of Hall's banking and other successes was started primarily as a history of the Citizens State Bank, founded in League City in 1906 and moved to Dickinson in 1935.

But writing a history of the Citizens State Bank became an impossibility without emphasizing the overwhelming efforts, foresight, integrity, imagination, perseverance, personality, workaholic habits, achievements and—yes, the brilliance—of the bank's guiding light during most of its existence.

There is no person in Galveston County who could possibly NOT have benefited from Hall's great work in several fields. The same is true for residents of many other areas.

Hall's story reflects a life of many major accomplishments. He has established, altered, improved, stabilized or even revolutionized more segments of life in his native state than almost any other Texan, living or dead. His influence in many fields, notably banking, communications, conservation, taxation, government, education and human rights, is being experienced each day in this state and, to some degree, in every part of the nation.

The writer of this history, then, completely surrendered any effort to produce a "pure" history of the Citizens State Bank and merged it with the colorful and often dramatic story of Walter Hall and his memorable achievements.

Such an effort, I am convinced, is very appropriate. And I also believe that the thousands of people who know and have been involved with Walter Hall in any manner—personally, financially, socially or politically—will agree.

Repetition, I hasten to admit, is abundant in these pages. For this I do not apologize, because I think it has been necessary to capture the full activity, personality and significance of Walter Hall in each individual section where such repetition is found.

Additionally, most of this book is written in such a manner that each chapter—and almost every section of each chapter—can be read as an individual part of the history of the bank or in the stories about Hall. A reader thus can read at any time a chapter or section of his or her own choice and refer to the table of contents to find an allied topic to read.

Thus it is not written as a typical history or biography. Some readers may consider it, perhaps, as more of a "Walter Hall Encyclopedia" or "Walter Hall Almanac."

Trying to find very much new to report and write about Hall and the Citizens State Bank in the 1990s would be almost impossible—even, I think, if Walter Hall would let me climb inside his brain and observe those fireworks for quite a while. Because Walter Hall has few secrets.

Thus much of this history, let me emphasize, is not as much probing and so-called investigative reporting or original writing as it is a collection of the writings and thoughts of many others who have known and interviewed Hall. This is responsible for much of the repetition; but I believe this repetitious material, revealing impressions and interpretations of others, adds interest to the book.

One of Hall's associates complained that I have failed to identify or emphasize an event or events in Hall's life which made a "difference"—something which separates him from the average citizen and gives him the spark to want to do so many things to benefit his fellow citizens.

I confess I have not found any one such particular, definable, spectacular spark. Instead I have found in Walter Hall the generous heart of a man who urgently wants to help his neighbors and friends in any way and every way possible. Most ordinary Texans, I think, have this desire also; but Hall discovered the means, at least partially, through his banking profession. Whether he could have done it in any other trade or industry might be debatable, but I would certainly answer the question in the affirmative. I think Walter Hall would have been a good—yea, a superlative—citizen in any business or profession.

In this book I have not dealt with what some readers might consider "faults" of Hall which they may think should be mentioned. Walter Hall would be the first to admit the truth to the basis for some of those criticisms: He does not regularly attend church, he has been known to enjoy an occasional alcoholic beverage, and his ability to curse might rival that of another great Texan, Sam Houston.

But obviously I have not attempted to emphasize anything other than the constructive accomplishments of Walter Hall. Those are the overwhelming facts and reflect the true story of this Texas giant.

I am positive that I have only scratched the surface on the tip of a very large iceberg in trying to tell the story of Walter Hall. A reader digesting the "Scope and Content" concerning the Hall papers in the Fondren Library at Rice University will recognize that fact. A copy of the "Scope and Content" is included in this book.

But I have tried to collect and report the best writings and quotations, along with some original material, about the many activities of Walter Hall and his Citizens State Bank.

Walter Hall has been my friend for almost 40 years, and I was employed by and worked under his personal supervision for several years. Yet, only when I started research on this book did I fully recognize the expanse and magnitude of his accomplishments. As a Texan and an American, I am grateful to him not only personally but as a U.S. citizen for his many outstanding works. I now realize the full extent to which he has made and is making my life a better one.

Despite the advice of most media stylebooks, I have had a difficult time throughout this book in trying to write only "Hall": I shall always think it really should be "Mr. Hall." Because my respect, admiration, amazement and love for this man have increased each day during the many months I have been involved in the project. I am grateful and humbled because he allowed me to attempt to write his bank's—and his—story.

I hope Walter Gardner Hall and his friends approve.

A. Pat Daniels
September, 1995

Dedication

While Walter Hall has been achieving goals that only heroes should dream about, he has maintained a commitment to live and work as an "ordinary citizen" in two small neighboring communities. Those communities are Dickinson (where his Citizens State Bank office has been his working base for 60 years, since he moved it there in 1935), and League City. He has considered League City his home since he was a small boy, and there he still pursues hobbies of woodworking, citrus-growing and diligently tending his home and grounds.

To citizens of those two communities; to all present and former staff members of the Citizens State Bank; to the bank's customers; and to Walter Hall's relatives, this book is dedicated.—apd.

Prologue

The Citizens State Bank of Dickinson in 1995 was the sixth oldest state bank in Texas.

According to records of the Texas Department of Banking in Austin, the only five state banks older than the Dickinson bank are the following, listed with their charter numbers and dates they opened for business:

First State Bank of Gainesville (Charter No. 11, Aug. 18, 1905)

First Texas Bank of Georgetown (Charter No. 17, Aug. 27, 1905)

First State Bank of Bremond (Charter No. 38, Nov. 28, 1905)

State Bank & Trust Co. of San Marcos (Charter No. 47, March 3, 1906)

Alvin State Bank of Alvin (Charter No. 54, Feb. 1, 1906)

. . .

The Citizens State Bank of League City was issued Charter No. 62 and opened for business March 1, 1906. It was moved to Dickinson in 1935.

The Alvin State Bank thus was opened for business one month earlier than the Citizens State Bank, on Feb. 1, 1906.

The Alvin and League City banks were organized by the same group of Galveston bankers. Walter G. Hall bought the Citizens State Bank from the Sealy Hutchings family in 1943, but the Alvin bank had changed hands before he bought controlling interest in 1953. He sold the Alvin bank in 1981.

The records indicate that although the charter for the bank at San Marcos was issued earlier than the charters for the banks at Alvin and League City, it actually opened after they did; so an argument could be made that the Alvin and Dickinson banks should rank fourth and fifth, rather than fifth and sixth, in the "oldest banks" category.

. . .

Almost 90 years after the Citizens State Bank was founded in 1906, it stands today as a proud and still vibrant financial monument. It can be considered a tribute to those citizens who organized the bank, to the men and women who developed it, to the hundreds of staff members who have presided over its growth and, most importantly, to the residents of the area and the bank's customers who made that growth possible.

The main bank is at 2401 Termini at Pine Drive in Dickinson; the West Side Branch is at 215 FM 517 West; and the Bacliff Branch is at 4021 Highway 146.

The bank in early 1995 had assets of $95,555,359, and total deposits of $84,458,435.

Directors, officers and other staff members totaling almost 100 accommodate the needs of thousands of customers in Dickinson and the surrounding area.

Chapter 1
History With a Dual Edge

Two Births in Texas

Not even a modern-day Nostradamus could have predicted how two unrelated events early in this century, one year apart, would affect the fate and fortune of Galveston County.

And no one could have imagined how those two events in two different communities would alter the political history of Galveston County and, to some extent, influence the political life of Texas and the United States.

In 1906, a group of enterprising Galveston bankers and businessmen founded a little bank in League City, Texas. It was not a unique financial event.

A year later, in Houston, the birth of a baby boy was one of many such natural events in that city. Thus it was unnoticed by anyone with recognizable political or business stature.

It would be many years before the convergence of those two events would be realized and the significance of such a union could be fully understood.

But an effective coalition for the future had been created by those events of 1906 and 1907.

. . .

Galveston businessmen always have been enterprising opportunists. But, generally, they were and are civic-minded opportunists.

This fact was demonstrated most effectively after the devastating 1900 hurricane, which claimed many Galveston fortunes as well as thousands of lives.

Those in the business community did not merely lick their wounds, camouflage their grief and let time play a passive role in the rebuilding and redevelopment of their city and of their economic lives. They began immediately salvaging what they could from the tragedies left by the tropical disaster.

The businessmen not only resurrected meaningful life on Galveston Island, but they also took an active role in assuring that all of Galveston County once again would be a healthy and financially thriving region.

Some of the progressive businessmen had the foresight to realize that neighboring areas also were ready for new economic development and needed the services they could provide.

A group of bankers led by those at Galveston's Hutchings-Sealy National Bank looked northward and westward and saw the area generally between Galveston and Houston as certainly among the promising areas for their activities.

After what now would be called market research, the group decided that the League City area was ripe for their efforts—as was Alvin, in nearby Brazoria County.

The Mainland of Galveston County at that time was primarily devoted to cattle-raising; and League City, on the banks of Clear Creek, was the headquarters for many of the larger ranchers.

This is believed to be the primary reason the Galveston group decided to locate a bank in League City rather than Dickinson, although Dickinson was the larger community.

These leaders were the founders, then, in 1906, of the Citizens State Bank of League City—now the Citizens State Bank of Dickinson.

Credited generally for being the founders of the bank were four Galvestonians and one League City businessman. They were Sealy Hutchings, George Sealy, John Sealy and W.L. Moody Jr. of Galveston and George W. Butler of League City.

It is safe to say that none in the group could have imagined the electrifying results their efforts would produce.

. . .

The event of May 30, 1907, in the Houston Heights—the birth of a son—while it probably was a happy occasion, was not particularly unusual for Samuel Emery Hall and Emmabelle Gardner Hall. This new citizen, named Walter Gardner Hall, was the youngest of seven children.

The Halls had moved to the Houston area in 1898 from Illinois (Springfield and Lincoln). They certainly had no indication of the unexpected, unusual and what some might even consider revolutionary changes their last baby would have on the development of the neighboring county and on "country banking."

The Halls, after their arrival in Texas, became intimately acquainted with League City and with the City of Galveston as well as with Houston.

A new resident of Houston, the infant Walter Gardner Hall played with his stuffed toy in either late 1907 or early 1908.
(Photo courtesy V. Lynn Morse, niece of Walter Hall)

Hall, an experienced mechanic, worked at a variety of jobs, and usually had at least two jobs to support his growing family. He alternated between Houston and the League City area and worked briefly in Galveston.

In the vicinity of what is now Ellington Field, Sam Hall and his wife—with the help of their children—operated a small farm.

After the Great Hurricane of 1900 interrupted that occupation by blowing their home off its blocks and destroying what little crops they had, Sam Hall was employed in Galveston. He and his team of mules helped to clean up the Island. Following that, the Hall family moved to East Texas and ran cafes in Lovelady and Crockett before moving to Houston.

Emmabelle Gardner Hall probably was very tired of moving by this time, but no record of her complaints is known. Apparently she was not too thrilled to leave Illinois earlier, however, because she was quoted as saying that people moving into new territory (enticed in advertisements as "home seekers") were really "home suckers," because they "fell" for the sales pitches of land developers and salesmen.

All nine members of the Sam Hall family—the parents and seven children—posed for this family photograph believed to have been taken about 1917 at their residence, 1309 Columbia, in Houston. Walter Gardner Hall, the youngest member of the family, is seated on the front porch railing, at the left. The parents, Emmabelle Gardner Hall and Samuel Emery Hall, are standing, second and third from the left. Walter would have been 10 years old if the 1917 portrait date is correct. Seated with him on the railing are Violet, 12, center, and Verna, 28. The other Hall children standing are Mora, far left, 22; Homer, third from the right, 24; Sarah (Mrs. Tom Burr), second from the right, 29; and Emery, far right, 23. The Halls at the time also owned the next-door house at 1311 Columbia, which they rented to another family. The entire area now is occupied by the John Reagan High School.

(Photo courtesy V. Lynn Morse, Walter Hall's niece)

The four sons of Sam Hall gathered for this photo in about 1930. From the left are Walter Gardner Hall, Mora Sylvester Hall, Emery Carl Hall and Homer Clyde Hall.

After the birth of Walter, the Hall family lived for a while in Friendswood. In the Friendswood-League City area, Sam Hall worked for Frank Brown, the founder of the Quaker village of Friendswood, operating Brown's fig plant.

Returning to Houston, Hall was employed by the engineering firm of Stone & Webster on its street car line. He also worked for Houston Lighting & Power Co.

Then, moving back to the League City area, Hall was employed in the construction of the power plant for the interurban line which the Galveston-Houston Electric Co. completed and started operating between Houston and Galveston in 1911.

The 1915 hurricane, comparable in strength to that of 1900, again damaged the Halls' house and ruined their furniture. The family returned to Houston.

Hall remained in the employment of the interurban line as a mechanic. This fact later would become a vital benefit for that son born in 1907.

Reflecting on the days of his youth, Walter Hall said the "first person who had a real impact on the way I see things" was his mother.

"Mother was one of the few women I've known who, in addition to being very sweet and very feminine, and with all the characteristics you expect to find in a very loving mother, was an extremely analytical person. During the Depression years, of course, we had problems.

"My father worked, and worked hard. He was not without work during the Depression, but he never made a large income. So we had financial problems—crises—from time to time. And it was always Mother's forte to come up with solutions. I saw how she would analyze things. She would visualize one approach and its possible and probable results, and then she would explore another one in the truly analytical process. I saw that was effective. So it did make an impression on me."

League City Was Ready

The residents of League City were ready and waiting—and probably somewhat surprised at one development—when their new bank opened in 1906.

They knew that some Galveston bankers were going to start a bank in Alvin, and had heard that one might be opened in League City. Many had doubts, however, about having their "own" bank. They thought a branch bank might be more likely.

And they had been "teased" with items about a branch bank in the

DEPARTMENT OF BANKING

CHARTER NUMBER 62

THIS IS TO CERTIFY THAT

The Citizens State Bank of Dickinson, Texas

IS DULY AUTHORIZED UNDER THE LAWS OF THE STATE OF TEXAS TO CONDUCT THE BUSINESS OF BANKING AT

Dickinson, Galveston County

TEXAS

IN WITNESS WHEREOF, I HAVE HEREUNTO SET MY HAND AND CAUSED TO BE AFFIXED MY OFFICIAL SEAL, AT THE CITY OF AUSTIN, IN THE STATE OF TEXAS, THIS THE 1st DAY OF March A. D. 1906

BANKING COMMISSIONER OF TEXAS

Charter No. 62 of the Texas Department of Banking in Austin was issued to the Citizens State Bank of League City, granting it permission to begin operating March 1, 1906. At some point a copy of the original charter was altered to indicate that the bank had moved to Dickinson. This is a reproduction of the altered "original" charter as it now exists in the department's files in Austin—without reference to its original site. A copy of the reproduction is exhibited in the bank building at Dickinson.

Texas Coast Promoter, League City's newspaper of the day. These items appeared in the issue of Jan. 27, 1905:

"If League City had a bank now to accomodate (sic) the buyers during strawberry time, money would be more plentiful in League City," and "How would a bank for League City suit those who are habitual 'knockers' and they will evidently knock their brains out when they see this in print."

Then this notice appeared, surely to the surprise and pleasure of its readers, in the Texas Coast Promoter on Jan. 12, 1906:

"WILL ESTABLISH A BANK"
"LEAGUE CITY TO HAVE A BANK WITHIN 60 DAYS"

"As have been noted in the columns of the Promoter recently that a bank would probably be opened here shortly as a branch of the Alvin Bank, the following letter was received by Mr. J.E. Walker Thursday from Mr. Robert Ingram, President of the Alvin Bank: We have decided to give League City a bank. Signed, Robert Ingram."

Finally, this notice appeared in the Texas Coast Promoter on Feb. 2, 1906:

"BANK OPENS ABOUT FEBRUARY 15"

"The new bank which will be opened in League City about the 15th of this month will be located in one of (T.J.) Dick's buildings. All arrangements have been made for its opening so that business can be started in time to handle the strawberry crop for all prospective buyers who expect to corner the berry market in this section. This new institution in business circles will be a great help to the town and surrounding country as it will be the only bank in this section between Houston and Galveston. The Promoter is unable to learn who will be placed in charge of the business here."

The newspaper was two weeks premature in its prediction; but that probably mattered little to area residents.

Ingram's letter obviously heralded an official change in plans of the group of Galveston bankers—they had decided to open a separate bank in League City rather than the anticipated branch of the Alvin bank.

They had received state Bank Charter No. 54 for Alvin, and opened that bank on Feb. 1, one month earlier than the Citizens State Bank opened in League City with Charter No. 62.

It is possible that one of the four Galvestonians and the one League City man mentioned as the founders of the Citizens State Bank provided most of the money and allowed others to incorporate the bank. This is

This is the earliest known photograph of the interior of the Citizens State Bank of League City and two men important in its early history. Taken bout 1915, it pictures J. P. Atkinson and E.D. Singeltary. (*Photo, first published in "League City: A History from Its Beginning to 1912," courtesy of Mrs. E.D. Singeltary*)

likely because the five persons listed in the records of the Department of Banking in Austin as the bank's incorporators were these: Sealy Hutchings and E.R. Girardeau of Galveston; Robert Ingram of Alvin; and George W. Butler and J.M. Alford of League City.

The bankers leased offices in League City in a small frame building at the southwest corner of Second Street and Michigan Avenue.

The Citizens State Bank of League City opened for business on March 1, with a capitalization of $10,000.

Initial officers of the bank were Sealy Hutchings, president, and Robert Ingram, cashier.

John Paxton Atkinson also was sent from Alvin to help with the opening. At least one report ("League City: A History from Its Beginning to 1912") says he was "the cashier since its organization."

John P. Atkinson did have a major role in the early years of the bank, whether as cashier or some other position. In November, 1906, his father, E.S. Atkinson, cashier of the Alvin State Bank when it was chartered, was elected county judge of Brazoria County and resigned his bank job. John P. Atkinson was drafted to return to Alvin to fill his father's old job.

In a game of musical chairs, W.E. (Ernest) Steele, who had been with the Alvin bank, was named cashier of the Citizens State Bank in League City.

"Mr. Steele," reported a notice in the Texas Coast Promoter of Nov. 16, 1906, "is perhaps the youngest bank cashier of the state being only 18 years old and was a graduate of the last term of the Alvin High School."

Later Steele would return to Alvin to become president of the Alvin State Bank.

And John P. Atkinson, according to notes of Mrs. Charles B. (Caroline) d'Etchegoyen, his daughter who still resides in Houston, returned to League City in 1908 or 1909 to serve as the bank's cashier until the outbreak of World War l, when he resigned to attend the First Officers Training Camp at Leon Springs, Texas.

Coincidentally, many years later the name of Walter G. Hall would appear as the president, at the same time, of the same two banks.

The amount of the initial capital stock of the Citizens State Bank in 1906, according to the Department of Banking records, was divided into 100 shares with the par value of $100 each. Those shareholders and the amount of stock subscribed were the following: Sealy Hutchings, 30 shares; E.R. Girardeau, 30 shares; Robert Ingram, 30 shares; George W. Butler, 5 shares; and J.M. Alford, 5 shares.

In addition to the founders and/or initial stockholders, the bank included among its stockholders and directors many other prominent Galveston County citizens. Among them were J.C. League (for whom League City was named), Harper Anderson, Henry Schroeder, J.H. Langbehn and P.G. Pauls.

Among others in the bank's early life who served as officers were W.E. Lewis and Elmo Singeltary.

Other early stockholders, according to records in the stock transfer book of the Citizens State Bank, included these: D.B. Henderson, Frank B. Moody, W.B. Wallace, J. & I. Ullman, Leon Lewis, Libbie Moody, J.O. Dyer, J.J. Davis, E.M. Hartrick, S.A. Kinner, M.O. Kopperl, J.P. Alvey and W.S. Keenan.

When an all-brick building, the Butler Building, was completed in 1909 on the southeast corner of the same intersection as that of the bank's frame building, Second Street and Michigan Avenue, the bank moved across the street.

The Butler Building in League City, erected in 1909, was the home of the Citizens State Bank for many years. *(Photo published in "League City: A History from Its Beginning to 1912," courtesy of King-Atkinson Papers)*

According to a report in the League City history book, the first floor housed the bank, a grocery store and a drug store. On the second floor were offices for a physician, a dentist and a real estate agent. The building, which was the home of the bank for many years, still stands. In 1995 it was being restored by League City architect David Hoffman, who bought it in 1994 from G.I. Butler, grandson of George W. Butler.

The Citizens State Bank was an important financial foundation for the cattle and farming industry of the Mainland.

The League City area also had a small railroad shop; and nearby, the Humble Tank Farm, on the north side of Clear Creek between League City and Webster, gave the struggling area much of its economic lifeblood.

The tank farm employed about 100 men and sometimes more during periods of construction. It included more than 100 oil tanks. A number of large pipelines converged at the site, and oil was pumped to refineries in Texas City and Baytown.

One writer described the tank farm as a form of "farming" that could exist only in Texas.

Dickinson was the center for vegetable growers of the area, and many farmers also were successful in producing and marketing strawberries.

Later League City farmers joined the strawberry marketing effort, and so did farmers in other communities. For several years, the towns of Pasadena, League City, Dickinson and Hitchcock vied to be known as the community which shipped the most carloads of strawberries. Each of the towns claimed to be the "Strawberry Capital of the World."

Oranges, pears and figs also were important crops. The following almost prophetic story appeared in the League City Herald on Sept. 29, 1911, concerning the League City-Dickinson area:

"But what does (the growth of Galveston and Houston) signify to such a district as the one about League City and Dickinson, just exactly half way between the two cities? It means that this interlying country becomes a part of these cities in the sense that thousands of real homes will be built by those whose business is in the cities, and that other thousands, whose interests are here, will find means of support in ministering to the needs of the population of these cities and those who work in them. It means, in fine, that these cities and their workers must look largely to the country adjacent for homes for those so fortunate as to get away from the crowded confines of city limits, and to this same country to afford them much of the means of living as produced from the soils of the fertile acres available."

It was in this rural area that Walter G. Hall at times played, attended school and later would choose as the place to make his start in the banking business. And many decades later, he's still operating in the same territory.

. . .

A bank statement for the Citizens State Bank dated June 30, 1906—after the bank had been operating four months—revealed its financial condition. Under the "Earnings" heading were these items: Interest, $381.15; exchange, $188.05; and loss, $114.38, for a total of $683.58. Under the "Expenditures" heading were expense, $310.78; salary, $260; and taxes, $112.80, for a balancing total of $683.58.

One of the first major changes in the bank's financial history apparently came in 1912. That year, according to records in the Texas Department of Banking's Austin headquarters, the capital stock was increased from $10,000 to $15,000.

The increase came after Sealy Hutchings, the president, subscribed to 50 shares of stock for the entire $5,000 increase.

. . .

The little bank had started its growth, the first stages in the major role it would play for many decades in the history and financial life of northern Galveston County. It has helped to unify the area, emphasizing the part of the smaller communities in the development and growth of the county.

At the same time, the Citizens State Bank has helped to spotlight the activities of its leader for a large part of its life, Walter G. Hall.

His role has been not only in the history and growth of his own business ventures, but in the development and growth of countless small business establishments of his neighbors and friends. He has had a similar role in several Texas communities. And, to a degree not imperceptible (despite Hall's protestations), because of his support of significant issues and individuals, Hall has had an influence throughout the state and the nation.

Walter Hall's Education

Young Walter Hall completed first grade in the school at League City. During the time the family lived in Houston, he attended second grade at Harvard Elementary School. One of his classmates that year was a girl who also became a banker and civic leader, Marcella Donovan Perry, who for many years was head of the Heights Savings Association and was a member of the Houston Port Commission.

Hall's family remained in Houston, following the 1915 hurricane, until 1919, when Sam Hall and his wife decided to again make their home in League City. Here Walter Hall went to grammar school through the seventh grade and to high school three years.

Because the League City High School offered only three grades of accredited work, young Hall took his last year of high school at Central High School in Houston, now named Sam Houston High School.

He was able to ride the interurban without charge because of his father's work. This ride, between League City and Houston each morning and the return trip each afternoon, consumed three hours' time.

So long hours became a way of life for Walter Hall as well as his father.

"When I was in high school," Hall recalled, "we did a small amount of farming—vegetables, corn, figs, that sort of thing. We developed a sizable dairy herd, and that was when I learned to detest milking cows, because it always came at the wrong time. If I wanted to get up early to go hunting, the cows had to be milked. If I wanted to go swimming in the afternoon, I had to get home early to milk the cows. But it proved to be important financially for my parents later because of the size the herd became. That was the time of free pastures and open range, before the stock law came to this country."

Hall graduated from his Houston high school in 1924 and the same year entered Rice University—at that time called Rice Institute.

Hall said he decided to attend Rice because of three facts: "Because it was my first choice; it was close to home and was tuition-free; and I could still ride the interurban without charge."

While he was at Rice, Hall worked two part-time jobs—he sold advertising for the Rice Thresher, the student newspaper; and he was a waiter and night sandwich "chef" for Houston's University Club.

During the summer months he was employed first by the Galveston, Houston & Henderson Railway, painting the lift bridge on the Galveston Causeway. This was only for about three weeks because he quickly got another summer job. The second job, working for what was then the Humble Pipeline Co. at the Humble Tank Farm near Webster, paid a little more money—about 45 cents an hour. Hall served as a "pipeliner," or laborer, adding or replacing pipes. Hall remembers that his two supervisors were H.G. Mobley and W.T. Guinn.

Hall said the experience he had working for the pipeline company was important.

"I made a lot of good friends and learned a lot," he said. Also during one summer vacation he sold advertising for an illuminated highway map; and at that time he first met Clark W. Thompson, who later would be a U.S. congressman from Galveston. Thompson, married to W.L. Moody Jr.'s youngest daughter, Libbie, owned a large department store.

"I didn't sell an ad to Thompson," Hall recalled, "but he did send me to the old Tremont Hotel, and on his recommendation I sold an ad there. Thompson was always a hero to me after that."

A short-time, part-time job Hall had in 1928 (immediately before he began work on his first "adult" job) was of particular interest to him: He was assistant night cashier for room service (for food) at the Rice Hotel for 10 days during the Democratic National Convention. Most delegates to the convention were headquartered at the Rice and held most of their caucuses there. Among the Rice Hotel's guests was Franklin Delano Roosevelt, who nominated Al Smith for the presidency. (Hall did not see FDR at the Rice Hotel. And although Roosevelt was a political favorite of Hall, the Dickinson banker never had the opportunity to see or meet Roosevelt.)

Those summer jobs enabled Hall to pay for his books and laboratory fees and buy clothes for the upcoming school years.

He was becoming convinced that hard work—along with long hours—was a real part of life.

"Part of the problem," Hall said, "was that I had to get up at 5 o'clock in the morning to milk cows, then catch the interurban to get to Rice in time for the 8:30 classes."

Each morning Hall would get off the interurban at Pierce and Jackson, walk over to Main Street and hitchhike a ride to Rice from there. The return trip to League City was similar—and also took about an hour and a half.

It is interesting to note that during two of the years Hall rode the interurban, 1925 and 1926, the Galveston Flyer and the Houston Rocket achieved fame as the fastest interurbans in the United States.

Hall attended Rice University, but his high school sweetheart, Helen Lewis, attended the University of Texas at Austin.

She was the daughter of an old Galveston County family. Her father, W.E. Lewis, was a brother of Had Lewis, who was Frank Brown's right-hand man. Had Lewis came to Texas at the time Frank Brown settled in Friendswood and established his Quaker colony there. W.E. Lewis ran a lumber yard in League City until he became Galveston County's tax assessor-collector.

Their difference in schools did not keep Walter Hall and Helen Lewis apart very long: They were married on July 4, 1927, one year before Hall received his bachelor of arts degree from Rice.

Walter and Helen Hall paused for a few moments in the spacious grounds of their home in League City. The year was about 1950.

Hall made a brief entry into politics in his student days—he ran for business manager of the Rice Thresher. A good friend, Moses "Goop" Hart, beat Hall for the job. Hart became a physician in Dallas.

As a student at Rice University, Hall distinguished himself by serving as a senior member of the Honor Council. He also gained some very great and lasting friendships.

His favorite subjects were history, economics and philosophy.

Hall greatly values what he learned at Rice, and mentions in particular the importance of tolerance of all ideas and how to obtain, study, organize and evaluate new information.

A few young professors in Rice at the time were championing the capitalist system, which some observers believed was "in tatters." In "bull sessions" with some of his friends and some of the young professors, Hall heard that Americans need not fear that communist Russia would survive for very long, because "it was contrary to the human characteristic of acquisition."

Undoubtedly his favorite teacher was Radoslav A. Tsanoff, one of his professors of philosophy. Hall's association with Tsanoff probably stimulated, more than anything else, Hall's interest later in his promotion of and contributions to Rice University.

Many of these philanthropic activities, both in the interest of Rice University and other institutions, are related in a segment of Chapter 3.

Hall Goes to Work

After his graduation from Rice University in 1928, Walter Hall in the fall of that year started work for the Texas Company at its Lena Clay Mine in Fayette County (county seat: La Grange). At that site a mineral known as bentonite, or clay, was mined for use in the oil industry. Hall handled the payroll, wrote purchase orders and "whatnot," he said. His salary was $125 a month.

Hall, a husband and young father—Walter G. Hall Jr. had been born a few months earlier—refused to go into debt for anything except a secondhand Model T Ford coupe.

Hall undoubtedly gained some basis for his fiscal and political philosophy while he worked at the mine and as a result of his first confrontations with those who failed to understand his beliefs concerning his fellow men.

Most of the workers were truck drivers who hauled the bentonite from open-pit mines. While Hall worked there the drivers were paid a maximum of 32.5 cents per hour.

Although they were not what Hall called formally educated or sophisticated workers, they were "fine people—honest and hard-working," he said.

Hall explained that to help ease the strain on their budgets, the drivers and other employees formed what they called "calf clubs." Five or six of them would pool their resources and buy beef on the hoof, which they would slaughter and divide equally among the "members."

At one point Hall was transferred to Houston by the Texas Company, but later was asked to return to the Lena mine to help with additional construction.

Hall was at the Lena mine in 1929 when the stock market crashed. He noted the distress of his immediate boss, who had some rather heavy investments in the market. He also noted that parents of some of his friends lost homes and businesses.

A photograph of Walter Hall, probably taken in the early 1930s, reveals him as a fashionably dressed, clean-shaven young man at the start of his banking career. He has never varied from his "clean-shaven" image except on hunting and fishing trips.

"The whole thing was rather chaotic and confusing," Hall said.

After observing the struggles of the families with whom he worked, Hall was transferred to the Houston office of the Texas Company as a permanent assignment in 1930.

"A large picture soon presented itself," Hall said, including the characteristics of big corporations.

As an example, Hall related that everyone in the Houston office respected the chief clerk of his office and admired the quality of his work. However, the chief clerk was passed over for a promotion in favor of a relative of a high official of the company.

Hall told his supervisor of his outrage and immediately resigned his position.

A week or so earlier Sealy Hutchings of the Hutchings-Sealy National

Bank in Galveston had offered Hall a job at the little Citizens State Bank in League City and Hall had rejected the offer.

"I couldn't see how anybody could make a living in a bank with assets of less than $100,000," Hall said. At the time the bank had less than $60,000 in total assets, with deposits of about $38,200.

Nevertheless, Hall called Hutchings and asked if he could still have the job. Although the nation was in a depression, and Hutchings told Hall he thought he was "crazy" for quitting any job at the time, he said the bank job was still open and hired Hall as cashier.

Robert K. Hutchings, a son of Sealy Hutchings, said later: "These were hard times and the bank was in need of an honest man to help with its operation. Mr. Hall was employed as the bank's sole employee."

Hall started work at the bank on Jan. 1, 1931.

The minutes of the board of directors dated March 28, 1931, indicate that E.D. Singeltary resigned as cashier and director and W.G. Hall was elected to the board of directors and was named cashier at a salary of $125 per month.

The president of the bank at the time was C. Harper Anderson. After he died several years later, Robert K. Hutchings was named president.

Despite the fact that Walter Hall had a new job, it was fortunate that he was an optimist. The 1931 facts and figures were anything but bright:

There were 7 million American workers unemployed that year, and the number was increasing daily. The population of the nation was only 123 million during the census count of 1930, and the number of unemployed jumped to 12 million in 1932.

And during Hall's first few months in the banking business, more than 1,800 banks throughout the nation failed.

But because of the financial strength and general reputation of the bank's principal owner, Sealy Hutchings, the Citizens State Bank never experienced a run. Hall said, however, that times were so poor that few citizens had money to bank or use otherwise.

A Back-Door Operation

In the depth of the Great Depression, Franklin D. Roosevelt had been elected president of the United States in 1932 and was inaugurated March 4, 1933.

As the entire banking system of the nation appeared to be on the verge of collapse, Roosevelt on March 6 suspended all banking operations.

A short time before the presidential order closed all banks, Hall, trying to ensure the life of the little Citizens State Bank, had gone to Galveston to obtain more operating money from the owners.

However, after Roosevelt's proclamation was issued on March 6, the Citizens State Bank management in Galveston told Hall to cooperate with the president.

Hall did close the front door, he said, "but I kept the back door of the little bank open, and we cashed small checks for food and medicine all during the bank 'holiday.' "

He said only checks of depositors in the Citizens State Bank were honored by the "back-door operation."

Hall related one instance of a customer very pleased with the bank's activity during that time:

"I had one customer, Ray Hanson, who was stranded in Atlanta and he needed funds to get home. There was a Western Union office in League City, and after he phoned me I wired him $100 in care of his hotel so he could come home. He told me later that he took those ten $10 bills around and shook them in the noses of his friends who were also stranded. He told them if they were just banking with the right bank they could get home, too."

The bank made many friends and gained major publicity as the result of Hall's clandestine operation.

"It was a very odd situation that our little bank, small as it was, was probably one of the very few completely solvent banks in the nation," Hall said.

The bank was saved partially because of its size. Many larger banks were closed because they could not pay their depositors. The Citizens State Bank, because of the limited number of depositors, had enough cash and government bonds to pay off all deposits if it became necessary, Hall explained.

The Emergency Banking Act of March 9 provided steps for reopening the sound banks of the nation.

Hall recalls that although League City struggled greatly in those early days of the Depression, the economy never reached the low point that it did in other parts of the nation. "We didn't have a soup line, for example," Hall said. "We had unemployed people, but not as many as most places. Nevertheless, the economy was very soft, and I would see a few old couples moving around from child to child."

With destitution for many citizens either real or imminent, Hall said, the Red Cross began distributing flour to families in need.

"The Red Cross asked me to keep the flour in our vault, because it was always dry," Hall said. The agency also designated Hall to see that those in need received it.

"Some of our citizens at first didn't want to be seen carrying Red Cross flour," Hall recalled. "Some people asked me from time to time to put sacks in the back of my car. I only lived about five blocks from the bank, and they would come by after dark to pick it up. After awhile, they'd come in broad daylight because their 'daubers' were down—they were discouraged and had lost some of their pride."

Growth: A Move and a War

The fortunes of the Citizens State Bank continued on a small but positive basis after Hall joined the staff as cashier in 1931.

"Mr. Hall...the bank's sole employee, with the help of his wife, Helen Lewis Hall, was able to work the bank out of its problem loans," said Robert K. Hutchings.

After the bank "holiday" crisis of 1933, the little bank progressed and made a little money for its owners.

At the same time, the owners, realizing that their salary scale for Hall would not be increasing at a jack-rabbit-fast pace, allowed him to conduct an insurance business and real estate business in the bank.

As a result Hall's Insurance Agency was organized the year Hall began working for the bank.

The area, too, was progressing under the policies of the "New Deal."

An oil field was developed near Dickinson in 1934, and it had gained substantial momentum by 1936. The huge Hastings oil field near Friendswood also was discovered in 1934. The mammoth oil and chemical operations of the Texas City area continued to expand.

The only bank near the Citizens State Bank, the First National Bank of Dickinson, had paid off its depositors and closed in 1932, leaving Dickinson without a bank for three years. Soon there was more money in the Citizens State Bank from depositors in Dickinson than from depositors in League City.

Hall was convinced that those improving economic factors would provide a greater opportunity for the bank in Dickinson.

The legality of such a move at that time was a consideration. Hall said he asked the State Department of Banking if state authorization was needed, and received no satisfactory answer.

"One of the directors, Tom Lain, and I then went to Austin to discuss such a move," Hall said. "I asked the banking commissioner if there were any prohibitions against us moving the bank and he said he knew of none. Then I told him, 'We will just move; and if that causes you any embarrassment, we'll organize another bank and take over the assets and liabilities of the old bank. That would put you in the clear, wouldn't it?'

When he had no objections, I knew we were clear. We did not get permission, but we were not prohibited from moving.

"A few minutes later, when Tom Lain and I were leaving the Banking Department, Lain said to me, 'I'll be doggoned. Here I am a lawyer with many years of experience, and I couldn't come up with the solution. And the banking commissioner couldn't come up with the solution. Then you, a country banker with only a few years of experience, came up with the answer.' "

The official move of the bank from League City to Dickinson was accomplished at a stockholders meeting through a bank charter amendment, approved on Dec. 28, 1934. The following stockholders voted: C. Harper Anderson; Hutchings-Sealy National Bank, guardian for the estate of Mary M. Butler; E.E. Cavin, E.R.Girardeau, W.G. Hall, Robert K. Hutchings, Sealy Hutchings, J.H. Langbehn, T.W.Lain, W.E.Lewis, Henry Schroeder; Fred W. Catterall and Mart H. Royston, under the will of John Sealy, deceased; George Sealy, H.O. Stein and W.C. Skinner. Anderson was president and Hall was cashier. Accordingly, on Jan. 1, 1935, three people moved the Citizens State Bank from League City to Dickinson. Involved were Hall; his wife, Helen; and a nephew, Clyde Hall.

"We borrowed a pickup truck, grabbed the posting machine, two desks and four chairs," Hall recalled. "I drove the truck. We moved the balance of the records in the back seat of our old four-door Chevrolet sedan. My wife drove it. My nephew helped us move in."

The Citizens State Bank of Dickinson opened for business on Jan. 2, 1935, at 2817 Main, in the building formerly occupied by the closed First National Bank.

Hall said there were some complaints from customers in the League City area because of the bank move, but that loss of business was negligible.

Good fortune continued to follow the Citizens State Bank in its new home.

In 1938 the League City oil field was discovered, and about this time the Hitchcock bank paid off its depositors and closed. The major portion of the Hitchcock and Santa Fe area business moved to the Citizens State Bank.

This increase in business made a new building necessary, and a new structure was completed in 1938 at 2810 Main. The bank opened for business there on June 30.

With the threat of the U.S. entry into World War II on the horizon, the U.S. Army in 1939 started building Camp Wallace between Dickinson and Hitchcock. It was called "Swamp Wallace" by many because of swampy land, heavy rains during the construction period and flood-control problems.

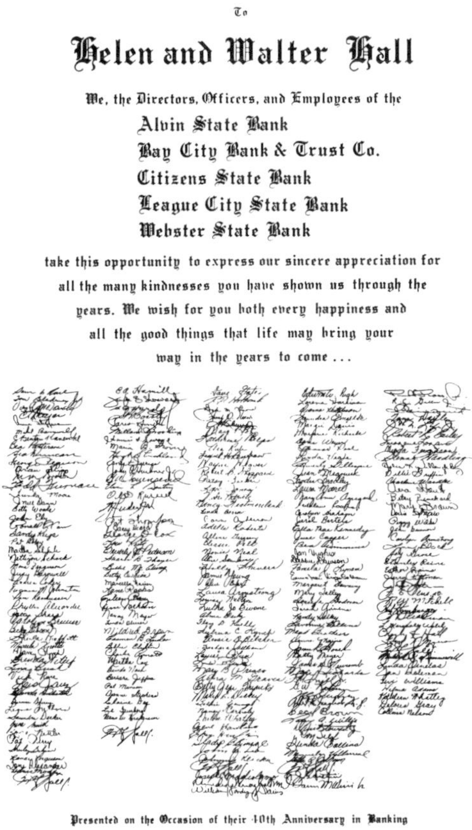

To

Helen and Walter Hall

We, the Directors, Officers, and Employees of the
Alvin State Bank
Bay City Bank & Trust Co.
Citizens State Bank
League City State Bank
Webster State Bank
take this opportunity to express our sincere appreciation for all the many kindnesses you have shown us through the years. We wish for you both every happiness and all the good things that life may bring your way in the years to come . . .

Presented on the Occasion of their 40th Anniversary in Banking

After Walter and Helen Hall had marked the start of their 40th year of banking, in 1971, the directors, officers and employees of the five banks the Halls headed at that time presented a plaque signed by more than 225 associates expressing their appreciation to the Galveston County couple.

Actually, the camp was named Camp Wallace by an act of Congress in honor of Col. Elmer J. Wallace, former commander of the 59th Coast Artillery Regiment, who was killed in France in World War I.

The Army's selection of that site of 1,600 acres of land for Camp Wallace and, to a lesser degree, the selection of a site near Hitchcock south of Highway 6 for the Hitchcock Naval Air Station, a blimp base, offered a great opportunity for the Citizens State Bank to be of service—and also to increase its profits.

Camp Wallace was a major operation. It had almost 400 buildings, 161 barracks, a capacity for 12,000 trainees and a payroll of $150,000 per week.

Camp Wallace originally was a training camp for the Coast Artillery (later Anti-Aircraft), then became a Navy boot camp in 1944 and finally, by the end of the war in 1945, was a discharge center for the Navy.

During its greater days as an Army training facility, at least 10,000 soldiers were quartered there daily. Initially, the Citizens State Bank received some deposits from the trainees and officers; but the real profitable business, from the camp officers' club and the post exchange, was going to a bank in Galveston.

However, late one Friday afternoon Hall received an SOS call from a high-ranking officer—Lt. Col. Elmer Block—asking if the Citizens State Bank could help solve a sudden and pressing problem: A troop movement had been ordered immediately, and the camp did not have sufficient cash on hand to send the necessary funds to transfer the soldiers.

The Galveston bank, despite all explanations and pleas from camp officials, was "closed" for the weekend. It was after banking hours, a switchboard operator told the camp officials, and no one would be available to help until Monday morning.

Hall and the Citizens State Bank, of course, were available and provided the necessary funds. The Camp Wallace troop movement for the U.S. Army proceeded as scheduled.

The following Monday, after a hurried but intense conference of Camp Wallace's commanding general with Colonel Block and others, the Citizens State Bank of Dickinson received the accounts of the officers' club and the post exchange.

The Camp Wallace and blimp base projects had filled every living unit in the area, and the bank was making loans for additions to homes and for apartments.

After the war, the Citizens State Bank had the distinction of making the first Federal Housing Administration (FHA) Title I home loan and was the first in a 16-county area to make FHA Title I home improvement loans. Other banks were slow in getting into this new program.

"But then," Hall smiled knowingly, "I didn't have the handicap of experience and outmoded ideas to tell me I shouldn't do it."

The bank's first FHA Title I home loan was to Ray C. Hanson of League City—the same Ray Hanson of League City to whom Hall had wired $100 in Atlanta during the "bank holiday" in 1933. The house was built on Kansas Avenue near the corner of Kansas and Walker Street in League City, near the intermediate school on that corner.

The bank also was active in making GI loans for homes until the program was curtailed by Congress in June, 1947.

The bank's first GI loan was to a former soldier who had been captured on Corregidor, Wiley Sloman. A survivor of the Bataan death march, he resided in League City until his death in the early 1990s.

The lack of sewers in the Dickinson area—the community was not incorporated at the time—was blamed for the rejection of many FHA loans.

About 1950, funds from a bond issue of the Galveston County Water Control and Improvement District No. 1, approved by the voters in April, 1947, became available. In addition to the water and sewerage work, some of the funds were allocated to paving the Alta Loma-Bayshore highway that runs throughout Dickinson. The city not only had its main street paved, but also had curbs and gutters installed along the route of the highway.

Following the installation of these improved water and sewerage facilities, FHA loans became easier to get. The Citizens State Bank prospered accordingly.

The Citizens State Bank also was one of the first to enter the field of automobile and other installment-type consumer financing. This business, together with other types of loans, some peculiar to the area, became specialties of the bank.

Close contacts with large city banks, utilizing a banking relationship referred to as "participation," enabled the Citizens State Bank to provide loans far larger than most country banks normally arranged.

Meantime, during the wartime activity in the community and the unusual growth registered by the bank, a sudden change had occurred. No longer was the Citizens State Bank an "outsider-owned" bank.

The Bank Changes Hands

The year 1943 probably was the most important year, bankwise, in the life of Walter G. Hall.

During that year he and a group of associates purchased from the Sealy Hutchings family of Galveston the controlling interest in the Citizens State Bank. The younger Sealy Hutchings, another son of founder Sealy Hutchings, arranged the transaction.

Considering the growth of the bank and its obvious bright prospects for the future, why would the group of Galveston bankers—who had owned the bank for almost four decades—suddenly sell the bank?

"Because the Hutchings family was a 'class' family," Hall said.

"They had made an adequate profit—not big for them, but big for me—and they were very conservative. At one time I told Bob Hutchings (who was president of the bank at the time), that I wished they would let me make some money for them. Bob's reply was, 'Walter, we're not so much interested in making money—we just don't want to lose any.'

"I told him, 'Bob, that's all right for you, because you're a member of a rich family; if I get any I have to make it.' They wouldn't let me make automobile loans; I knew the value of automobile loans, both for the customers who needed and wanted them and for the bank. I knew that if we didn't start making auto loans and other consumer loans it would be an opportunity and money down the drain.

"I didn't tell Bob this, but I knew if I didn't buy this bank I was going to start one in La Marque. I had a lot of business from La Marque, and La Marque had no bank.

"So I asked him if he'd sell me the Citizens State Bank." Robert Hutchings joined the Army in June 1942, and then his brother, the younger Sealy Hutchings, became involved in the discussions.

A short time later, Hall said, a deal was struck so that the Galveston group got a fair price and Hall did not pay a big premium for the bank.

Hall's associates were successful and respected businessmen in several communities in Galveston County.

They were A.J. Pollastrini, Dickinson merchant; Ernest Brown, president of the Dickinson Lumber and Supply Co.; Cecil Brown, owner of the Brown Fig Co. of Friendswood (the son of Frank Brown); Roy Lambden, Arcadia dairyman and manager of the Farmers Co-Operative Association; Lawrence Henckel, owner of the Henckel Motor and Lumber Co. of Hitchcock; and W.R. Blackburn, resident of Kemah, who had been assistant cashier of the bank since 1938.

Immediately after the purchase of the bank from the Galveston interests was completed, a special stockholders meeting was held, and those businessmen were elected as directors of the bank and the following officers were elected: Hall, president; Henckel, vice president; Blackburn, cashier; and Paul H. Leonard and Marie Yedel, assistant cashiers.

At the time Hall became an employee of the bank in 1931 as cashier, deposits were about $38,200; when his group purchased the bank in 1943, deposits were more than $1 million.

By the end of 1945, the bank had almost doubled in size. Hall stressed that this growth of the bank was primarily because of the growth of the area.

Post-War Growth

By the time World War II ended in 1945, the Citizens State Bank building at 2810 Main had outgrown its quarters.

The Dickinson Post Office for several years had been occupying space in the bank building; in 1949 the post office moved to a new building across the street.

Renovation of the space the post office had occupied gave the bank much needed room for expansion.

Still it was not enough.

So the bank launched a major expansion and modernization project which amounted to the construction of a new building.

The building at 2810 Main Street was enlarged to 2 1/2 times its former size and a drive-in window and night depository were added.

Concerning the plans for the new building, Hall was quoted in Galveston magazine, the official publication of the Galveston Chamber of Commerce, as saying that officers of the bank, "at that time, as they do now, have every confidence in the area they serve, and felt the need to expand with the ever-growing Mainland area. The chief motive behind the new bank building is to give the people a bank designed especially for service, prompt and efficient in a comfortable manner."

"Ben Milam of Galveston was the architect, and he stressed comfort...throughout the building," the magazine reported.

The opening of the new bank building in 1950 provided the Galveston County Press with an opportunity for a special advertising section marking the opening of the building, but Editor William Law also offered news coverage with the lead story on Page 1 concerning the open house. He detailed some of the facts concerning the building:

"The opening of the new building will afford patrons of the bank many new services and conveniences. The entire building, which includes over 6,600 square feet, is completely air conditioned and heated.

"...Herman Ostendorf of Dickinson was general contractor. Subcontractors include James A. Manning, mason contractor; H.D. Winkler, plumber; Ernie's Electric Service, electrical contractors; Hawk's Sheet Metal Works; Kelley Truck Service, excavation; J.E. Rourke, Galveston, plastering; A.A.Pruitt, Texas City, cement contractor; and Hull and Smith, Texas City, painting."

The Galveston County Press story also included information concerning some of the personnel of the bank. Included was the following:

"The bank's active officers now, in addition to the president (Hall) are Vice President D.L. Gates, who has been with the bank since 1943.

Mr. Gates was graduated from Southwestern University and came to the bank from League City, where he had been superintendent of the schools for several years. Mr. and Mrs. Gates and their son, Dave Jr., reside in Dickinson.

Two of the major officers and their wives posed after a reception following a meeting of stockholders of the Citizens State Bank in 1978. They are Walter and Helen Hall, left, and Frances and Dave Gates.

"Vice President R. Lee Vanderpool, Jr., is a native of Galveston and has been vice president only for a short time. He joined the bank in May, 1946. He is a graduate of Tulane University and spent five years in the U.S. Navy, from which he was discharged as lieutenant commander in March, 1946. He became cashier of the bank in January, 1947, was made a director in January, 1949, and elected vice president on June 20, 1949. Mr. and Mrs. Vanderpool and their small daughter, Janet Ann, reside in Dickinson.

"Cashier C.A. Deese assumed those duties at the bank in August, 1949. He previously served as cashier of the Security State Bank in Navasota. Mr. and Mrs. Deese and their small son reside in Dickinson.

"The bank's two assistant cashiers are Mrs. Lorena Harbison of League City and Miss Grace Lewis of Dickinson. Other employees are Wayne Weaver, Mrs. Darelle Best, Mrs. Mary E. Klotz, Gerald Hoff, Mrs. Mary Katherine Broussard, Mrs. Kay Kirby, Mrs. Sammy Morgan,

Miss Joan Palmer, Miss Gay Brown and Mrs. Margery Norris.

"In addition to the president and two vice presidents, the directors of the bank are Cecil Brown of Friendswood, Ernest Brown of Dickinson, A.J. Pollastrini of Dickinson and Mrs. Helen Hall of League City."

When the new building was completed, total assets of the bank were more than $3,000,000.

Hall said at the time it was "interesting to note that the capital account of the bank has grown from $10,000 as originally capitalized in 1906 to the present amount of $174,500."

The years passed more rapidly than Hall likes to remember. The Citizens State Bank observed its 50th anniversary with an open house Friday, Jan. 27, 1956.

In a special invitation to his friends and customers, Hall said:

"We're particularly proud of the fact that we do have many friends in the Mainland area. Cooperation has made possible the tremendous growth and development of the resources of the area, and we want our friends to join us as the oldest financial institution of the area crosses this half-century milestone."

Officially recognizing the significance of the occasion in the history of the area, the president of the Dickinson Chamber of Commerce, Earl J. Leeney, proclaimed the day as "Citizens State Bank Day."

Hundreds of well-wishers descended on the bank that day to congratulate Hall and his staff.

Among the publicity received on the occasion was a photograph published in the La Marque Times recording a meeting of bank officers' wives, employees and others closely associated with the bank. Those pictured were Mrs. R.L. Carmon, bank staff member; Mrs. Raymond (Margery) Norris, secretary to Hall; Mrs. W.G. (Helen) Hall; Mrs. Joseph C. Magliolo, wife of a director; Mrs. A.J. Pollastrini, wife of a director; Mrs. Wayne Weaver, wife of an officer; Mrs. Dave L. Gates, wife of an officer; Mrs. C.A. Deese, wife of an officer; and Mrs. Cecil Brown, wife of a director.

With the growth of Dickinson from a village of 2,704 people in 1950 to a city with more than 10,000 people in 1970, and with bank deposits growing in the same period from $2,849,853 to $18,071,115, time for a new building was almost past due.

So Hall and his associates broke ground in 1972 for a new building at 2401 Termini at Pine Drive. The fine new building was completed in 1973—the first new location for the bank in 35 years. It was officially opened on September 24.

As usual for the completion of an architectural achievement at one of Hall's banks, a round of festivities, including an open house and other special events, marked the opening of the new building.

One of the most popular public events associated with the opening was a drawing for prizes.

Winner of the grand prize was George Vaughn, who drove away from the bank in a new 1974 model Pontiac automobile.

Other major winners and their prizes were the following:

Mrs. Bessie Frank, $100 a month for 12 months; James A. Tennyson, $50 a month for 12 months; Doris Marselli, an antique commode; Joann Robinson, a chest filled with choice meats; and Andrew Slutak, Mrs. A.H. Pressley, Phyllis Maude, Mrs. Marianne Hieronimous and Rosemary Johnson, $50 savings bond each.

George Vaughn's experience with Walter Hall was not complete after his name was selected as the winner of the automobile.

R.D. (Bob) Holcomb, at that time executive vice president and later president of the Citizens State Bank, remembers that new autos at the time did not come "gassed up," and Vaughn was warned to fill up at the earliest opportunity and get insurance as soon as possible.

Wary Hall, however, was not satisfied with the warning: Before Vaughn headed for the nearest service station, Hall insisted that his Hall's Insurance Agency cover Vaughn and the new car until Vaughn could make his own arrangements the following day.

Vaughn then drove away, Holcomb said, and just as he was pulling into a service station on the Gulf Freeway, another car struck Vaughn's auto—causing primarily fender damage, but making Vaughn appreciative of Hall's cautious nature.

The new Citizens State Bank building had floor space of 37,775 square feet and five drive-in lanes.

One of the major features of the bank was—and is—its community room, where many civic and service organizations hold their meetings.

A community meeting room has been a feature for each of the banks which Hall has directed.

The Dickinson bank building also provides rental space for Hall's Insurance Agency.

Total assets at the time the new bank building opened were $25,150,338.

An expansion program in 1977 included the installation of data processing equipment.

"AnyTime Bank," an automated teller machine, or ATM, was introduced at the Citizens State Bank in 1979.

Drive-in lanes were expanded to a total of 10 in 1981, and the bank's vault was enlarged.

The bank celebrated its 75th anniversary in 1981.

The West Branch of the bank was added in 1989 at 215 FM 517 West.

A trust department was added in 1989.

The Citizens State Bank in June, 1990, purchased the Bacliff National Bank, a branch of the Mainland Bank of Texas City, and the Bacliff Branch of the Citizens State Bank opened in 1990 at 4021 Highway 146.

Time Capsule

An object familiar to many residents of the Dickinson area—and a subject of curiosity for all visitors to the bank—is a time capsule buried in the foyer of the building.

The time capsule, or vault, was included in the foundation when the bank was completed in September, 1973.

In it are more than 200 envelopes of customers containing messages to their friends and relatives, to be delivered after the capsule is opened.

Newspapers and other publications of the day also are included in the capsule.

Hall also buried a case of champagne with the other material, to be opened and consumed when the capsule is opened.

That date, according to the inscription on the floor of the foyer, will be June 15, 2000.

"I'll be there," Hall says emphatically.

The Bank Becomes a Football Expert

The Citizens State Bank became an expert in football in 1990.

The lobby of the bank has been the showcase for a variety of interesting exhibits—including new automobiles, boats, paintings, school posters, photographs, quilts and other items which were being displayed or promoted by Dickinson organizations, schools or individual citizens.

None has ever created the interest which was generated in 1990 by an exhibit offered to the bank on a "tentative" basis.

Gwen Neugent, vice president for marketing for the bank, graphically described the exhibit and the excitement it created:

"The eyes of the world were on Citizens State Bank in 1990...not so much for what we did but what we allowed to have happen—the housing of the famous Heisman Trophy. This event literally ruled over us after its placement in our bank on Jan. 5, 1990.

"I don't think any of us realized the impact it would have when the mother of Andre Ware approached me to ask if she could place the trophy in our bank, telling us her son Andre had a better-than-average chance to receive the award. With some degree of doubt, we informed her we would be happy to house the trophy in our lobby. (Ware, a quarterback at the University of Houston, had an outstanding collegiate career and was favored for the award.)

"Suspense hovered over us until that eventful night on Saturday, Dec. 1, 1989, when it was announced worldwide that Andre was the recipient. A local boy from Dickinson...a high school athlete who played on the Gator football team. It was like the shot that was heard around the world to us. We knew immediately we had to make gigantic plans and soon.

"Thanks to Mr. Hall we had access to a glass case he had built for another purpose some months prior, and we quickly obtained the aid of an excellent cabinet man to build the base for the glass case which would hold the trophy.

"Sounds simple? That was just the beginning. We felt research needed to be done on the Heisman with regard to its origination and purpose. This threw our marketing department into first gear...calls to the Downtown Athletic Club in New York and other places soon brought the answers we needed. Additionally, calls began coming in wanting to know when the trophy could be viewed by the public. It was a hectic but interesting time, bringing all our efforts into fruition within a 3-week period. We were ready!

"On the morning of Jan. 5, 1990, with approximately 300 invited guests present, Andre Ware placed his most prized possession in the lobby of Citizens State Bank. News coverage of the event was nationwide and Citizens State Bank found its name on the front page of USA Today as well as other nationally known publications, including the prestigious Sports Illustrated magazine, which descended on us one day in June, 1990, and shot pictures for four hours in the lobby.

"Because of the tremendous interest in viewing the Heisman and because of our limited hours open to the general public, we felt it would be a nice gesture for Citizens State Bank to open its doors on a Sunday afternoon from 1 to 4 p.m. to allow school children and working people to see the Heisman. On Sunday, Feb. 11, 1990, we had a record crowd of more than 1,000 people visit our bank to see the trophy. It was a welcome gesture by the public who told us how appreciative they were.

"During the two years the trophy remained in the lobby, we had a daily stream of visitors from all over the United States and some foreign countries.

"It was a very exceptional experience for us as a people and as a bank. Little did we realize that by agreeing to accept the display would it generate so much interest. It was a very positive force for Citizens State Bank.

Andre Ware, University of Houston quarterback, placed the Heisman Trophy in a special case for display in the lobby of the Citizens State Bank in 1990. President R.D. Holcomb, at left, observes.

"The Heisman Trophy has now found its proper place in the home of Andre Ware; but even today we continue to have people inquire about the trophy. It was a wonderful experience for all of us at Citizens State Bank."

Ware, as a University of Houston Cougar, set 26 NCAA passing and total offense records and 15 more Southwest Conference records. He was the first Cougar to receive college football's most cherished award.

Ware was drafted to play professional football with the Detroit Lions, where he saw limited service through the 1993 season. He was signed in 1994 by the Minnesota Vikings as a backup quarterback to Warren Moon, former Houston Oilers star. Later in the year he signed a contract to play with the Ottawa Rough Riders of the Canadian Football League.

The display of the Heisman Trophy was a personally nostalgic experience for Hall. The sports figure for whom the award was named, John W. Heisman, was an early head football coach at Rice Institute.

"His first year as coach was the same as my freshman year there," Hall recalled. "I, of course, was not a football player, and the only contact I had with him was when I was taking the routine physical education classes in the gymnasium. The first important game in that year, 1924, our team beat Texas 19 to 6, and at that time it meant a great deal more than football does now."

Heisman coached the Rice football teams until 1927. He later became director of the Downtown Athletic Club of New York City, which now sponsors the award of the Heisman Trophy.

Heisman Trophy winner Andre Ware and his mother, Joyce, right, posed with the Citizens State Bank's Gwen Neugent during a reception at the bank.

Heisman's name was featured in a 1994 column of L.M. Boyd in The Houston Post with this question-and-answer exchange: "Q) Why didn't football coach John Heisman ever stand up at games during the playing of the National Anthem? A) He died in 1936. Playing of the Anthem at sporting events didn't start until 1942."

A Bank With a Heart

Walter Hall and all staff members of the Citizens State Bank have always been happy because the bank is what their customers and others consider a "good citizen" of the community.

That fact was recognized statewide in 1992 when the Citizens State Bank was declared the winner of the "Best of Community Banking Award" in the community programs category (for a bank in a community of its size). The competition was sponsored by the Independent Bankers Association of Texas.

In its award-winning entry, "Adopt-A-School" program, the Citizens State Bank reported that it was assigned, by the Dickinson Independent School District, the Hughes Road Elementary School as its adopted school.

"The response to our efforts have been positive," Gwen Neugent, vice president for marketing, wrote in the report to contest judges.

"The Citizens State Bank has a keen interest in the welfare of our community and the future," Neugent wrote, echoing the spirit of the bank. "We recognize the future is in our children, and our goal is to be a partner with the schools to build character and good citizenship in our children...The...program our bank has developed is gratifying to our employees, officers and board as we have first-hand evidence of the improvement in the desire of many 4th and 5th graders to be winners. Dickinson will be a winner in the future as the children we reward now become responsible citizens."

Another school program that Neugent considers important is this:

"Beginning in 1990 the Dickinson Independent School District instituted the H.O.S.T.S. Program at Silbernagle School, which houses the 2nd and 3rd grades. H.O.S.T.S. is an abbreviation for 'Help One Student to Succeed.' It is a mentor-tutor reading program and to be successful, the program needed more than 200 volunteers to spend one hour per week teaching students to read. The one-hour constitutes teaching two students 30 minutes each.

"...For the past two semesters, Citizens State Bank has allowed eight of its...employees to participate on a weekly basis, devoting one hour per week per employee to this program. The...program has been so successful in our district that it has become a model program for other schools across the nation."

Citizens State Bank staff members who participated in this particular program are Grace Lewis, Vickie Stumpenhaus, Gwen Neugent, Cynthia Valencia, Stella Coffman, Mary Prisco, Stacy Fields and Diana Anderson.

As a further indication of the bank's belief in the importance of education in the community's life, in 1993 the bank made loans to 174 Dickinson-area college students.

Of course the efforts of the Citizens State Bank to be of service to its customers and the community did not start nor did they end with the award-winning educational effort in 1992 or other educational endeavors.

Those efforts are traced to 1906, when the bank accepted its first deposit and made its first loan; but the efforts are more measurable in later years of the bank's history.

One of the first precedents for public service to the community may have been established a year after the bank's founding, as reported in the Texas Coast Promoter, in its issue of June 14, 1907:

"About three months ago, a few of the citizens of League City met in the office of the Citizens State Bank and discussed the proposition of several creamery men to establish a creamery here."

Ever since that time, citizens of League City and later Dickinson have met in the buildings of the Citizens State Bank for a variety and multitude of purposes.

Officials of the bank, early in its history in Dickinson, established a community room in the bank, and the bank provides the use of the room, its heating, air conditioning, security and janitorial services...and even coffee. The community room is used several times a week.

Officials of the bank, many years ago, started keeping a record of the use of its community room. That record, staff members say, is both amazing and gratifying in reflecting the bank's service to the community, its organizations and its citizens.

As an example, the Pilot Club of Dickinson, a women's service organization, started holding semimonthly meetings in the bank's community room in 1974—and is continuing to do so today.

For the last few years, Gwen Neugent's records reveal, about 200 meetings have been held each year in the community room.

This partial list of the groups which have met or held functions in the community room is an indication of the diverse usage:

Dickinson Little League Basketball, Communications Workers of America, Bay Area Pioneer Club, Spanish Club, Bayou Chantilly Civic

Club, Chamber of Commerce Seminar, Dickinson Youth Baseball, Texas Parks and Wildlife, Casa Rio Home Owners Association, Speech Club, Parents Action Committee, Galveston County Beekeepers Association, DISD Parent Action Committee, Bayou Realtors and "general use by the public"—including such things as baby showers, retirement parties, weddings and wedding receptions.

The bank also permits the use of its lobby display area to organizations which request it for civic endeavors.

The organizations and citizens of Dickinson have indicated that they appreciate the services of the Citizens State Bank.

H.C. Lewis Jr., vice president of the bank, has voluminous files of "thank you" notes and letters from customers and other citizens who express thanks for the use of the community room and for other services of the bank.

In response to a questionnaire to customers to tell the bank how it could better serve their needs or the community's needs, these replies were typical:.

"Do not change. I've been with your bank over 27 years."

"I think you're doing great already. Continue the good work..."

"I've never had to apply for a loan but if the need should arise I wouldn't hesitate. Your staff has been helpful and kind in many other ways."

The bank's service as a place to congregate has gained what the staff considers deserved recognition with helpful publicity. Through the years gatherings of many groups have been recognized with photographs in local newspapers.

One such example came several months after the bank moved into its present building in 1973. The Suburban Journal chronicled the event with a large photograph on its front page with these cutlines: "The Dickinson Chamber of Commerce and Citizens State Bank held an art show at the bank building during the week of November 18-29 (1974). Open house was held on Sunday, and several of the Red Coats (service representatives) served as hosts for the show. They are pictured from left to right: Bob Potter, Bart Trotta, Jan Foley, Walter Hall's secretary and hostess; Bob Holley, president of the Chamber of Commerce; Gwen Neugent and Bob Holcomb."

One other "extra" in service which the bank provides for the comfort of its customers: a covered area where they can park their cars in times of bad weather.

Walter G. Hall, on the speakers' platform, presided at ceremonies opening the new Citizens State Bank building, at Termini and Pine Drive, on Sept. 24, 1973. A group of bank directors, officials, stockholders, Hall family members and other friends listened. From the left are Darvin M. Winick, Dr. Amedeo Magliolo, A.J. (Tony) Pollastrini, John Lee, Gloria Hall, Johnnie Klecka, Randy Hall, Dr. Joseph Magliolo, Kim Hall, Helen Hall, Kathy Hall, William Hardy Davis, Dave Gates, Bob Holcomb and W.G. Hall Jr.

'Help' Is Offered in Many Ways

The Citizens State Bank, during its nearly 90 years' existence, has developed highly sophisticated, modern financial services expected of a bank in a suburban area such as Dickinson.

Of course the bank provides normal services such as checking accounts, savings accounts, motor banking, personal and commercial loans, wire fund transfer, traveler's and cashier's checks, trust services and many more.

Few services are offered by banks in metropolitan areas such as Houston and Galveston—or even New York City—which cannot be duplicated or obtained at the Citizens State Bank.

However, Vice President H.C. Lewis Jr. reported the story of a development of one unusual service not offered to every customer.

"Several years ago," Lewis related, "one of our residents came into the bank and asked me for a loan in the amount of $21,000 to purchase a Buick automobile.

"On his loan application he stated the following:

"ADDRESS: HEAVEN

"EMPLOYER: GOD

"POSITION HELD: HEAVENLY WORK

"I told him that this was certainly a fine job; however, it did not pay enough to purchase the car.

"The next day he came into my office and told me that he had not disclosed his proper identification the previous day. He then stated, 'I AM God,' and he held up his hands to show me some imaginary nail holes. Somehow I got him out of my office again.

"The third day I received a call from a car dealer stating that the man was again coming to get the money—or else."

This time, Lewis, with the help of understanding police officers, was able to have the man restrained. Later, proper mental treatment for the man was arranged.

Bank Security and Safety

The Citizens State Bank has been blessed because it has been relatively free of armed holdups or similar types of losses.

There never has been any hint of misappropriation of funds by a bank staff member.

And certainly no problem with financial security has been experienced at any time in the history of the Citizens State Bank.

Only one holdup has been recorded in the bank's history. That came several years ago when a lone gunman took a small amount of money from a teller.

The only other known illegal loss of funds came when a visiting bank messenger gained access to a night depository bag and was able to leave the bank with unauthorized funds.

Friends and other bank officers attribute Walter Hall's sensitive selection of bank officials and the inquisitive screening of prospective staff members for the internal safety record.

Hall's banking philosophy is given most of the credit for the enviable record the Citizens State Bank has established in maintaining its reputation as a safe, reliable depository for its customers' funds.

That basic philosophy is the policy of lending against cash flow, not assets, to assure that the bank can at all times meet any demands of customers for deposited funds. (This philosophy is examined in detail in Chapter 4.)

Probably the best confirmation of Hall's belief that this is a wise policy for the Citizens State Bank is in the report for the bank released by Veribanc, Inc., of Wakefield, Mass. Veribanc has been called the "leading research firm of its kind in the United States" reporting on the strength and safety of the nation's financial institutions.

The Citizens State Bank of Dickinson has received, for Veribanc's "equity test" and "income test," the firm's "green classification"—the highest classification possible.

In addition to the color code, Veribanc classifies banks through a star rating system (considering future trends and contingencies not accounted for in the color classification), and the Citizens State Bank received three stars—the highest rating possible.

"This institution," Veribanc reported, "is currently listed in VERIBANC'S compilation of BLUE RIBBON BANKS."

There is no higher rating.

Other bank rating organizations also have always given the Citizens State Bank high ratings.

Hall's Other Banks

The banking life of Walter Hall has not been limited to the bank at Dickinson.

His loyalty to his hometown of League City has never wavered. Although he moved the Citizens State Bank from League City to Dickinson early in his career because of the economic considerations involved, as soon as the opportunity arose he started another bank in League City.

Hall also has successfully operated banks in Alvin, Bay City and Webster. The bank in Webster is still under his direction.

Prudent Bank Practices

An indication of Walter Hall's prudent business practices is reflected by the success of each of the five banks with which he has been associated—the one he joined as an employee and later bought; the two he organized; and the two he purchased from others and later sold.

Each bank gained strength—and profits—under Hall's leadership and with his ability to delegate authority to others.

The little bank he joined in 1931 as cashier—the Citizens State Bank of League City—had $38,200 in deposits when he was first employed.

When he convinced his bosses in 1934 to move the bank to Dickinson, deposits were $78,186. (The bank opened in its new home on Jan. 2, 1935.)

Hall and his associates bought control of the Citizens State Bank in 1943. At the end of that year, deposits were $1,397,808.

By the end of 1994, deposits of the Citizens State Bank were $84,458,435.

Hall purchased control of the Alvin State Bank and became president and chairman of the board in 1953. The deposits were $6,359,459. He sold the controlling interest in 1981. Deposits on Dec. 31, 1980, were $92,773,236.

Hall opened the League City State Bank (now League City Bank & Trust) on March 15, 1956. Initial deposits were about $1,400,000. Deposits at the end of 1994 were $91,719,121.

Hall opened the Webster State Bank (now Bay Area Bank & Trust) on Nov. 8, 1963. Total reserves on Dec. 20, 1963, were $1,750,365. At the end of 1994 deposits were $84,545,740.

Hall bought controlling interest in the Bay City Bank & Trust in 1966, when deposits were about $14,000,000. Hall sold the bank in 1974, after deposits had climbed to $24,533,677.

An Unrealized Plan for Bay City

Walter Hall was not involved in the bank at Bay City—Bay City Bank & Trust—for a great length of time, but the hand he held was a heavy one, and the bank grew solidly and substantially under his leadership.

One dream Hall had concerning the Bay City bank was never realized, however.

He and the architect, Tom Price of Galveston, carefully laid their plans for a new building for the Bay City bank.

Each of the bank buildings Hall built had one feature which made it outstanding. The bank at Dickinson has as its outstanding feature the interior lighting fixtures. The Alvin bank has a mammoth lobby fireplace display.

For the Bay City bank, Hall and the architect determined that a huge chandelier at the entrance, which faced one of the main thoroughfares in Bay City, would be most effective.

The chandelier would be an exact replica of an elaborate and highly praised fixture the architectural firm had installed in a Boston church.

Before the chandelier was installed in the new building—an impressive facility for Bay City—Hall had an opportunity to sell the bank to a friend, who in turn sold it to others who were not impressed with Hall's building ideas. The plans for the chandelier were dumped.

Chapter 2
Other Hall Enterprises

A Battle of Permanent and National Significance

One experience in the professional life of Walter Hall may be making a more profound and more lasting impact, nationwide, than anything else he has ever done. And strangely, it had nothing to do with the banking business.

This unusual episode in Hall's career was an 11-year legal adventure that started in 1969, spanned all of the 1970s and ended in 1980.

Hall's incursion into a completely unknown field for him—television—extended into another state—Mississippi; but it did involve an element with which Hall was vitally concerned, that of human rights.

A participant in that venture, Weyman Walker, said that as a result of Hall's participation, "Broadcasting was forever changed. It was a landmark proceeding; without him, it would not have taken place, and has got to be one of the most important things Walter Hall has ever done in his life. Maybe THE most important thing."

Walker, who at that time was manager of a television station in Meridian, Miss., had become concerned because a major Mississippi television station in the state's capital, Jackson, was, he said, conducting outrageous editorial racial practices.

As an example, Walker said the station, WLBT, Channel 3, an NBC affiliate, would black out, from the network news, coverage of Martin Luther King's activities. "Network Trouble" slides would be flashed when such news was being aired, Walker said. Additionally, he said, during the integration troubles at the University of Mississippi, the station practically "invited" violence by reporting untrue statements such as "Negroes are going to kill and rape students on the campus at Oxford" and other bigoted and racially inflammatory falsehoods.

Information about these reports infuriated Walter Hall; and when Walker, a fellow Texan whom Hall had known earlier, asked for his help, Hall was amenable.

The stage had been set, a few years before Walker became involved, when leaders of the United Church of Christ became incensed for the same reasons Walker and Hall were furious.

The United Church of Christ had petitioned the Federal Communications Commission to vacate (revoke) the license of the Lamar Life Broadcasting Co. of Dallas (a Murchison organization) to operate the station. The FCC had rejected the petition, and the church appealed the decision to the U.S. Court of Appeals for the District of Columbia. However, the church had offered no alternative to the FCC for the operation of the station.

Walker said his appeal to Hall for financial help to intervene in the case brought immediate action.

Hall and Walker retained the services of a Washington communications law firm; and attorney Martin Firestone, now a practicing lawyer in Florida, directed the legal battle for more than a decade. Hall and Walker both give major credit to Firestone for his effective handling of the case.

The group organized by Walker and financed by Hall, Civic Communications Corp., intervened and offered the necessary operation alternative—that the license be vacated and additionally that new applications be received from others who desired to own and operate the station.

The appellate court ruled for the intervenors. The ruling, incidentally, was written by Warren E. Burger. He chaired the panel that considered the entire proceeding, Walker said, and this was his final decision as a federal appeals court judge. A few minutes after the decision was issued, Burger became the chief justice of the U.S. Supreme Court in 1969.

Burger's decision ordered the FCC to invite new applicants for the Channel 3 license.

The decision was quickly upheld by the U.S. Supreme Court, Walker said.

The FCC then invited applications from new bidders for the station's license.

Five applicants were received. Included were Lamar Life, which eventually was eliminated from contention, and Hall's Civic Communications Corp. The four surviving applicants battled in the courts and negotiating sessions for 10 years over the license.

The station, in the interim, was operated by a non-profit group established by the church through a plan devised by the Hall group. Under this plan, profits were distributed to charitable, educational and not-for-profit organizations.

Burger's decision ordered, in effect, that if the initial applicants

Ceremonies marking the opening of the new Citizens State Bank Building in 1973 were broadcast over KGBC Radio in Galveston. Steve Cowan, center, station manager, and Roger Rother, technician, observe as Walter Hall discussed the new building.

could not reach a compromise, the FCC would receive petitions from other applicants.

It was during this 10-year period, Walker said, that Hall was most effective.

"His testimony as a witness was unbelievable," Walker said. "His negotiating talent is unmatched."

Finally, a settlement was reached in 1980, and Hall's group became a partner, with the other three applicants, in the operation of the Jackson station.

The combined group operated the station for several years before selling it at a handsome profit.

Others involved with Walker and Hall in the Civic Communications Corp. were Greenville, Miss., newspaper editor Hodding Carter III, who later became assistant secretary of state for public affairs in the Jimmy

Carter administration; Patricia Derian, national Democratic committeewoman from Mississippi, who later was named assistant secretary of state for human rights in the Carter administration; Aaron Henry, president of the National Association for the Advancement of Colored People in Mississippi; Charles Young, a black cosmetics manufacturer; and Charles Evers (brother of slain Mississippi black leader Medgar Evers), a civil rights leader and mayor of Fayette, Miss., who withdrew early in the negotiations. Concerning the significance of the case, Walker said: "A good deal of broadcast history was made. For example, Warren Burger wrote about the potential effect of broadcasting on American life. He was suspicious of the power of broadcasting and the mass media. He didn't like it personally; he was afraid of it, and he wanted broadcasting to be responsive to the needs and interests of the citizens of the republic."

As a result, Walker said, "(Much of what) you see in communications today—the changes that were made—were made as a result of those proceedings."

Those changes, Walker said, are in the field of employment—including non-discriminatory hiring practices—and editorial treatment of news and public affairs.

"What we stopped," Walker said, "was the worst example of irresponsible, reckless, dangerous, racist, inflammatory broadcasting in history."

Without Walter Hall, Walker said, "nothing would have ever happened. With his persistence—he stayed with it, unflinchingly, day after day, year after year—he made things happen. He was the most amazing person that you can imagine."

Attorney Martin Firestone has added a most effective, legally incisive, technical and historically enlightening insight into the Mississippi television affair:

"When (the historical and political context for Mr. Hall's activities in Mississippi) is considered, what Mr. Hall did and accomplished...becomes even more remarkable and admirable.

"When the application for WLBT-TV was filed by Mr. Hall and Weyman, the Lyndon Johnson 'Great Society' era was coming to an end. The resentments which the Great Society programs created in Mississippi still burned feverishly and the opposition to them was as fierce as ever. WLBT-TV, the most powerful media voice in Mississippi, stood as the symbol of the state's resistance to integration and civil rights. Into this climate, came Walter Hall and Weyman Walker not merely to challenge the renewal of the station's license but to obtain that license for a group which was comprised of a majority of black civil rights workers complemented by well-known Mississippi white civil rights advocates.

"The fierce, and often violent, opposition to that which Mr. Hall and Weyman were trying to accomplish can best be exemplified by Weyman's experience, (when Walker's station in Meridian) was the first in Mississippi to telecast a racially integrated children's program...The response to the program were numerous threats of violence against the station and Weyman. The FBI extended protection to both the station and Weyman. You can imagine, then, the reaction to the challenge of WLBT-TV's license by a 'bunch of civil rights radicals.'

"The hostile environment in Mississippi was fueled by the obvious animus of the newly installed Nixon administration toward the civil rights movement; and, more relevant to our challenge to WLBT-TV, the blatant politicization of the federal regulatory agencies, among them the FCC, by the Nixon administration. The best evidence of the latter is that after some three years of administrative litigation involving multiple applicants, the initial decision of the FCC's administrative law judge awarded the license to the patently Republican applicant, two of its major principals being the two-time Republican candidate for governor of Mississippi and the incumbent treasurer of the Republican Party of Mississippi.

"Mr. Hall never gave up the fight or his principles. He kept up both his intellectual, moral and financial support. As a consequence, I was able to discover new evidence which resulted in the initial decision being set aside and the case being reopened for further hearings. It was the prospect of these further extended and costly hearings that forced the remaining competing applicants into settlement negotiations.

"Directly through Mr. Hall's unwavering effort and support, watershed changes were accomplished in the telecommunications industry. No longer could the facilities of a federally licensed broadcast facility be employed in the manner described by Weyman and go unchallenged by those who were the victims of such conduct. Perhaps more significantly from its historical impact, the negotiations which Mr. Hall's efforts precipitated and which he personally conducted resulted in a settlement which created the first black, minority-controlled network-affiliated VHF television station in the history of U.S. broadcasting.

"Mr. Hall, in my opinion, was primarily responsible for forcing open the door to minority ownership and operation of telecommunications facilities in this country. Also, in my opinion, Mr. Hall has never received the recognition he deserves for this accomplishment. Knowing Mr. Hall as I do, I am sure that this does not bother him one whit; but, it bothers me that what he did does not seem to have made a footnote in the history of the civil rights movement in the South."

Broadcasters are still studying Justice Burger's ruling, which warned: "The infinite potential of broadcasting to influence American life renders somewhat irrelevant the semantics of whether broadcasting is or is not to be described as a public utility. By whatever name or classification, broadcasters are temporary permittees—fiduciaries—of a great private resource, and they must meet the highest standards which are embraced in the public interest concept."

Hall said that he received many plaudits for the amount of time, effort and money he had expended on this 11-year venture, but none gratified him as much as this from his wife, Helen:

"I knew you had guts, but I didn't know you had that kind of guts."

A Few of Many Other Hall Interests

Walter Hall has had what many consider spectacular success in businesses other than the banks and the unexpected venture into the television industry.

He had made excursions, of course—as most bankers have—into some rather unusual fields because of the broad range of investments and loans that banks make. Hall's included, for example, periods of managing (or advising the management) of a newspaper, a radio station, a restaurant and a carpet retail store.

Hall had even gone beyond the field of his own insurance agency to found an insurance company, the Statesman National Life Insurance Co. Hall also acquired controlling interest in the Sentinel National Life Insurance Co. of Dallas.

Hall said he sold both companies for a profit.

A license was granted to the Statesman National Life Insurance Co. in January, 1955, and it was sold in about January, 1964, and the headquarters office was moved to Houston. The records in the office of the Texas Department of Insurance in Austin indicate that the company changed hands since Hall sold it, but it is still in existence.

The Insurance Department's records do not indicate the disposition of the Sentinel National Life Insurance Co., but it is not now licensed in the State of Texas.

Another major financial organization headed by Hall is the Citizens Investment Co.

"Early in 1948," Hall said, "we felt there existed here a field for profitable credit considerably in excess of that which our bank could supply."

Loans to get a major supply of capital enabled Hall and other bank officers, including Dave Gates, Dr. Joe Magliolo and Lee Vanderpool, to organize the investment company. It was a service to customers who could not be accommodated by loans from the Citizens State Bank—those who desired large loans for purchases of such things as homes, furniture and automobiles.

CIC has had spectacular success, Hall said.

Hall and several other partners had another successful undertaking in organizing and promoting a subdivision, Inter City Place, between La Marque and Texas City. His partners in this effort were Louis Pauls of Galveston, an investment banker; Tony Bogatto of La Marque, an automobile dealer; and William P. (Pat) Sweeney of La Marque, owner of a dredging and marine construction company.

"Because we were using my personal funds—and those of my partners—in these outside ventures, there was absolutely no risk to the funds deposited in the Citizens State Bank," Hall said.

R.D. (Bob) Holcomb, now-retired president of the Citizens State Bank, presented a plaque to Walter G. Hall in 1990 from the employees of the bank recognizing Hall for his lengthy service to banking and the community.

(Beverly Miller photo, courtesy The Galveston Daily News)

Chapter 3

Hall's Service to Others

Expanding Horizons

Walter Hall's life in banking, despite his dedication to it and success in his primary profession, has never completely captured his time or interest.

His first financial expansion, as reported, was in the field of insurance. Since that time his economic horizons have recognized few limits, and some of his experiences are recorded in Chapter 2.

Parallel to his work in the fiscal field has been Hall's far-reaching service to his neighbors.

The Need for Health

Possibly the first evidence of Walter Hall's public service foresight and acumen came a few years before the United States entered World War II.

Many of the residents of Galveston County's Mainland were saddled with septic tanks and individual water wells and, as a result, they existed with completely unsatisfactory, insanitary and unsafe living conditions.

One of the federal government's New Deal measures provided most of the funds needed for municipalities and districts to construct water and sewer plants, with local communities providing only a small part of the balance of the funds.

At Hall's insistence, the first county water district, Galveston County Water Control and Improvement District No. 1, was formed in the latter 1930s in Dickinson.

A short time later, in 1939, WCID No. 2 was organized in League City, and Hall was elected president, bringing the first sanitary facilities to his hometown.

The League City WCID actually began operating earlier than that at Dickinson, Hall said.

City officials, Chamber of Commerce executives, bank officers and other friends helped with the ribbon cutting ceremony when an expansion program was completed by the Citizens State Bank in November, 1981. In the front row from left, holding the ribbon, are Earl Leeney, Dickinson civic leader; Willie Matthews, Lew Stephens, Gwen Neugent, Juanita Johnstone, president of the Dickinson Chamber of Commerce; Walter G. Hall, Bert Trotta, Bill Brown, R.D. Holcomb, Ann Bragg and Jay Morris.

One story Hall tells indicates the difficulties WCID No. 2 encountered in locating a sewer plant and Hall's willingness to go an "extra mile" to assure the success of the district.

"We sought $50,000 worth of revenue bonds and sold $47,500," Hall said. "The balance of the funds came from a federal grant. We were pressed to economize in every possible way.

"We told everyone from whom we needed easements that they would have to give them, because we could not afford to pay for them. One man from whom we needed an easement was a neighbor of mine who lived next to my five-acre tract. His house was about 50 feet from the property line which separated his land and mine. He did not want to see a sewer plant built on the other end of his property, about 300 yards from his home. And he knew he could force us into condemnation proceedings; and although we would get the easement, we would have to pay the court costs. He knew we did not have the money to do so.

"It reached the point where I felt there was only one way to get him to sign, and I made it clear that if we did not get the easement from him, we would build the sewer plant on my land, which would put it about 125 feet from his home. He did not believe I would do that."

But the alternate preparations for the sewer plant, including the actual delivery of gravel to the site near Hall's home, convinced Hall's neighbor that the banker was serious; and the neighbor finally executed the easement to the originally planned site.

Hall served with the League City district for four years, resigning in 1943 to accept a place on the board of directors of the San Jacinto River Authority.

Because of Hall's experience in the water districts at Dickinson and League City, he was asked by other communities to help obtain information and assistance from the government. That led to improved health services on much of the Mainland.

Among the other cities which Hall aided in creating WCID organizations were Kemah, La Marque, Hitchcock, Alta Loma and Friendswood.

Several of these organizations eventually were taken over by the cities after they were incorporated.

The Need for Water

One of Walter Hall's major contributions to the welfare of his fellow citizens involved the need for water, both domestic and industrial, and Hall's work with the San Jacinto River Authority.

In the early years of the Authority, after it had been organized in 1937, the San Jacinto River Authority was little more than a paper authority.

In the 1940s, the City of Houston was planning a dam on the West Fork of the San Jacinto River near Conroe.

Immediately a dispute arose between the City of Houston and the San Jacinto River Authority: The City of Houston claimed that because the water was held by the city's dam, the water belonged to Houston; the San Jacinto River Authority said the water was San Jacinto River water and the Authority had priority under state law.

According to files of the San Jacinto River Authority, "The controversy with the City of Houston had not yet been worked out (during World War II) and, accordingly, the Federal Works Agency built a water supply system on the lower San Jacinto to supply the war industries of the area. This system consisted of a pumping plant, with a canal and reservoir system on each side of the river.

"The Authority," the files reflect, "cooperated with the federal government to the fullest extent during the war years and postponed its own plans. The board of directors met on June 4, 1943, and adopted a resolution assigning to the Federal Works Agency the Authority's water rights for the duration of the war and twelve months thereafter. In return the Authority was to receive $1 per year, and all water rights were to be returned at the end of the designated period of time."

Hall had been appointed to the San Jacinto River Authority by what was then called the State Board of Water Engineers. At the first meeting of the board of directors after his appointment, in August, 1943, the directors named Hall president of the Authority.

Hall explained his interest in the state's water circumstances that led to his appointment to the Authority:

"Texas has a vast amount of waters that go down the rivers into the Gulf. Much of those waters should continue to go down to the sea because of the marine life they play a part in. But the floodwaters and some of the normal flow should be conserved for industry, farm, and a thirsting people and a thirsting land. And so I indicated a very keen interest in a water supply for our own area, including our own county. The City of Galveston was having to constantly drill new wells farther and farther north to supply its people and industries. Other industrial, farming, and domestic needs clearly existed in this county.

"It was the conviction of many of us who had studied it some and who had the benefit of good engineering information that the San Jacinto was then the logical source of supply for Galveston—logical largely because of the quality of the water. The Brazos River water was cheaper to obtain and to bring in but it was of inferior quality and it was not cheaper for a domestic supply. The treatment was too costly."

Hall's history as president of the Authority reflects the tenacity with which he tackles—and usually solves—his problems.

Other officers of the Authority were Frank N. Read of Baytown, vice president; Charles R. Scott of Houston, secretary; and A.R. Woodson of Conroe, treasurer. Doyle F. McAdams of Huntsville was sworn in as a board member and James V. Allred, the former governor, was retained as legal counsel. Later C.A. Deese of Plantersville was appointed a director and was elected secretary of the board. Deese later became a major cog in Hall's banking operation.

"Negotiations between the Authority and the Federal Works Agency continued throughout the war years," the Authority's records related, "and the Authority also sought to effect some sort of workable compromise with officials of the City of Houston. In 1945, the FWA advised both the Authority and the City of Houston that if the two could come to an agreement, the FWA would consider the sale of the water supply system."

Hall recalls that negotiations between the Authority and the City of Houston were stalled. Allred, the Authority's attorney, insisted on a man-to-man meeting between Hall, as the Authority's president, and the mayor of Houston, Otis Massey.

Accordingly, Hall said, he agreed to the meeting and went to the mayor's office to keep the appointment.

"When Mayor Massey escorted a man out of his office," Hall said, "he saw me sitting in the waiting room and said to the receptionist, 'Tell that hard-headed SOB to come in.' " To which Hall replied, "Tell that stubborn b——— I'm on my way."

Hall said he and Massey "got along famously," and the Authority's history records the results thusly:

"Such an agreement was finally reached, and on April 25, 1945, the Authority purchased that part of the system east of the river and the City of Houston purchased the west half of the system. The pumping plant, which supplied both canals, was to remain FWA property and be operated by the City of Houston, with operation expenses shared by the Authority and Houston.

"At last the Authority was actually 'in business,'" the Authority's files reported, "and thought was turned to the expansion of the water business and getting soil conservation practices, reforestation and recreation facilities into operation as soon as possible."

It was during the period of negotiations for the system that Hall had his only confrontation—and one that was unexpected—with Roy Hofheinz. Hofheinz at the time was county judge of Harris County. Later he was elected mayor of the City of Houston and still later conceived and built the Harris County Domed Stadium—the Astrodome.

Hall and Allred both considered Hofheinz their personal and political friend, and were greatly surprised to find him in an antagonistic role.

The occasion was during what presumably would be the final meeting of officials and attorneys of the FWA and the Authority to complete the legal transfer.

Hofheinz made an unanticipated entrance to the meeting, Hall said, and told the presiding FWA official, a retired federal judge:

"Judge, I'm the county judge of the largest county in Texas, and I resent having our water supply controlled by a little dinky river authority, and I'm asking for a postponement of this action until we can get it squared away and until it is right."

Allred, Hall said, was prepared to answer legal questions concerning the contract but was unprepared for Hofheinz's sort of attack. So when the official asked for the Authority's answer, Hall countered with his remarks.

"I resent very much the interruption of this procedure," Hall told the FWA official. "We have dealt in good faith with your agency; we have come to an agreement; we have put up our earnest money to guarantee it; and we are here to close the agreement.

"And here comes this man, Judge Hofheinz, with no legal authority to be here. He must get legislation passed before his county can get into the water business. He doesn't know whether he can get Harris County to do anything; he doesn't know whether he can get the Legislature to do anything. Our Authority is here, ready to go."

"Roy was a great speaker—one of the best I have ever heard," Hall said, "and I was no match for him. But I had the facts on my side."

Hofheinz was angry, Hall said, but he lost that fight. Later, of course, Hall and Hofheinz resumed their friendly relations.

Hall gives much credit for the successful negotiations to the FWA official with whom he usually worked. He was Jim Bradner, who later became a prominent citizen of Galveston and owner of Radio Station KGBC. His widow still lives in Galveston. (See also Chapter 5.)

The contract with the City of Houston assured a permanent supply of high-quality water to the cities in Galveston County, and Hall resigned from the Authority in 1954.

The Need for Leadership

One of Walter Hall's favorite topics is soil and water conservation, and obviously he has had an insider's opportunity to practice what he believes with several important projects.

In addition to his involvement with the local water districts and the San Jacinto River Authority, Hall also had an unmatched opportunity to study and influence the growth and activities of the National Association of Soil Conservation Districts. In the 1950s the headquarters office of the organization was established in League City. The national president, Waters S. Davis Jr., was a director of Hall's League City State Bank.

David Stewart Jr. of League City, an official of the NASCD from 1960 to 1987, said, "Walter Hall could...make as good a speech or pitch for soil conservation as anyone in America."

Hall said he first became interested in water supplies because of the need in the area for fresh water, especially for industry, which needed far more than wells could supply.

"Water supply has been the ceiling for every civilization," he told John Rainey of The Houston Post in 1962. "The need is now, and it will increase in the future...

"It can be said, perhaps with logic, that the people will see the need when they become sufficiently educated. This may be true, but I point out that we have many well-educated people now and only a few of them seem to be much concerned about all of the aspects of taxes and water development.

"While the educational process is going on—and I hope being improved—considerable damage is being done in the state through neglect of soil and water development.

"For instance, there goes down the rivers of Texas into the Gulf of Mexico enough of our soil each year to create 8,000 farms, 100 acres each, with soil 6 inches deep.

"The leaders must lead. But the fact that the masses are not greatly concerned over these problems is a reflection on the leaders."

Post-War Planning Committee

By the 1940s the power structure of Galveston County was becoming more and more aware of the clout which Walter Hall was wielding in the northern part of the county.

It was wartime, but Hall was continuing to make big strides which were attracting the attention of more than just his neighbors in Dickinson and League City.

Hall had gained enough personal and financial strength to purchase control of the Citizens State Bank from a well-regarded Galveston banking group in 1943; in the same year he was named president of the San Jacinto River Authority.

The increasing personal and political success and growing financial strength of the young banker (in 1943 he was only 36) led the members of the Commissioners Court to tap him for an unpaid, time-consuming but strategically important task.

By early 1945, most observers believed, the nation was near the end of the war. And many citizens of Galveston County realized that some of the major problems facing the county would grow to catastrophic proportions by the end of the war if they were not confronted and at least partially solved immediately.

The commissioners created what they called a Post-War Planning Committee, authorizing it by a unanimous vote at the meeting of March 5, 1945.

Citizens appointed to the committee—many of the leaders of commerce, industry and finance in the county—were the following:

H.S. Autrey of Galveston, president of the Galveston-Houston Breweries; R.C. Bouse Jr. of Port Bolivar; T.H. Dodson of Galveston; W.G. Hall, a banker from Dickinson; A.A. Horne, a banker from Galveston; E.A. Johnson of Texas City; I.H. Kempner, a banker from Galveston; T.M. McCormick of Texas City; J.W. McCullough, a banker from Galveston; George W. Smith of High Island; and W.C. Steed, mayor of Texas City (1940-1947).

At the insistence of Mayor Steed and banker Kempner, members of the committee designated Hall as chairman.

Names of others, who apparently were added to the committee—or represented members—and appear on later records, are those of Roger J. Seaman and L.H. Jolley.

During the next few months the committee met many times, usually in the Cotton Exchange Building in Galveston.

Hall then appeared before the county Commissioners Court on Aug. 13, 1945—two days before the surrender of Japan during World War II. He was accompanied by Seaman, designated as acting secretary of the committee.

The commissioners heard Hall's plea for funds for the committee's work, and approved a resolution allowing the committee to seek federal planning funds.

Then Hall's committee, on Nov. 26, 1945, approved a final draft of its recommendations. The committee made its final report to the Commissioners Court on Dec. 6, 1945.

The committee had considered many needed improvements for the county, but recommended only four immediately urgent projects. They were a new courthouse and jail; extensions of the Galveston and Texas City sea walls; additions of county roads and drainage systems; and the creation of a hospital on the Mainland of Galveston County.

Voters of the county, in bond elections, approved all of these projects. Many have been completed; and some never-completed public works undertakings, such as road and drainage systems, received a healthy boost.

The first road bonds, for $3.3 million, passed July 10, 1948.

A series of sea wall bonds was authorized, starting in 1951.

The new jail was built and the new courthouse erected in Galveston.

Work for the hospital for the Mainland—with the first bond issue approved in August, 1947—is particularly noteworthy.

Hall was asked to serve as chairman of a committee to promote the bond issue necessary to build the hospital at La Marque. Hall agreed, recalling that the tragic Texas City explosion in April, 1947, spotlighted the desperate need for a Mainland hospital. Hall reminded the voters that many severely injured persons died en route from Texas City to Galveston and undoubtedly lives could have been saved with prompt attention.

The bond issue passed, and the Galveston County Memorial Hospital was constructed and opened in September, 1952. It has been of great benefit to the county since that time. (It is now known as the Mainland Center Hospital.)

Hall also had a major role later in further development of the hospital. In 1959, when the rapid growth of the installation necessitated additional space and other improvements, he was asked to head a campaign to obtain voter approval for another bond issue.

As usual, he accepted—with the stipulation that the doctors of the area demonstrate their support of the hospital and the bond issue. The doctors responded with some financial help and with promotional material in their statements to patients supporting the bond issue.

In addition, a major public relations campaign followed, with Hall himself financing much of the cost of publicity and television, radio and newspaper advertising used in the campaign.

The bond issue for $2,500,000 was approved by the voters of Galveston County on Sept. 26, 1959.

Other than satisfaction for the realization that such a campaign is successful, Hall said, there are few personal benefits for such an effort.

However, he said, after this particular campaign he received a letter that he will never forget. It was from Bob Sullivan—now Dr. Robert E. Sullivan of La Marque—who wrote him a few weeks after the bond issue for the hospital was approved. The letter follows:

"This note is doubly belated.

"First of all I would like to thank you and your bank for the courteous treatment I received during my years as a medical student. You had loaned me money on several occasions, when Galveston banks refused to even consider my application.

"Believe me, this was and is appreciated.

"Secondly, thanks for taking time, effort and money to successfully push over our hospital bond campaign. I am glad that there are men in the community like you and your associates, who are willing to work to make this a better place to live."

Immediately after the passage of the bond issue, County Judge Ted Robinson, speaking for the county Commissioners Court, asked Hall to serve as president of the hospital board of directors.

Hall declined, on the grounds that he simply lacked the time to serve. The judge then asked Hall to recommend some other citizen for the position. To the surprise of many—including the citizen himself—Hall recommended John Richardson for the post. Richardson had been the leader of the opposition to the hospital bond issue, but accepted the nomination. Hall said that Richardson served very capably in the position for many years.

The Saibara Incident

Possibly nothing Walter Hall has ever accomplished or attempted to do for an individual exhibits more strikingly his respect and compassion for a fellow human being than did his efforts for Kiyoaki Saibara. Saibara was a Japanese colonist and a naturalized American citizen who lived in the Webster area.

Saibara came to the United States, perhaps under duress because his father, Seito Saibara, asked him to come.

The younger Saibara at the time, 1903, was an 18-year-old engineering student in Japan. The father, who had come to the United States in 1901, visited the Webster area two years later, liked what he saw, and leased and later purchased a 300-acre tract of land.

The father asked the son to bring his mother, grandparents, belongings and hired men to Texas, which the traditionally duty-bound son did.

Kiyoaki Saibara also brought with him a variety of superior Japanese native rice that proved to be more productive than the rice then growing in the United States.

Kiyoaki Saibara began farming with his father, and the younger Saibara, who became known as "Mr. K.," and his friends soon owned about 900 acres of farm land.

The father, Seito Saibara, died in 1939 at the age of 78—perhaps a blessing because it was only two years before the Japanese attack on Pearl Harbor.

That attack, on Dec. 7, 1941, had tremendous repercussions in Webster.

The FBI and Houston police, reacting to the terror which swept the country, arrested "Mr. K." Saibara and other Japanese and placed them in a detention camp in San Antonio.

When Hall learned of Saibara's plight, he immediately telephoned U.S. Sen. Tom Connally. Hall had campaigned for Connally in the last election, and it was, perhaps, the first time he had sought to use his political influence to gain a favor for a friend.

Saibara, Hall recalled, was released "rather promptly." Other Japanese seized in Webster were not as fortunate.

Walter Hall stands beside a mannequin dressed in the Japanese garment that once was worn by Kiyoaki Saibara to a formal ceremony with the emperor of Japan in Tokyo. Saibara presented the kimono to Hall as a token of his appreciation for Hall's help in freeing Saibara from imprisonment after Pearl Harbor. Hall presented the garment to the Bay Area Museum in Webster.

Several years after the end of World War II, Saibara was invited to Japan to be recognized for his efforts to re-establish warm relationships between the people of Japan and the people of the United States.

Saibara received the "Order of Sacred Treasure," the highest honor a non-citizen of Japan can receive.

At the ritual in Tokyo, Saibara wore a heavy, black silk kimono, a ceremonial garment, in his appearance before the emperor of Japan.

When "Mr. K." returned to the United States, Saibara presented the robe to Hall in appreciation for his work to correct what Hall considers a "terrible injustice."

To be certain that the injustice would not be forgotten, Hall had an artist re-design a male mannequin to look like a Japanese, placed the kimono on it, built a cabinet to house the mannequin and presented it to the Bay Area Museum in Webster. The museum is in the old building of the Webster Presbyterian Church, which Kiyoaki Saibara attended and where he and his wife were married.

Hall later observed that the treatment Saibara received when he was incarcerated after Pearl Harbor revealed to him the emotional attitude of U.S. citizens about other races for no reason other than that "they were of a different race."

Hall mentioned that Saibara had one son in the U.S. Army and one in the U.S. Air Corps. The latter son lost his life in a flying accident. The older son, Robert, after graduating from Texas A&M University, served as an officer in the U.S. Army. As part of the Nisei force in Italy during World War II, he and his troops played a major role with the 32nd Division, many of whom were from Texas. Robert Saibara retired from the Army as a lieutenant colonel.

The Tax Evaluation Program

In the course of making home loans, Walter Hall in about 1948 began noticing that there was a discrepancy in the tax program of Galveston County.

He discovered that GI and FHA home owners were paying county and state property taxes on the basis of 25 percent to 40 percent of the values of the homes; while at the same time most business properties, including the multimillion-dollar oil refineries and chemical plants of Texas City and some major properties in Galveston, were being taxed at from 5 percent to 12 percent of their fair value.

"When you handle GI or real estate loans," Hall explained to the Texas Observer, a weekly Austin political newspaper, "you come across information on taxes paid. Among GI homes which I knew were comparatively equal in value to each other, I found a wide discrepancy in assessed values. I was of course in a quandary as to why that was. I began a more or less casual investigation. The more I investigated the more convinced I was that there was simply no rhyme or reason in the assessed valuations—that there were wide discrepancies in every type of property.

"Anybody with any sense of justice couldn't tolerate that," Hall said in the interview in September, 1959.

Hall also noticed a few other things:

His Citizens State Bank in 1953 paid $1,262 in state and county taxes on $203,000 in capital, surplus and undivided profits; but the Galveston banking firm of W.L. Moody & Co., with a declared worth of $11,048,000, paid only $846 in taxes.

Hall realized, as a result of his earlier chairmanship of the Post-War Planning Committee, that Galveston County was desperately in need of money. Despite the fact that some bond funds had been voted for some of the improvements recommended by Hall's committee, Hall knew that there were simply inadequate funds in the hands of the county government to cover its basic needs. The reason, he concluded, was unequal, unfair and inadequate tax income.

Hall's observations led to what many believe is the greatest accomplishment of his career in banking, because it was of great service not only to his bank customers but also to every citizen in Galveston County.

He conceived a plan to remedy the tax situation for all of the county.

He said he went to the directors of the Citizens State Bank and asked them to approve necessary expenditures to start a campaign to reform the county tax rolls. He warned the directors that costs might run into many thousands of dollars, but argued that the bank had a duty not only to its customers but to its area. The directors backed him, and he hired George Byess, a Houston certified public accountant, to make a study of the county's tax rolls.

Ronnie Dugger, editor of the Texas Observer, reported the details of the involved negotiations after a conversation with Hall and two lawyers for the bank, Cecil Palmer of Dickinson and Ralph Crawford of Galveston. Dugger's story continued:.

"'When the results of our survey were revealed to our board of directors,' Hall said, 'they without exception took the position that not only in justice to our stockholders, but also because of the far larger thing that we owed a duty to the people who were banking with us, the people of this community, we should use the resources that were available to us to rectify the obvious inequities of the tax structure.'

"'We found properties valued at around 2 percent all the way up to 127 percent,' lawyer Crawford said. 'Those reports,' said Hall, 'did show a general condition of homes being taxed at from 25 to 40 percent of value, whereas business properties were being taxed at just a fraction of that—from 5 to 12 percent—of those amounts.'

"But Hall did not feel he was in a position to say whether the big industries were not pulling their weight, he says, 'because there was no accurate information as to what they were really worth.'

"'I set about doing what I could to find out who in Texas had a sufficiently large organization of sufficient skill and professional ability, and a background of experience and integrity,' Hall said. 'There was one that stood out above all others, and that was Pritchard & Abbott of Fort Worth.

"'My interest, then, was to have Galveston County enter into a proper contract with the best qualified firm to do this work.'

"Crawford said that Hall decided the average county valuation was about 15 percent of value, 'so Walter assessed his bank at 15 percent of value.'

"'It's supposed to be 100 percent,' Palmer remarked.

"The tax assessor refused to accept this value. In a hearing before the board of equalization, Palmer, Crawford and Hall 'raised a lot of hell,' Crawford recalls, but the board refused the valuation, too.

"Thereupon, said Palmer, the bank brought an injunction suit to enjoin the county judge and Commissioners Court from placing the bank's property on the delinquent rolls. The suit also contained a general charge against unfair and unequal taxation. 'We had the stage lighted and we walked into court.'

"After much disconcerted byplay the court granted the injunction against the county officials. 'They just finally folded up and accepted the taxes we offered,' Hall said. The three believed that the county did not want to have to defend against a lawsuit which asked for a court order that they equalize county taxes.

"The next year the bank reported only 10 percent of its true value. 'It was strictly ridiculous,' said Hall. 'Incidentally,' Palmer said, 'some of these other banks were getting kind of hot under the collar.' The lawyers prepared another lawsuit like the one of the year before. Obviously the county officials couldn't accept the 10 percent valuation, but they didn't want the lawsuit.

"What happened then must remain a subject of conjecture, but there is little doubt that the county politicians came around to Hall's plan.

"Crawford said it amounted to them telling Hall, 'Walter, if you'll not raise any more hell, and pay taxes the same as other banks, we assure you that we will have experts to revalue every piece of property in the county.'

"'Walter polled 'em just like polling a jury,' Crawford said of the county Commissioners Court. Each one of the five agreed. An official minute was entered committing the court to the program. The county assessor-collector, Johnny Oberndorfer, wrote the court a letter approving the program.

"Hall said the court was 'willing' in the matter. 'After different lawsuits and conferences and whatnot,' he said, 'the court did enter into a proper contract' with Pritchard & Abbott."

County records show that the county's contract with Pritchard & Abbott was dated April 18, 1955.

Another story in the Texas Observer backtracked to report some of the more revealing details of the fight:

"The findings (tax inequities) about the banks, and about the anarchy evidently prevailing in assessments—outraged Hall. In a Houston Press story he charged a 'rotten tax mess,' blamed the county commissioners, and determined on an 'expose of the whole filthy tax situation.' And he laid down his next line of argument: 'The main sufferers of the tax inequalities are the home-owners.'

"Fighting for attention then, Hall appeared before the county court (sitting as an equalization board) and protested the bank's assessment. In a radio interview afterward, he said:

"'It is the "little man" that is getting the rawest deal on tax assessments in this county. We have found cases where veterans who have recently purchased homes under GI loans are being assessed from 45 to 55 percent of what they paid for their homes, and of course this ratio is completely out of line with most assessments.'

"Asked why he was getting mixed up in such a fight, the banker replied to the radio interviewer:

"'The little folks are my kind of folks. Our bank's customers are, on the whole, little folks. We have watched them receive this mistreatment for years, and, frankly, we are fed up; and if it is within our power to help bring about the equalization of taxes in this county or contribute to that end, we are going all out to do it.

"'There is no other solution than to complete revaluation on tax values,' he said."

The Texas Observer concluded:

"Hall is enjoying the role of giant-killer, but he is anxious he not get too much credit.

"But for a county judge and county commissioners who stood behind Pritchard & Abbott's professional appraisals without a flinch, the program could have caused much more stir than it did or could have been sold out, he (Hall) says. Instead, the county officials backed P&A on every new valuation."

The county judge at the time was Theodore R. Robinson, and the county commissioners were Edwin Dantin, Jimmie Vacek, Bob Palmer and Jack Lawrence.

By 1959, then, Galveston County had completed what is probably the largest county revaluation program in the state's history, with every piece of property in the county reappraised "from scratch."

Hundreds of millions of dollars were added to the county tax rolls.

The values of about 98 percent of the GI and FHA homes in the county were decreased—most of them from about $600 to $1,000.

The values of large businesses were increased, many of them dramatically.

And the powerful Moody bank in Galveston began paying taxes on the same basis as the little Citizens State Bank in Dickinson.

"All we had on our side," Hall said, "was the law, the facts and the right.

"We have every reason to believe," he said at the time, "that the assessed values will be kept current, which is, of course, necessary if the program is to live. If this is done, these officials have rendered a great service to Galveston County not only for now but for years to come and, in addition, have set an example that may have far-reaching and greatly beneficial effects throughout Texas."

As events proved, Hall at that time was overly optimistic.

The Tax Program Setback

The death of County Judge Theodore (Ted) Robinson on Aug. 1, 1961, drastically changed the complexion of the tax evaluation program of Galveston County.

Walter Hall and one of his political friends, Al Grospiron, a leader in the Oil, Chemical and Atomic Workers Union at Texas City, disagreed over Robinson's successor.

Hall feared that one of the contenders, state Rep. Peter J. (Pete) LaValle, would not continue to support the tax assessment program.

Hall explained that LaValle had been elected by the liberals to the House of Representatives on the grounds that he was opposed to the sales tax. LaValle, however, Hall said, got himself appointed to the committee considering the sales tax and supported amendments introduced in committee favoring the tax.

When the bill got to the floor of the House, Hall said, and LaValle knew that his vote was not needed to assure passage of the bill, "He voted against the bill, thinking he could stand in our eyes as a strong opponent of the sales tax. So he lied to us."

The labor leader, Grospiron, told Hall, however, that he had LaValle's word that he wouldn't disturb the county's tax assessment program. So reluctantly, Hall said he withdrew his opposition to the appointment of Pete LaValle as county judge.

LaValle's appointment by the county Commissioners Court as county judge came on Aug. 8, 1961. LaValle was elected to his first full term on Nov. 6, 1962.

Hall's fears were justified.

"Very shortly after his appointment," Hall said, "Pete generated enough pressure on members of the Commissioners Court through use of various means—the details of which I, of course, don't know—so that the contract with Pritchard & Abbott for the equalization of taxes was not renewed."

County records reflect the fact that the contract with Pritchard & Abbott expired in April, 1962; and Judge LaValle, following conversations with John Richardson, a representative of the major industries of the county, recommended that the county hire Hugh Landrum to conduct industrial appraisals. Landrum, records indicate, negotiated an agreement for 55% lifetime value on the industries. Judge LaValle recommended the agreement and the county commissioners approved it.

Hall continued his story during a 1976 interview with Connie and Jim Simpson, conducted for an oral history project for the library of the College of the Mainland at Texas City:

"In view of the expansion going on in many parts of the county—principally in the Texas City industrial area—it was essential for those property assessments to be made fairly and kept current," Hall said.

"Of course, I was extremely disappointed that the tax equalization program was abandoned because county employees could not be fairly paid except with the orderly increase of county tax income. Many things that needed to be done could not be done except through this program. But nonetheless, it went out the window and...years followed when it was quite clear that the tax favoring of certain groups was keeping the county in bad financial trouble.

"Then, a young man from Texas City by the name of Ray Holbrook decided to run for county judge (in 1966) and I was convinced that conditions were such that a good man running a good campaign could be elected county judge in opposition to Pete LaValle."

Hall said that he was concerned because the day after he had promised Holbrook he would support him for the judgeship, a very good friend and an able attorney, Andy Baker, told Hall he would like to run for the office and asked for Hall's support.

"Nevertheless," Hall said, "I had pledged my support to Ray, and I could not renege on my pledge."

Hall's report of the campaign gives some idea of his involvement in the county election process.

"Of course," he was asked by the College of the Mainland questioners, "it is always difficult to hope to unseat an incumbent county judge, is it not?"

"Yes," Hall replied, "and Ray Holbrook was a comparatively unknown man. He was a graduate engineer and had made his living that way. He had also become an attorney but had only practiced law a short time. He gave me complete assurance that he would work hard and I knew where the little pockets of opposition to Pete LaValle were. I felt that Ray Holbrook could organize those into enough votes to give him victory. In the primary, Andy Baker was eliminated, and the runoff was between Pete and Ray." In the Democratic runoff election on June 4, 1966, Holbrook defeated LaValle: Holbrook, 10,889 votes, LaValle, 8,275 votes. Holbrook subsequently was elected in the general election with no opposition on Nov. 8, 1966, and took office on Jan. 1, 1967.

(Additional details of the Holbrook-LaValle campaign are included in Chapter 5.)

Under Judge Holbrook's leadership, the Commissioners Court adopted a new contract with Pritchard & Abbott on April 24, 1967.

For the benefit of the College of the Mainland interviewers, Hall answered a question he said he has been asked many times: Why would Walter Hall, a banker with extensive holdings, try to have property re-evaluated, knowing that this would probably result in an increase in his own taxes?

Hall's answer: "Really, I think the answer is very simple. A bank usually reflects the strength of the economy of the area. It is true it contributes to it in a substantial way, but if the basic economy of the area is weak, there is not apt to be too strong a bank there. For Galveston County to have reasonably good growth and people to have jobs in the area and to be able to have proper homes close to their work, it is necessary, in addition to good schools, to have county improvements—

primarily roads, the drainage of those roads, sea walls, hospitals, parks, proper protection through the Sheriff's Department and local constables, and all of the other services. I felt then, and I feel now, that the events have demonstrated clearly that progressive county government is good for all of us."

Possibly one of the greatest tributes to Hall and his work in the tax fight came from a staunchly conservative banker in Houston, Oscar Weyrich, at that time chairman of the board of the Houston Bank & Trust Co., whose letter Hall has in his files:

"...you must have delegated your bank work to someone else while you went in and cleaned up the tax mess...I wish you had one of your banks in Houston."

Ronnie Dugger, in what might be considered a "P.S." to the tax fight, wrote in the Texas Observer:

"The complexity of the tax tangle in Galveston County might have fazed a less tenacious or a less well-situated man than banker Walter Hall of Dickinson. But in two years he used the practical tools at his command—his bank's position as a taxpayer and its access to accountants and lawyers, his own status as a political figure, and his willingness to round-house county officials when they played cat-and-mouse with him—to convert a situation characterized by indifference and lack of firm information into a reform program greased and churning."

Service to Youth: School Reorganization

Walter Hall has been a major player for many decades in endeavors of finance and power politics. A casual observer thus might imagine that service to the youth of the community would be a minor consideration for such a financial giant.

Certainly this is not true in the case of Hall.

Many citizens in northern Galveston County and southeastern Harris County remember when four independent school districts, as separate entities, were struggling for quality. Those were League City, Kemah, Webster and Seabrook. Hall's determination, finances, and work at a critical time in 1948 were invaluable in gaining the creation of a single consolidated school district, now known as the Clear Creek Consolidated Independent School District—recognized as one of the finest in the state.

Hall, however, gives major credit for the creation of the Clear Creek district to two other area citizens, Gail Whitcomb Sr. and Haydn Ross.

Whitcomb, the father of Gail Whitcomb Jr., president of the Houston Chamber of Commerce in the 1960s, was president of the board of trustees of the Webster School District. Ross was president of the school board at League City.

The law at that time, Hall recalled, provided that a school district which had a minimum number of students was required to consolidate with another school district within a certain time or an adjoining district could absorb it.

Within its territory the Webster school district had the Webster-Friendswood oil field and also the Houston Lighting & Power Co. plant. Thus it had an extremely high average assessed valuation per student. On the other hand the League City, Kemah and Seabrook school districts were poor.

So here was this very rich school district of Webster which, because of its small number of students, was threatened with absorption by either South Houston or Pasadena.

So Whitcomb and Ross, Hall said, conceived the idea of a consolidated district by involving the four neighboring school districts.

"They had no trouble in Webster or League City," Hall said. "But they ran into some opposition in Seabrook and Kemah. That's where I came in. Ross came to me, explained the situation and asked for my help with Seabrook and Kemah. All I did was to hold two little meetings in Seabrook and one in Kemah."

Historically, the formation of the district is traced to a joint meeting of the boards of trustees of the independent school districts of League City, Webster and Seabrook on April 20, 1948. The trustees of the three districts voted to petition for elections within the three districts. The consolidation was approved by an almost unanimous vote. Kemah, at that time a common school district, voted to join the consolidation on July 7, 1948.

Hall also aided in converting the Dickinson Common School District to an independent school district.

He later had other major roles in the history of the Clear Creek schools.

Among the notable events was the $1,850,000 school bond election on Jan. 30, 1960. Many of the schools of the district were overcrowded and antiquated. Again Hall contributed money and manpower to publicize and promote the need for the bonds, which were approved by the district's voters.

In 1970, in recognition for Hall's dedication to education, he was the recipient of the "Red Apple Award" given by the Clear Creek Teachers Association.

Hall's help to youth extended beyond the school campuses. In 1980, Walter and Helen Hall donated to the county all of the land for the Paul Hopkins Community Park on Pine Drive (FM 518, between the Gulf

Freeway and the business district of Dickinson). Hopkins, a longtime friend of Hall, is a former county commissioner and later was a member and chairman of the Texas Water Commission.

The park has been beautified and is enjoyed daily by many children and other citizens of Dickinson.

Covered elsewhere are events leading to the naming of Walter G. Hall Park.

Even more recently, in March, 1993, Hall recognized the fact that between 400 and 500 Little Leaguers in 68 teams in League City had no practice field facilities.

Hall solved part of the problem.

He made available to the Little League 10 acres of land in front of his home for practice fields.

Walter Hall's neighbors decided that they did not want to wait until he died before they expressed their appreciation to him for his work for the youth of the community.

The board of the Clear Creek Independent School District named its new elementary school, in Hall's hometown of League City, the Walter Hall Elementary School. This was despite his protests that he thought it should be named for someone other than a live citizen.

In their decision to name the new school, members of the board cited Hall for his continued interest in the schools of the district, and also for his constant philosophy of promoting good education.

"I told the school board to name it after someone who was dead," Hall said. "That way they would never get criticized. But it does make me happy to know that I beat out John Wayne by a 3-to-1 vote."

The new $2.7 million school was dedicated May 18, 1980.

Dr. John F. Ward, Clear Creek superintendent of schools, served as master of ceremonies and Dr. Ned E. Dudney of League City, one of Hall's great friends and a director of his League City bank, delivered the dedicatory address. Music was provided by the Clear Creek High School Chorale and a choir composed of Hall Elementary School students.

Members of the Clear Creek Board of Education on the program were Dr. Dean Woodruff, who gave the benediction; board President Floyd Myers, who introduced other members of the board and special guests; James Larrabee, assistant superintendent of elementary education, who officially presented the building to the school principal, Jane Coomer.

The tremendous effect Walter Hall has had on education in general and students in the Walter Hall Elementary School in particular was emphasized three years later. A newspaper story written by Kathleen

Mayse, editor of the League City News, poignantly tells the story. The report, headlined "Happy Third Birthday, Walter Hall Elementary!" follows:

"When he was growing up League City was grassy, unfenced and open country; a person could drive a wagon from Alvin to League City and open only one gate; Kemah was the local swimming hole and Dickinson beat the local basketball team 79-2.

"But despite chores like milking cows and helping keep the family garden, young Walter Hall survived.

"'I thought my chores would be fatal and I've never been the same since, but I survived,' he said. And survive he did, to watch a sleepy little community turn into a booming, growing and thriving city.

"He also survived long enough to see a multi-million dollar elementary school named in his honor, and it was to those students at Walter Hall Elementary School that he spoke recently about the history of the community.

"The occasion was the third anniversary of the opening of Hall Elementary that was marked by birthday cake, bright decorations and a kite contest last week.

"The highlight of the anniversary celebration was a visit from the living legend himself, the man behind the name of the school, Walter Hall.

"Hushed whispers of 'Is that him?' could be heard from third and fourth graders as they filed into the library looking, pointing and guessing that this was the man.

"Unprepared for his wit and easy manner, the children were all prepared to be bored—this was going to be another speech from another adult. The fidgeting, the nudges, the conversations were typical of the age group.

"But when he spoke, they got quiet. And as he continued, they were still.

"He regaled them with stories of life before automobiles, times before cities and school 'before your grand daddies were born.'

"He recounted fishing stories, found a common bond with not liking chores as a child and had them spellbound with stories of banking during the Depression, going to school on a train, and numerous trips to the White House.

"But more than talk, he listened. He encouraged them to ask him anything and said he wasn't afraid to say he didn't know.

"So they asked. Everything from 'Do you really know how old you are?' to 'How many times did you visit the White House?' were covered in the two-hour visit. It was informal and informative, it was candid and refreshing. In the end, they gathered around Hall to take tips on flying a kite and to hear one more fishing story.

Walter Hall stands beside a plaque at the Walter Hall Elementary School in League City—a school named in his honor.

"They never really understood why this seemingly ordinary and grandfatherly person had a school named after him and they kept asking him why.

"Hall told them he had been surprised by the decision and had told the school board to name the school after someone who was no longer living.

"'There is nothing so dignified as a corpse,' he told the students, who apparently thought this Walter Hall wasn't solemn enough to have a school named after him.

"But the smile was unmistakable—he is glad the board didn't take his advice.

"'This is one of the finest schools in one of the finest school districts in the state,' Hall told the students. 'I'm proud of it and I'm proud of all of the fine facilities you have,' he added.

"Maybe they didn't understand why the smiling, witty man was a living legend and maybe they didn't understand life before NASA, and maybe they didn't know he was one of a handful of leaders who helped in the birth of the Clear Creek Independent School District.

"But they didn't care—they loved him anyway. And long after they have graduated from Hall Elementary and long after their children and even grandchildren have attended the school, they will know something.

"They will have known, touched and hugged a piece of history."

Aid for Rice University and Other Institutions

In honor of Radoslav A. Tsanoff, one of his Rice University professors of philosophy, Walter Hall and his wife, Helen, endowed, with a seven-figure sum, the Tsanoff Chair of Public Affairs at Rice's Jones School of Business Administration.

Hall said they endowed the chair not only from respect and appreciation of this "great teacher and philosopher, but with the hope that it would provide outstanding persons at Rice to promote interest in public affairs."

Among those who have occupied the chair are Covey Oliver, former U.S. undersecretary of state for Latin America; U.S. Ambassador (and former Texas Railroad Commissioner and former U.S. Sen.) Robert Krueger; former Texas Lt. Gov. Bill Hobby; and former Houston Mayor Kathy Whitmire.

Dr. Tsanoff's influence on Walter Hall's philosophy—and Hall's desire to "spread the gospel" as expressed by Dr. Tsanoff—lasted long after Walter Hall left Rice University as a student.

A speech delivered by Dr. Tsanoff at Rice University in 1953 has been widely distributed by Hall to many of his friends, associates, libraries, schools and the media. And it so attracted the attention of U.S. Sen. Ralph Yarborough of Texas that he introduced the speech on June 27, 1966, for inclusion in the Congressional Record. The speech was titled "Intellectual Freedom."

In his introductory remarks, Yarborough said:

"...Dr. Tsanoff stressed the importance of free inquiry, stating that 'Truth does not need police protection, but only support by adequate evidence.' He wants the individual professor to be able to explore all ideas without restriction.

"Perhaps the thought in Dr. Tsanoff's speech most relevant for us today is this:

"The principle of intellectual freedom applies in college teaching just as truly as it does in scientific or scholarly research. If ecclesiastic or civil authorities or well-organized factions in our society should succeed in forcing on teachers the obligation to teach certain definite ideas and to oppose certain other books, then the whole process of education would be compromised.

"No real training of young minds in the pursuit of truth would be possible if the students saw in their teachers men who were obliged to teach them the way they did, or otherwise they would lose their jobs and get into further trouble."

Yarborough's introduction to Tsanoff's speech included this foreword by Walter G. Hall:

"In this address before the Rice students the distinguished Dr. Tsanoff states brilliantly the case for Intellectual Freedom. His emphasis on the obligations which go with it are particularly timely as we see freedom assaulted under the guise of protection and its defense neglected through failure of appreciation of the duties it brings."

Hall said he greatly appreciates the conclusion of Dr. Tsanoff's speech:

"And if you want a short oath of loyalty to the spirit to which the true universities are dedicated, here is one...by Thomas Jefferson: 'I have sworn upon the altar of God eternal hostility against every form of tyranny over the mind of man.'"

Hall also has endowed the Walter and Helen Hall Lectureship in the Rice Sociology Department. Hall said in view of his contacts and friendship with that department's Dr. Chandler Davidson, he feels the contribution has enabled Davidson and others to deal with helping students understand the growing problems of society.

Among those who have lectured at Rice under this program are Liz Carpenter, author and former aide to Lady Bird Johnson; U.S. Rep. Bob Eckhardt; Ross Perot, businessman; Jim Hightower, former agriculture commissioner of Texas; Robert Maddox, executive director of the Americans United for the Separation of Church and State; Julius Chambers, executive director of the National Association for the Advancement of Colored People's Legal Defense Fund; Dr. James Q. Wilson, professor of the University of California at Los Angeles; and columnist Molly Ivins.

Hall also has been a benefactor to Rice's Shepherd School of Music. Dr. Michael Hammond, dean of the school, related this incident:

"In the spring of 1988 I spoke with Walter about his participation in our fund-raising efforts for Alice Pratt Brown Hall, the new home of the Shepherd School. He was eager to respond with a very generous gift that allowed us to honor him in a rather unique manner.

"The Shepherd School was about to acquire an historic Steinway concert grand piano that had been autographed by all the major artists of this century. Walter was fascinated by this instrument and its legacy in Steinway Hall, so President George Rupp and I thought it appropriate to name the piano in recognition of his building gift."

One newspaper writer exclaimed that the piano is one "whose keyboard has felt the touch of notables such as Artur Rubenstein and Vladimir Horowitz."

Hall also has made sizable contributions to Rice's Fondren Library (including his voluminous and historically valuable personal papers dating from 1923 to 1979); and many of his friends have contributed funds for the purchase of books for the library in Hall's name.

Rice University, however, is not the only institution of higher learning to receive the benefits of Walter Hall's benevolence.

Texas City attorney James P. Simpson, a member of the board of trustees of the College of the Mainland for 22 years, said that Hall was a major early contributor to the development and growth of that school. He has offered encouragement, advice and financial help, and aided in passing a bond issue for the creation of the school, Simpson said.

Dr. George M. Fleming, now a Houston consultant in hospital and health care administration, reported an unusual way in which Hall—with the help of a political friend—aided another area school.

"In 1964, as administrator of the county hospital, I called Mr. Walter Hall and asked him for his help," Dr. Fleming wrote. "The president of Alvin Junior College (now called Alvin Community College) had worked with me to develop an associate in science degree program in nursing in affiliation with Galveston County Memorial Hospital. This was the first associate's degree program in Texas approved by the State Board of Nursing Examiners as a direct result of community interest and resolve.

"The president of Alvin College brought me a letter from the State Board of Nursing Examiners advising that nursing was a profession and junior colleges were not to accept vocational education funds from the federal government in the future. I advised the Alvin College president that we would use this letter to educate the Board of Nursing Examiners. Mr. Hall had Sen. Ralph Yarborough notify the State Board of Nursing Examiners the federal government had supplied collegiate vocational programs since 1936. Also, Texas A&M had many college-level vocational programs in agriculture, medicine, mechanics and engineering that received federal support, and nursing was one of them."

The college had no further problem from the state board.

Hall also has provided support for the University of Texas Medical Branch in Galveston as well as the city's Rosenberg Library.

His most recent gift to the Rosenberg Library—in 1994—was money for a new computer system for library users which allows patrons to download information from the library files (such as a listing of books in print and information in a dictionary) onto their own personal discs. A unique feature of the sophisticated system is that more than one person can access the same information at the same time. And it is indexed in so many different ways that the user can access information faster than through a book.

In recognition of that gift, Hall was honored at a reception at the library in August, 1994.

Immediately after Hurricane Carla struck its disastrous blow at the Texas Gulf Coast in 1961, Walter Hall called Lyndon Johnson, then vice president, to suggest that he make an inspection tour of the Kemah area, which was devastated by the storm. Johnson, at the right, was greeted on his arrival at Ellington Field by U.S. Rep. Clark W. Thompson of Galveston, left, and Hall. Relief efforts were begun almost as quickly as Johnson returned to Washington.

Service to the Elderly

The elderly, too, whether rich or poor, have felt the friendly hand of Walter Hall.

"A few years ago," Hall recalled, "two of my black friends came separately to my office to ask me to help do something about the steps on the frame building they were using to receive free lunches for the elderly citizens in the program operated by the county.

"I sent two carpenters out to check the steps, and both told me the building was about to fall down and not worth new steps.

"The president of the Citizens State Bank at the time, Bob Holcomb, had an idea: He suggested giving the Senior Citizens Program a building on Highway 3, just north of the downtown area, that we had just acquired.

"I told him that was a great idea and that I would discuss it with County Judge Ray Holbrook.

"Holbrook agreed that if the bank would donate the land and the building, the county would renovate it, add a new roof and install heating and air-conditioning equipment.

"Then my family and I furnished the building.

"Now, to the high credit of the Galveston County Commissioners Court, the senior citizens have a nice place, have a hot meal daily, with transportation provided if needed. And after the meal is served, the men often spend the afternoons, enjoy fellowship or play dominoes. The ladies frequently spend the afternoons talking and sewing or working together on other common goals."

The food, Hall added, is prepared by a central county kitchen in La Marque and delivered to the senior citizens house in a "food wagon."

The center, operated under the auspices of the county's Senior Citizens Program, can serve 100 people nutritious lunches and also offers health screening.

Shortly before Christmas each year, Hall said, many women bring bedspreads, serapes and other objects they've made to the Citizens State Bank and place them on sale in the lobby. They usually are sold very promptly, he added.

"I don't know why," Hall said, "but I have a certain fondness for old folks."

Johnson Space Center

Many observers of the Texas Gulf Coast believe that Walter Hall's friendship with Lyndon B. Johnson had a great influence in bringing NASA's Manned Spacecraft Center (later named the Johnson Space Center) to this area. Hall denies this.

When several congressmen visited the Manned Spacecraft Center (later the Johnson Space Center) on March 5, 1965, Walter Hall sponsored a luncheon for a group that also included space center officials and astronauts. The group entering the dining room at Lakewood Yacht Club at Seabrook included, from left, U.S. Rep. George Miller of California, chairman of the House Science and Astronautics Committee; Dr. Robert Gilruth, director of the space center; Hall; U.S. Rep. Olin Teague of Bryan; and George M. Low, deputy director of the space center. Others at the luncheon included U.S. Rep. Bob Casey of Houston and astronaut Scott Carpenter. Hall told the group: "Nothing has ever happened here that has affected us in so many ways as this installation has. The people who have come to conduct it have brought quality to our communities, and reason to cause pride they are here."

Many residents also give him much credit for the massive economic growth of the Bayshore area as a result of the space center location.

Joe Henkel, president of First City Clear Lake Bank, told Steven Long, writer for the Houston Chronicle, that he thinks it was Hall who influenced LBJ to "bring the space industry to a prairie near Webster in the early '60s. If so, Hall was responsible, at least in part, for the tremendous economic growth that followed."

"He (Hall) denies being responsible for the Johnson Space Center being here," Long quoted Henkel as saying, "but he was a longtime friend of Lyndon Johnson, and you can't deny that."

Credence is gained for that view in the fact that in 1961, two days after Hurricane Carla raked the upper Texas coast, Hall urged then-Vice President Johnson to come to Texas. Johnson, U.S. Rep. Clark W. Thompson and Hall toured the damaged area.

A trio at the Nassau Bay Motor Hotel on May 5, 1967, discussed the progress of the nation's space program. The occasion was an appreciation party honoring Alan B. Shepard Jr., who made the first suborbital flight into space for the United States in 1961. Participants in the "miniconference" were, from the left, Mrs. Sue Hurley, wife of Marvin Hurley, executive vice president of the Houston Chamber of Commerce; Dr. Robert Gilruth, director of the space center; and Walter G. Hall.

Hall remembers the telephone call he made which resulted in the vice president's tour:

"I called Lyndon from the Lakewood Yacht Club at Seabrook, where the telephones were working two days after the hurricane. 'This area is devastated,' I told Lyndon. 'Kemah is washed clean.'

"'What do you think I ought to do?' Lyndon asked me, and I replied, 'You ought to get your a— down here.' I shouldn't have talked that way to the vice president, but I did."

This action resulted in the rapid establishment of government relief facilities that greatly lessened the losses and suffering caused by Carla. Walter and Helen Hall were honored by Kemah for their work in the community.

Hall described even earlier work for the Bayshore area, shortly after

Science, society and Walter Hall converged on NASA's space center on Oct. 12, 1966. The moment was recorded by this official NASA photo and reported in the caption: "Perle Mesta, famed Washington, D.C., hostess and close friend of numerous political notables, gets a briefing on an Apollo/Saturn V space vehicle model from Paul E. Purser, special assistant to the space center director, during a tour of the center. On right is Walter Hall, who accompanied Mrs. Mesta on the tour." Gossip columnists called Mrs. Mesta "the hostess with the mostest."

(NASA photograph)

World War II, for Houston Post reporter John Rainey in a 1962 interview:

"The people trying to develop the Bayshore area were considered wharf rats by many. I felt that the rapidly expanding population in Houston and along the coast would create a boom someday in the recreation business.

"I didn't consider it going out on a limb to help these people get started," Hall continued. "Some of the first loans in that area were no more than $100. And the same people who borrowed these small amounts are pretty well off today."

Concerning the location of the Manned Spacecraft Center in this area, Hall also gives great credit to another official—U.S. Rep. Albert Thomas of Houston—as well as Vice President Johnson.

Schwartz Defense for a Banker

The conversation at the Galveston cocktail party many years ago concerned a small-town banker.

"How does that piss-ant banker have so much influence?" asked the real estate agent. "Walter Hall acts like he runs the entire county."

"Oh, I don't know," replied the Island banker, "but he does have a lot of power."

A.R. (Babe) Schwartz, at that time a state senator from Galveston and a loyal friend of Hall, overheard the conversation and moved over to the pair.

"I'll tell you exactly where he gets his power," Schwartz said. "You consider the fact that he owns banks in Dickinson, Alvin, League City, Webster and Bay City, and add up the deposits in those banks, and you'll discover that he's the biggest banker in Galveston County.

"Additionally," Schwartz continued, "he gets some of his power because he gets things done. As a matter of fact, the water in that glass of scotch and water you're drinking is there because of Walter Hall. He forged a contract with the City of Houston when he was president of the San Jacinto River Authority to guarantee this city a desperately needed addition to its water supply."

Hall was—and is—very appreciative of that defense, because he considers Schwartz one of the most able state senators in Texas' history.

"Babe Schwartz is not only one of the ablest that I have ever seen, " Hall said "but the press has repeatedly labeled him as if not the ablest, one of the most able members either of the House or the Senate. The adversary newspapers have begrudgingly editorialized about him on many occasions that while they disagreed with him, his ability and integrity were beyond criticism. He has been in the minority most of the time in Austin and yet his effectiveness has been very, very great. It is hard to understand how a man in the minority could be as effective as he has been."

Service to His Own Profession

Walter Hall, of course, has not been a "do-gooder" only for his favorite politicians, political causes, government reform and community activities: His profession has not been neglected. He has acted when he thought action was advisable. He has been a "mover and a shaker" when he thought a mountain needed moving.

He has served as an official in several professional banking organizations, as detailed elsewhere.

One of the most notable examples of Hall's leadership and effectiveness among his peers came in the early 1960s, when Hall and other Texas bankers felt that tax inequities that burdened state banks should be addressed.

At that time, the State of Texas was collecting franchise taxes and sales taxes from state banks. This created an unfair advantage in the state for national banks, since the franchise taxes and sales taxes were not applicable to national banks under federal law at that time.

Hall was among a group of almost 40 independent state bankers who met in Austin on June 27, 1962, at the Villa Capri Motor Hotel to discuss their problems.

Among the leaders of the meeting was J.M. Faulkner, banking commissioner of Texas, who was a longtime friend of Hall and who understood thoroughly the problems of the state banks. It is probable that Falkner and Hall had discussed the problems on one of their fishing trips near Galveston.

The group at the Austin session decided to organize a permanent association of state-chartered banks. P.B. Garrett of Dallas was named temporary chairman, Sam 0. Kimberlin Jr. of Austin was designated as secretary and Hall was named to the steering committee.

Later that year the Association of State Chartered Banks in Texas was formally organized. Hall was represented on the board of governors by L.B. Manry, executive vice president of the Alvin State Bank, which Hall owned at the time.

Hall credits Kimberlin with much of the success of the organization in accomplishing most of its goals, primarily through passage of about 20 bills by the 58th Texas Legislature at its regular session in 1963.

In 1964 the Association of State Chartered Banks in effect was merged into the Texas Bankers Association, and Kimberlin became executive vice president and chief executive officer of that organization.

Kimberlin has told Hall that the Dickinson banker had a "paramount role" in getting the legislation passed.

Kimberlin wrote the following to Hall:

"Without your support and contacts with members of the Legislature who considered you to be not only their banker but also their counselor on banking matters, I doubt that we could have gotten H.B.16 passed. I remember Bill Heatley (chairman of the House Appropriations Committee)... wanted to hold up the bill, but your legislative friends, along with others who were not in the so-called establishment group, gleefully ran over his objections."

And Kimberlin added:

"I have never had more fun than calling you to call a member on a certain point, then sitting back and watching the light of understanding illuminate his actions after your call...You were the most effective banker-lobbyist I have ever known."

A Record-Setting Party

Social events always have been an important part in the banking history of Galveston County, although not widely publicized.

However, a social party sponsored by Walter Hall, in contrast to parties of many other banks, usually had a community objective for its purpose.

For example, for many years Hall's home in League City was the site of an annual reception for members of the volunteer fire departments of the communities served by his banks and insurance agencies.

Then the sports communities occasionally were invited to parties at the Lakewood Yacht Club in Seabrook, at which football coaches from some of the Southwest Conference schools were invited to speak, exchange barbs and meet with Hall's other guests.

New teachers of the community also were beneficiaries of Hall's welcome and hospitality.

Such parties did not always have noble conclusions, although Hall personally could not foresee the end results.

One party in particular was a record-setter, one which astounded even the host.

Later, Hall might have recalled a story written by Galveston banker I.H. Kempner, in his 1961 book, "Recalled Recollections." Kempner wrote that in 1937 he hosted a party at his home for press representatives who accompanied Franklin D. Roosevelt to Galveston. FDR was on a fishing trip to the Texas Gulf Coast.

"We gave these correspondents a garden party at our home," Kempner wrote, "where Hennie (his wife) personally mixed over one hundred mint juleps."

That party, it seems, was a piker compared to Hall's "record-setter."

One of Hall's staff members had been elected president of the Press Club of Galveston County in the 1950s; Hall apparently was impressed, and suggested that an installation banquet be held at the Lakewood Yacht Club, with Hall serving as the host.

Accordingly, members of the media not only in Galveston County but those in Houston as well were invited. They accepted in great numbers and appreciated the free food and booze provided by host Hall. More than 300 "media-type" citizens and their spouses attended.

The following day Hall called in the new Press Club president and demanded: "What in the world happened? For the first time in the history of the Lakewood Yacht Club, the bar bill was larger than the food bill."

He is still awaiting an answer.

Directors of the Citizens State Bank honored a longtime employee of the bank, Alice Saunders, when she retired in April, 1988. Seated, she is flanked by Walter G. Hall, left, and Dr. Amedeo A. Magliolo. Other directors are standing, from the left, Charles E. Yoes, John T. Creden, Charles L. Hutchins, William Hardy Davis, Darvin M. Winick, Robert V. Holley, Charles F. Hall, Madeleine Rogers and R.D. Holcomb.

Chapter 4:

Walter Hall's Philosophy

Capsule Quotations of Walter G. Hall

"I (have been) regarded by the 'establishment'...as something of a liberal when they were kind, a radical when they were irritated, and a communist when they were mad as hell, none of which bothered me in the least."

"I have been called a liberal and I suppose by some measure I am. This is because I know that change is inevitable, and orderly change is the most desirable kind."

"Democracy is a sensitive form of government—it must be nurtured and protected by the people it benefits."

"Democracy has only just started on what it can do for the masses."

"Our democratic society will succeed to the degree that those in it discharge their responsibilities, which are in direct ratio to their capabilities."

"After decades of handling other people's money, I feel I have taken a 'pragmatic' approach to problem-solving that includes reviewing all the facts and taking action."

"A bank prospers only in relation to the prosperity of its customers. You can play a part by extending credit as best you know how. When you see kids go off to college because of a loan or you see a business grow, you know you've helped. If you would take that sort of thing out of banking, it would be a sorry business."

"When a nation spends a large part of its productivity for non-productive things, such as war or war machines, either the products are used in a non-profitable effort or they become obsolete. The country is poorer as a result. It is, of course, obvious that our nation must remain strong, but not without necessary limits and not to the extent that the military industry has great influence on the nation's affairs."

"Like the six-shooter was for the little man in the movement West, the atomic bomb is now the equalizer of little nations."

"The big trend is toward concentration of funds into too few hands.

Many of these large money-center banks make high-interest loans abroad which means that money is not available to American consumers and small businesses when they need it, and when loans made by such big banks go 'sour' they seek help from the International Money Fund and the American taxpayers through the U.S. Treasury. Of course, as long as local banks provide good aggressive service, there will be a place for them in the banking industry."

"I don't think I would have fit in a big city. I've always been a non-conformist. And there's no place for a subordinate (and that's what I'd have been) to go contrary to the rules of a big bank. When you're bull-headed, opinionated and cocky, you shouldn't be working for somebody else. At least I know my many failings and try to keep them subdued."

"I don't brood over defeats and I don't exult over victories. And I can't stay mad after a fight."

"The trust and the kindness that the people of this area have shown to me and my family are gratifying and I have always tried to do what I feel is right."

Quick Explanation of Hall's Philosophy

Walter Hall has explained the development of his banking philosophy and practices in this most uncomplicated way:

"My idea of sound banking started in 1931 in a very, very small bank. I was brand new to banking. I had received a little education in economics, but not much.

"Quickly I learned that no matter what else happened, if a borrower was absolutely honest, and continued to work hard in one way or another, be it in a profession, or business, or farming, the bank's chances of repayment were excellent.

"There was no way that a bank could 'win,' shall we say, dealing with people whose honesty was questionable. I observed that from some of my friendly banker friends, who were very much disappointed when some of their customers had not been true to their pledges.

"So early on I learned that a customer, whether he was a doctor, or dentist, farmer, shopkeeper or whatever, if he was honest, if we would 'hang in there' with him, through good times and bad, the chances were that we would recover our money.

"That was what we did and that was what proved successful."

Hall's 'Mixture' of Banking and Politics

Walter G. Hall has a quick explanation for his mixture of conservative banking and liberal politics, and his statement has been quoted often in newspaper and magazine stories:

"I am a citizen first and a banker second."

Bankers, Hall explains, serve the public trust; they are custodians only of the public's money. Therefore, he believes, they have a moral responsibility not to gamble with their banks' deposits.

"In banking," Hall said, "the basic principle seems to me to be when depositors are kind enough to leave their money with you, you as a banker are actively in a trust or fiduciary capacity, and their funds should be handled with safety and availability. That should be the first consideration.

"What one does with his or her personal funds is not here considered, but when caring for funds of others there can be no appropriate substitute for safety and availability."

One rule of thumb that Hall adopted early in his banking career is that lending should be based on cash flow, not security (assets).

"We want to get paid; we don't want to sell property," Hall explains.

Hall believes too many banks in Texas failed to remember this rule of lending and were saddled with heavily discounted real estate when agriculture and oil prices collapsed in the 1980s.

Another time-honored principle of Hall's banks which has earned him and his banks customers and friends is to lend locally and invest primarily in the immediate area of the banks.

Hall tells those who are puzzled by his success in business and activity in political matters that he simply does not mix the two. He says he tries to show others the respect for their ideas and opinions that he hopes to receive for himself. Many who have differed with him politically also have been his business associates.

Media Writers Discuss Hall

Stories in four publications—Houston Business Journal, Bankers Monthly magazine, the Houston Chronicle and The Houston Post—clearly and succinctly define Hall's philosophy and political beliefs.

The interpretations of interviews with Hall also offer interesting perspectives of the banker's personality.

With some repetition, excerpts and some complete quotations from these stories follow:

Houston Business Journal:

"...an atypical banker."

"Hall's political views run liberal in a traditionally conservative field of Texas bankers. And Hall has been happy to remain an independent banker outside of holding company-intensive Houston.

"He has also been able to turn a profit as a small bank owner in a less than desirable economy."

Hall was asked by the writer, Jim Greer, to compare or contrast the recent financial industry failures and the crash that began more than 50 years ago. The newspaper recorded these thoughts of Hall at the time—1989:

"I'm one of the few who was around for both. With the great market collapse of '29 we had no deposit insurance and people lost confidence in their banking. The industry cannot stand runs—it's just fundamental. Business generally was in a chaotic situation. Banks were afraid to lend and businesses were going broke, some of them because they couldn't get reasonable credit.

"The market collapsed because smart buyers began to realize that the country was inflated, in one sense of the word. It was overbought and overinvested. But at that time, we had two good things that we don't have now. We had all the oil we needed. We were not a captive to the Middle East or any other group of foreign oil producers. Also, we didn't have to go to Japan or Germany or any place else. We had enough capital in our own country to capitalize and finance our reconstruction."

Asked which factors will help the country in the midst of these current problems, Hall replied, "Now we have Social Security. We have the FDIC (Federal Deposit Insurance Corp.). People have not lost confidence, generally, in the banking industry."

Hall also pinpointed the difference between the banking industry when he started and that of today, and said, "In many, many cases the ownership and control of the banks stayed in the major cities and towns. Right now, there's not a major holding company in Texas that is controlled in Texas. The big five are controlled elsewhere."

Hall emphasized that he has never been impressed with the idea that bigness is goodness.

"I never was enchanted with organizing a holding company and getting to be big," he said. "I had no ambition in that direction."

He admitted at least one shortcoming: "We were never smart enough to foresee the collapse of oil prices."

Explaining how his banks stayed afloat despite many regional problems, Hall again emphasized his basic philosophy: "A very, very important aspect of credit is cash flow. We are concerned with a high degree of liquidity and a high degree of equity in our bank operations. In making loans, we want cash flow. That means we have to operate at reduced profits in tough times. But that's OK, because we think when people have money in a bank they ought not to have to depend on the FDIC."

Bankers Monthly magazine:

"A champion of conservative banking and liberal politics."

"A New Deal Democrat who thinks deregulation stinks."

"A successful banker who made his profits by thinking small and reinvesting in the communities of Dickinson, Webster, and League City. His example might be a good one for beleaguered banks in Texas and elsewhere to follow."

In a story in the October, 1989, issue of the bank magazine, writer Tim Loughran captured Hall's philosophy of both banking and politics in a few pithy paragraphs:

"Hall's banking and personal philosophy was born during the New Deal. He champions a compassionate government that will protect the common man and his modest American dream...

"Almost a traitor to the modern thinking of fellow bankers, Hall favors an excess corporate profits tax and the termination of deregulated interest rates.

"He scorns those who worship at the shrine of bigness..."

Concerning deregulation, the magazine reported: "Hall says that if deregulation hadn't clouded bankers' traditional conservative judgment—and a Republican administration hadn't encouraged it—the nation's financial system wouldn't be in the multibillion-dollar mess it is today. Banking is the only business where you're using other people's money. It seems clear as a bell it ought to be regulated...You can't separate greed from handling of money; that's why you need regulation.

"Hall's traditional views on bank lending and deregulation," the magazine continued, "are accompanied by a further recommendation about how the (government) might be able to rehabilitate the nation's weakened banking sector. Hall suggests a revival of the Reconstruction Finance Corporation (RFC) which bought bank debentures from ailing banks to restore their capital. The RFC was instituted (sic—See parenthetical material below) as part of FDR's campaign to revitalize and restore public confidence in the nation's banks after the 1933 banking crisis.

"Hall suggests that the same stringent requirements of the original RFC be applied today. He suggests that RFC-like debentures would reassert a healthy control over local banks, returning smalltown efficiency, restoring smalltown responsibility of bankers to their customers—a standard that has been forgotten in recent years and perhaps should be remembered in years to come."

(Clarifying both a historical reference and his remarks, Hall later said: "The RFC was formed by Herbert Hoover, not FDR, but FDR did expand it and it became more effective. It was of great benefit and in the nation's best interest because many big firms, just as little firms and individuals, needed help. The RFC also cooperated with the FDIC in many ways in dealing with making the banks stronger after the 'holiday.' The RFC has in the last several years been replaced by the FDIC and the National Banking Department and at all times the requirements should be 'what is in the best interest of the public, the depositors, and then the banks.' The present tendency has been for the regulators, the FDIC and the national bank regulators, to practically force banks, particularly small banks, to merge rather than supplying temporary funds through secondary stock and loans, which permitted many, many banks to survive following the great banking 'mess' which came to a head in 1933. One of the great benefits of the measures of the RFC in the '30s was that many banks earned out of their loan position, and ownership or control remained local. The U.S. government's policy gave birth to the true comment: Banks are too big to fail.")

. . .

Steven Long, writing in the Houston Chronicle's Texas Magazine edition of March 26, 1989, said of Walter Hall:

"He's a survivor and not just as a banker. One of the few remaining political kingmakers from the heyday of the once all-powerful Democratic Party in Texas, Hall is a diehard Democrat, a man who might have been governor once, and one who can claim among his departed friends the likes of Sam Rayburn and Lyndon B. Johnson.

"The Dickinson banker has outlived many of his political enemies and banking associates from the past. What's remarkable is that he has managed to do so by practicing an unusual combination of conservative banking and liberal politics for the last 50 years..."

"...perhaps the most telling symbol of Hall's success—given the sad state of the banking and thrift industry in Texas—is that his banks have weathered the current financial storm so well."

Long also called Hall "a keen observer of Texas' economic problems, particularly bank failures."

Long wrote:

"'So many other banks in this area and many parts of Texas participated in oil and gas and agricultural loans through participations, which means participating in loans by obtaining a portion of a loan made by banks in other areas,' he (Hall) said.

"'The other factor that has to be recognized is that many banks were so anxious to have growth and profits that they perhaps paid too little attention to soundness and liquidity in general and too little to cash flow of the loan applicants. We learned that sound cash flow is equal to, or in many cases more important than, collateral.'"

The Citizens State Bank always has included what are believed to be the strongest and most conscientious group of officers available. Present officers include those in this photo taken in early 1994. Standing, from the left, are Charles F. (Chuck) Hall Jr., secretary of the board; R.C. Green Jr., senior vice president; Frances Carter, administrative assistant; H.C. Lewis Jr., vice president; Walter G. Hall, chairman of the board; Madeleine Rogers, vice president and auditor; Ronald C. Lemon, president; Michael K. Richardson, executive vice president; Ron Trail, Bacliff Branch manager; Clint Karm, West Side Branch manager; Charles E. Yoes, executive vice president and cashier; and Miranda L. Sandstrum, operations officer. Seated, from the left, are Barbara Liefert, trust officer; Gwen Neugent, vice president; Vicki Stumpenhaus, personnel officer; and Stella Coffman, assistant auditor.

Long quoted a banking competitor, Joe Henkel, president of First City Clear Lake: "I respect him. He's an excellent banker, and a tremendous citizen of this area. He's survived for a number of years because he's avoided the extremes. Overall, he's been a high quality survivor, and a bank can't do its job unless it is making money. He hasn't sucked all of the profits out of the bank to pay himself dividends. He's kept the money in the bank."

"That's Hall the banker," wrote Long, "—savvy yet prudent, possessing a comfortable blend of old-fashioned common sense and conservative fiscal responsibility. But the other side of Walter Hall bears a different stripe—Hall the political activist, the dogged, unbowed supporter of liberal Democratic leaders in Texas."

John Rainey of The Houston Post observed that Hall "has broken the so-called cardinal rules of banking, has become the image of a man most bankers refuse to be—and he's still solvent."

"This has confused his financial and political opponents no end. They can't figure out how he manages to remain solvent."

"Some bankers laugh at me for making small loans of $50 and $60," Hall told Rainey in a 1962 interview. "Yet, I know when people need money in a country town they have no other place to go. Loan sharks have tried to move into the towns where my banks are, but they don't stay long."

Hall also discussed with Rainey his views concerning his involvement in politics that were captured in this portion of the interview:

"People, especially businessmen, can't understand why I should be so interested and also mixed up in this business of politics.

"I do not consider myself a politician at all. We approach all problems through some political unit, generally. I like to see the efforts of meeting changing problems made by applying reason and using the best information possible.

"All of us—the busy businessman included—should see that tax money is spent efficiently and for the things the taxpayers want it spent. That there may be some penalty risk by businessmen participating in politics as I do, I do not question...But I do know a man is or at least should be, a citizen first, and a banker, engineer, farmer, or whatever, second.

"I respect politicians because I realize we cannot have a democracy without them. While democracy may have its defects, it is so far superior to anything yet devised that to me there is no alternative.

"I have been called a liberal and I suppose by some measures I am. This is because I know that change is inevitable and that orderly change is the most desirable kind. I do not fear change and it wouldn't mattter if I did because it would still be with us—and I would have to meet it.

"It is my feeling that all citizens should take an informed interest and have some participation in politics. I believe good government is almost in direct ratio to the percentage of people engaging in it as voters and in political activities.

"People scream about the federal government invading the states, taking away states rights. While I do not regard the federal government as some sort of enemy as do some folks, I do not think it is good, in a state with the basic wealth of Texas, to have development of these resources depend upon federal financing.

"I think it is a poor trade to exchange some degree of state control for federal dollars.

"Yet, we have seen, countless times, people who constantly criticize federal taxes and expenditures go all out for federal aid to finance state projects. In some cases this is necessary—it is not in Texas. And yet, there is nothing now to cause anyone to believe there is any basic change in sight."

Rainey also offered these observations about Hall: "Hall does not demand that others listen to his opinions, only that others be tolerant of them.

"His politics is not a company policy, he once observed, and mentioned that his secretary at that time was a Republican.

"Those who differ with him rarely become bitter over the differences.

"He likes to have ideas on problems come out in full play, regardless of their nature. He likes to philosophize and mix economics with the philosophy.

"One of his friends sums him up this way: 'He has listened to the small because he considers them important. But the listening has not made him small. If he has a banner, it is one of individualism. He carries it high. It is, though, the kind of higher individualism that grows out of looking for meanings in the human drama.'

"He is still a country boy at heart. He knows the people in his area personally."

Leon Hale Discusses Walter Hall

Leon Hale, one of the premier writers of the nation, elicited, and superbly reported, details of some of Walter Hall's philosophy as a result of a conversation the writer had with Hall in 1970.

Hale, now a columnist for the Houston Chronicle, at that time was a columnist for The Houston Post, and his column appeared in the Post on Sept. 25, 1970. Permission to reprint the column was obtained from Leon Hale.

The column follows:

"Politicking Texas banker

"A damp day at Seabrook. Early afternoon. Walter Hall sat in the dining room of a yacht club on Clear Lake, eating filet of redfish and talking. About hurricanes and mules. About jacks and jennies and stud horses and bulls. And politics. Mostly politics.

"Hall is what Texans call a country banker. But he doesn't look like one or sound like one, even when he talks about bulls. He's all tanned and trim and still full of scat in his mid-60s. Speaks fast. Moves quick. If I'd never met him, if I saw him scooting along the street I'd think, well, there goes a fellow who once played halfback at college and married the head cheer leader and now coaches the varsity.

"Instead, Walter Hall owns five banks. Or at least he owns controlling interest in five. At Dickinson, League City, Alvin, Webster and Bay City. Total assets, $90 million.

"Which makes him wealthy but it doesn't make him unique. What makes Hall a curiosity among bankers is that he is so openly involved in politics. If there's a race in his vicinity, Hall is apt to enter it, whether it's a presidential campaign or some free-swinging, over-heated local election. He goes forth and stumps for his candidate, runs the race right out there in the sun where everybody can see him, and nobody has to wonder which side he's on, for crying out loud.

"So naturally you ask him, whether this hurts his bank business.

"'I don't know,' he said. 'How's a man going to tell? One of those Houston bankers asked me not long ago, "How can you afford to get involved in those controversial local elections? It's not good for banking." Well, I don't see how I can afford to stay out of politics. It's too important. These men we elect, they make our laws, they levy taxes, they do so much that controls our lives. I can't stay away from politics.

"'I insist on being a citizen first and a banker second. And I'll make this clear—I'm not at all sure that's very smart. If I hadn't gotten into politics, maybe I'd have 10 banks instead of five, with assets of $150 million instead of $90 million. But I can't eat more than three meals a day and I'm eating too much already.

"'Sometimes I talk to these young businessmen in small towns. I don't know anything about the big cities. I've never been there. But I tell these young men that if their main concern is achieving the highest possible success in business, then maybe they ought to stay out of politics.'

"What he's saying, you know, is that a man in a vulnerable financial position can get hurt in politics. He's also saying Walter Hall just doesn't worry about that, because he was dang well financially secure when he began jumping into political battles.

"'It would take a pretty big operator to cut me,' he said, which may be the plainest sentence I ever heard out of a banker.

"Some of the little stories Hall told over that redfish provide a hint of the reluctance many bankers have to stand up and be counted in politics. He'll be at a bankers convention, Hall said, and a banker will come up and hand him a check and say, 'Use this for Ralph, but don't say anything about it.'

The board of directors of the Citizens State Bank represents not only a cross-section of the area, but the business leaders who represent the strength and character which have made Dickinson a near-model community. This photo of present directors was taken in early 1994. Seated, from the left, are Ronald C. Lemon, bank president; Madeleine Rogers, bank vice president and auditor; William Hardy Davis, banker; Walter G. Hall, chairman of the board; Darvin M. Winick, management consultant; Robert D. Holcomb, retired banker; and Michael K. Richardson, bank executive vice president. Standing, from left, are Charles E. Yoes, bank executive vice president and cashier; Charles F. Hall, insurance executive; Charles F. (Chuck) Hall Jr., bank executive; Charles L. Hutchins, industrialist; and Robert B. Holley, pharmacist.

"Hall is a down-the-line Democrat. A liberal, he says, by Texas standards. He's an FDR man and an HST man and an LBJ man. An Adlai Stevenson and a Hubert Humphrey man. And a Ralph Yarborough man. He's one of The Faithful. He goes out to The Ranch sometimes. He's a personal friend of The Rancher.

"I suppose a liberal Democrat banker is anyway a mild rarity. It's always seemed clear that most bankers have conservative, Republican tendencies. Isn't that right, Mr. Hall, at least in the big cities?

"'Yes,' he said, 'and most of them in the small towns are the same way. I think it's just because they like to equate themselves with all those big shots.' Hoo boy.

"Other Hallisms I remember:

"'I can't stay mad after a fight. It's a waste of energy.'

"'I've lost plenty of battles. I'm the world's greatest authority on losing.'

"'I've never supported him (this about several politicians) but he's a close personal friend.'

"Then this, how about this: A banker who can gig and then laugh when he's gigged back? Hall told me how the Austin attorney Ed Clark once introduced him at a banquet as 'a country banker who's just as honest as present conditions will permit.'"

Dismantling of a Gambling Empire

An outstanding example of Walter Hall's belief that principles as well as profits should have a leading role in banking is related by James P. Simpson.

Simpson is a highly-respected Texas City labor and personal injury attorney. He gained fame during Texas Attorney General Will Wilson's successful efforts to rid Galveston of gambling in the 1950s. Simpson became a disciple of Hall when he was a young attorney on the staff of Cecil J. Palmer's law office in Dickinson. Palmer was the lawyer for Citizens State Bank.

Simpson had been a special agent for the Federal Bureau of Investigation in Minneapolis, Minn., for two years and decided in 1952 to return to Texas—where he had received his law degree from the University of Texas at Austin—to practice law.

"It was then that I first became completely aware of the pervasive nature of the criminal underworld in Galveston County," Simpson said. "I made up my mind that I was going to do something about the rackets while I was still young."

It was then that Simpson decided to run for district attorney of Galveston County.

"I knew that Walter Hall had long held disgust for the corrupting influence of the rackets," Simpson continued. "With Walter and with me, it wasn't necessarily a moral thing. I've always believed that what folks want to do with their money and their time pretty well comes under the heading of their business. But when it gets to the point where it's corrupting local law enforcement and in fact corrupting statewide politics, then it did come under the head of my business.

"You simply cannot operate a widespread criminal syndicate without the help of the district attorney, the sheriff, the Texas Rangers, the state attorney general and the governor. Unless you've got their consent, you simply cannot survive. And so when you look about you and you see that there are as high as a hundred illegally operated establishments here within the confines of the county, then you know that somebody is bound to be getting paid off.

"When (public officials) become the advocates of the criminal underworld, they cease to be the advocates of those of us who come under the Declaration of Independence where it says 'We the people.'

"Things had gotten to where we had government of the Maceos, by the Maceos and for the Maceos.

"Of course the Maceos were not the only racketeers in Galveston County," Simpson said.

"There was a nest of them in Dickinson and other places—(including) Texas City. They pervaded almost all of Galveston County. Kemah had a large nest of them.

"This was frankly offensive to me, and I knew Walter shared that.

"Walter is the most devout advocate I know of democracy. And he knows that those kinds of conditions cannot coexist with the democratic form of government."

Simpson said that when he first announced that he was running for district attorney (called the county attorney at that time) in 1954, he made it very plain that his mission was to shut down the rackets and stick the racketeers in the penitentiary.

"Running a campaign then and now is an expensive proposition. And Walter made...the heaviest contribution I ever received, I believe, in that race as soon as he learned I was running."

Simpson said the interesting thing about the campaign was that it was widely known in Dickinson and around the county that he and Walter Hall were good friends, although Simpson was much younger than Hall.

"But we both were hard-rock liberal Democrats. We both had supported Adlai Stevenson; and before me, Walter had supported every progressive, fundamentally decent, honest person that ever ran for office within his bailiwick. He had supported Jimmy Allred for governor and later supported Ralph Yarborough for governor.

"So it was well known that Walter and I were good friends; so some of the racketeers started saying that the way to get me out of the race was to go through Walter Hall...

"So the racketeers went to Walter and told him, 'That young guy is messing in our business. We don't think he can win, but meanwhile he's giving us a lot of hell and a lot of bad publicity.'"

Hall, of course, refused the request to try to convince Simpson to quit the race. Then, Simpson said, one of the main racketeers, who for years had been a heavy depositor in the Citizens State Bank, went to Hall and tried to get tough. He told Hall that if he didn't "get Jim Simpson out of the race" he would withdraw his funds from the Citizens State Bank. Hall again refused.

As a result, Simpson said, the racketeer withdrew $60,000—"a pretty good chunk of money in 1954 for a country bank"—and deposited it elsewhere.

"Walter just wasn't going to give in to blackmail," Simpson said.

"This illustrates the granite, hard-rock integrity of Walter Hall.

"One of the first lessons he offered to me—I love to talk with him and learn from him—was this: 'If you've got to choose between a fellow's friendship and his respect, take his respect. Because ultimately you may gain his friendship.'

"Walter practiced this," Simpson continued. "He knew he had to have the respect of people. This integrity of Walter and his bank (has been) important to his success. So he wasn't going to be blackmailed."

Several years later, Simpson said—a fact confirmed by Hall—the gambler returned to the Citizens State Bank and did business with the bank until his death.

Simpson lost that election in 1954, in a runoff with Galveston attorney Marsene Johnson, by eight votes—the smallest margin of votes in the county's history. Because he was only 30 years old, Simpson had planned to run again in 1956. The need to support his family with his law practice changed his mind, but he was determined to continue his fight against the syndicate.

When Will Wilson was elected state attorney general in 1956 (and assumed office in 1957), Simpson saw his opportunity and devised the plan that ended the gambling era in Galveston County. Wilson agreed to Simpson's plan: Secretly gather evidence against the gambling establishments and secure temporary restraining orders. Through this civil injunction process, after seven months' undercover work, 62 gambling establishments and bawdy houses were closed.

During the time Simpson and his two aides—James (Buddy) Givens and Carroll Yaws—were working, only those three and Attorney General Wilson knew of the plans.

"The work was totally secret," Simpson said.

"Once it became public, Walter called to congratulate me and said in effect that he thought it was a major breakthrough for restoring honest government. He was delighted and said that this would have a very cleansing effect on public 1ife."

"The boss takes a break in his Dickinson bank," reported the Houston Chronicle's Texas magazine in this 1989 photo. With Walter Hall are, from the left, Gwen Neugent, Barbara Liefert, Frances Carter and Madeleine Rogers. ***(Betty Tichich photo, illustrating a Steven Long story about Hall, courtesy of the Houston Chronicle)***

Simpson said he found it very interesting to note that Walter Hall's advice has been sought for more than half a century by people running for office from drainage commissioner to president.

Describing Hall's political beliefs, Simpson called the banker a "philosopher—not just a student."

"When I first met him, or soon after, he gave me a monograph—a speech or published paper—of his Rice professor of philosophy, Dr. Radoslav A. Tsanoff. The title was 'Intellectual Freedom.'

"That was in the time of (Sen. Joseph) McCarthy, where people were pilloried if they simply believed in the Social Security program or that the mininum wage law had some merit—you became a communist.

"As a matter of fact, I had two or three people here in the county try to convince me, when I first came here, that Walter Hall was a communist. And I told (one of them), "You dumb SOB—here's a guy who could buy the Mainland if he wanted to. He's the absolute epitome of the free enterprise system. On a shoestring he took a little bank, built it up—and I believe by that time he had two banks—and you have the unmitigated gall to call him a communist. Do you think he wants to split with you his hard-earned wealth? You're the dumbest b———I've met in years."

Simpson said Hall was always helpful to him as a banker as well as a friend. "Because a lot of the time," he explained, "most of what I was doing paid either absolutely nothing, like running for district attorney, or paid very little, like when I was assistant attorney general under Will Wilson. And I really wasn't the greatest prospect for loaning money to. But Walter would always find a reason to loan me whatever money I needed to keep my law practice afloat or put bread on the table."

Simpson has become one of the most influential lawyers in Galveston County and is in heavy demand by some of the nation's largest corporations because of his legal ability and particularly his skill in selecting juries for civil lawsuits.

"So long as a breath of life is in me there will always be an account (of mine) at Citizens State Bank," Simpson says.

. . .

"When I became reasonably active in the county, business-wise and otherwise, illegal gambling was rampant," Hall has said, to reinforce Simpson's remarks about the "Free State of Galveston" era. "It was a menace. I knew people who would lose their entire pay checks in slot machines and in the gambling joints...The business establishments in Galveston and even the churches, in the main, would not lift their hands in opposition. I knew that it was beyond my power to correct. The illegal gambling crowd had been headed up in the main by Sam and Rose Maceo, who were bright men. Some of their coterie were not. And they (the second-rank gamblers, not the Maceos) made statements, I was informed, that claimed they already had the sheriff and the county (district) attorney and they were going to take over the rest of the courthouse. Of course, that was offensive and intolerable to me and a lot of people, including Jim Simpson."

Concerning the 1954 election, Hall said it was stolen from Simpson.

"He lost it by only eight votes, even with (the gambling crowd) stealing about 200 votes."

Most of those votes, he explained, were in what they called the "waterfront box," where Simpson's foes were voting, illegally—sailors and seamen under what was called the "Sailors' and Seamen's Voting Act."

Challenging the results of an election was not practical, Hall said, because of the use of voting machines: The testimony of a witness concerning his vote could not be questioned because it was impossible to prove that he was lying.

In addition to the difficulty of contesting an election in those days, Hall added, "it wasn't feasible to try to contest an election for an office that had only two years to run."

But because of Simpson's great work under Attorney General Will Wilson, Hall said, "the back of illegal gambling was broken in Galveston, and it has never been re-established."

TEXAS SALUTE

AN APPRECIATION DINNER

honoring

UNITED STATES SENATOR

RALPH W. YARBOROUGH

Program

Mr. Walter Hall, Toastmaster

INVOCATION .... Reverend John Barclay
Central Christian Church, Austin, Texas

STAR SPANGLED BANNER

WELCOME .... Honorable Lester E. Palmer
Mayor of Austin, Texas

Dinner
Fresh Fruit Cocktail
Charcoal Broiled KC Steak
Idaho Baked Potato   Kentucky Wonder Green Beans
Assorted French Rolls
Spring Garden Salad with Gourmet Dressing
Old Fashioned Apple Pie
(with Apple Pie Sauce)
Coffee

REMARKS .... Honorable Jack Brooks
Congressman from Texas

REMARKS .... Honorable Henry Gonzalez
Congressman from Texas

REMARKS .... Honorable Olin D. Johnston
Senator from South Carolina

REMARKS .... Honorable Lee Metcalf
Senator from Montana

REMARKS .... Honorable Ernest Gruening
Senator from Alaska

REMARKS .... Honorable Daniel K. Inouye
Senator from Hawaii

REMARKS .... Honorable Frank Church
Senator from Idaho

ADDRESS .... Honorable John A. Gronouski
Postmaster General of the United States

MESSAGE ON FILM .... The President of The United States

ACKNOWLEDGMENT .... Honorable Ralph W. Yarborough
Senator from Texas

BENEDICTION .... Reverend Baxton Bryant
Arcadia Park Methodist Church, Dallas, Texas

THE EYES OF TEXAS

One of the exhibits in the political memorabilia collection of former U.S. Sen. Ralph W. Yarborough of Austin is a program from the Statewide Texas Salute to Yarborough in Austin on Oct. 19, 1963. This page from the program records the fact that Walter Hall was toastmaster, reflecting, Yarborough said, "the importance of Walter Hall in my political career."

Chapter 5
The Political World of Walter Hall

A First: A Political Speech

Walter Hall's first political speech was made in 1934 for U.S. Sen. Tom Connally, who was running for re-election after his first term in the Senate. Connally, who had been a U.S. congressman since 1917, in 1928 challenged—and unseated—the incumbent, U.S. Sen. Earle B. Mayfield.

In his bid for re-election six years later, Connally's opponent was the son of former U.S. Sen. Joseph Weldon Bailey—Joseph Weldon Bailey Jr., called "Little Joe" Bailey.

It was in that campaign that Connally sought Walter Hall's help.

The occasion for Hall's speech was a political rally in Galveston.

Hall explained that he had written to Connally about several matters, so the senator knew of the banker's political activities on his behalf.

"I had never met him, except for a handshake once in Galveston," Hall said.

Hall was still a very young man and had held his banking job at the Citizens State Bank in League City only since 1931. But Connally obviously had confidence in the young banker.

Connally called Hall, told him about the Galveston rally and said he could not possibly be there; his invitation arrived too late. He asked Hall to represent him at the rally and make a speech for him.

Hall agreed to do it.

Walter Hall had actively entered the political arena; a precedent had been established; and a habit had been created.

The record reflects, however, that as early as 1928 and 1932 Hall had already indicated a political preference for the Democratic Party—vocally if not as actively as he pursued his challenges later.

Also during those years Hall was a strong supporter of U.S. Rep. J.J.

Mansfield of Eagle Lake, who represented the 9th Texas Congressional District in Congress from 1916 to 1947.

Hall related many of these events during his 1976 conversation with Connie and Jim Simpson for their College of the Mainland project.

Hall was living in the little Texas town of West Point (near the Texas Company's Lena Clay Mine) when Al Smith ran for the presidency in 1928.

"Always being somewhat of a loudmouth," Hall said, "I made it clear that I was going to (support) Al Smith. I think out of a total in that community of some 300 votes, Al Smith got seven."

Hall told historian and author Dr. David G. McComb, in a 1974 interview for the Lyndon Baines Johnson Library at Austin:

"I have been a Democrat, not particularly by inheritance, but by interest...ever since studying American history under Dean Robert G. Caldwell at Rice University. Incidentally, he later became minister to Portugal and to Bolivia and also dean later at MIT (Massachusetts Institute of Technology). He was a great historian and a great teacher. So I was an Al Smith Democrat for my first vote..."

Then came 1932, in the depth of the Great Depression, after Hall's banking career was started.

"I saw the parents of some of the boys and girls I went to school with go completely bankrupt and jobless," Hall said.

"...I became clearly convinced that there had to be major repairs to our system for it to be what we all hoped it would be," Hall told the Simpsons. "I became convinced that it wasn't a good system when people who wanted jobs would have to stand in line to get a little bowl of weak soup or maybe an apple or something of that sort, or maybe peddle apples.

"Having a nature of just not believing everything I am told and having to revise some of my earlier ideas in view of the clear facts before us, I became convinced that we had to make some basic changes. That is why I was so active in the election that brought Franklin Delano Roosevelt into power."

Hall said that although he saw "the system we had was breaking down...I had no idea of what could be done to put it back into running order. I knew something had to be done, so I applauded the early moves that Roosevelt made...I think anything comparable to (the economic situation existing at that time) now, instead of bringing bread lines, would have people mobbing the supermarkets."

So, Hall said, when he saw the collapse of what "we had been led to believe was a near-perfect system...it made me, if not a cynic, at least a skeptic. And since that time, I have not been willing to accept an idea just because some newspaper or commentator or politician or banker or labor leader or somebody else said it was so. I've seen great experts proved to be quite, quite wrong."

Hall continued:

"When you see a nation with warehouses full of wheat and rice and corn, and warehouses full of cotton that could be spun into goods, and lumber yards stacked with lumber, and in those same communities you see people who are hungry for bread and need those clothes that could be made from that cotton and need the houses that could be built, you recognize that our problem is not so much one of production as one of proper distribution. We see the desperate need for the training of people so that they will have salable skills so they can contribute in a way that will enable them to have the things they need—in other words, education. Even though I was rather young then, those issues first seemed to become clear to me...People called me somewhat unorthodox, to put it mildly.

"I then became involved from time to time in county politics," Hall said.

"It was clear our county needed a lot of things, and our county Commissioners Court was greatly influenced by people who wanted little, if any, increase in taxes. They wanted the county budget held quite low even while neglecting fair wages and the needs for roads and proper ditches to handle the water from those roads. A multitude of county services were being denied because of the Commissioners Court's unwise policy.

"I had supported County Judge E.B. Holman through two very hot elections that he had lost on the Island, but had won on the Mainland," Hall continued. "He was again faced with an election (1938) and it was obvious that he was going to have a tough time. A group of my friends from Santa Fe were bitterly opposed to him because they had been neglected from the standpoint of desperately needed roads. Their commissioner contended, and was able to demonstrate to them, it was because the budget officer (who was the county judge) wouldn't provide the funds necessary and he could not get the other commissioners to amend the budget. But, nonetheless, on the judge's word that he would provide the funds for those roads in the next budget, I urged my Santa Fe friends to support the judge because he had been, on the whole, a good, honest public official. To my utter dismay, after he was re-elected again by a small vote that was provided by the Mainland, he literally broke his word to us and again provided a budget without doing what he said he would do. I told him that I wouldn't support him again and he said very frankly that he didn't believe that I could go against the man who had been friendly with him for so many years, and I told him that I would have to. And so, sure enough, the next time he was again defeated on the Island; and that time we had the votes on the Mainland to beat him and we had a new county judge, Ted Robinson."

Holman was defeated in November, 1942, and Robinson became county judge on Jan. 1, 1943.

It was while Robinson was county judge that Hall forced the county's adoption of the tax evaluation program.

Hall expanded on some of his early political activities for McComb for the LBJ Library project:.

"...in 1940 we came pretty close to capturing our county convention in behalf of FDR when the 'establishment' in the City of Galveston was for Jack Garner...

"It soon became clear to me that our county was of such comparatively small size that the Mainland, which was growing far more rapidly than the City of Galveston, (with) organization...could soon come to have a consequential political effect in this county and thereby change some political conditions in the county, all for the good.

"My interest was largely because of the lack of roads for my friends and my customers; a very poor school system in many parts of the county; a neglect of the Mainland by the 'establishment' of Galveston who knew we didn't have enough votes to run the show. And so we were kind of a frustrated minority that sought means to do something about it, and this group soon came to be called the Unorganized Organization. It consisted of labor groups in Texas City and La Marque and some in Galveston on certain issues; of rural people, namely, dairy farmers and...cattlemen; small businessmen who were in the small towns or the communities."

Hall's activities and effectiveness now are well known throughout Galveston County and documented in the fact that he has served, for the Democratic Party, as precinct chairman, county chairman, member of the State Democratic Executive Committee, and delegate to both state and national Democratic conventions.

Hall recalls, without any great amount of pleasure, some of the opposition he met locally.

During the campaign for the water district in League City, Hall said, "We faced the usual amount of opposition, much of it based on completely false information about how we were going to tax people out of their homes—when, as a matter of fact, (it) didn't involve any taxes at all. That was when I started getting scars on me politically...I was perhaps too active in supporting the positions I felt were in order, and I received some pretty good blows in the process. But I tried to mete out a few and we did prevail."

It may have been during those first few years of political activity that Hall started getting his reputation as "a liberal Democrat and solvent banker."

A Few Galveston County Battles

Undoubtedly one of the most intense major political battles which Walter Hall waged in Galveston County resulted in the election of Ray Holbrook and/or defeat of Peter J. (Pete) LaValle. The campaign was that for county judge of Galveston County in 1966.

Hall had become upset with LaValle partially because, Hall said, of a deal LaValle apparently had made with huge taxpayers on tax values and failing to renew the Galveston County revaluation program with Pritchard & Abbott, as recorded in Chapter 3.

Hall also believed that LaValle had mistreated some of his friends, including labor, and some employees in the County Courthouse.

Ray Holbrook was a young patent attorney at the Monsanto Chemical Co. plant in Texas City. He had graduated from Texas A&M University and been an engineer for Monsanto before becoming an attorney.

Although Holbrook had served on the State Board of Education since 1960, he was considered a political unknown. After a hard-fought campaign, Holbrook beat LaValle overwhelmingly.

"I had Walter's unequivocal support," Holbrook said. "He loaned me a lot of money, and he gave me a lot of money."

Holbrook defined in more detail Hall's part in that campaign:

"(Walter Hall) was one of the principal reasons why I ran for county judge of Galveston County in 1966...He helped me financially and he helped me with advice and counsel all during the campaign. He was very definite that in his opinion based on his 'vast political experience,' I would conduct the campaign as he recommended if I wanted to win. Although it was impossible to do everything that he asked and suggested, I did campaign almost exactly as he suggested up to the limit of my capabilities. And it was a successful campaign."

It was also a very bitter campaign. The Galveston News, in an unusual editorial on May 31, 1966, defended the integrity of Walter Hall against the charges that were being made during the campaign.

The editorial, titled "Our Runoff Recommendation: Cold Showers for All, Then Soapy Tub Baths!" follows:

"The News views with shocked disbelief the depths of personal attack and vituperation to which the county judge runoff campaign has degenerated. Certainly we do not condone the violent personal attacks being made on Walter Hall Sr., a Dickinson and League City banker.

"Neither side can take much pride in the tone of the campaign. If the candidates haven't personally hurled the mud, their supporters certainly have. And Hall has been subjected to unprecedented abuse.

"Walter Hall's interest in politics is not new. Nor is his interest in Democratic politics. Nor are his frequently unconventional (in the eyes of many of his friends and business associates) political views. Nor is his well-publicized alignment with Sen. Ralph Yarborough in the senator's obsessive contest with Gov. Connally to control the Texas Democratic Party.

"None of these facts makes Hall a dishonest man. Nor a power-hungry political boss. Nor a would-be dictator. They do make him a tough and resourceful political scrapper (with whom we are in frequent disagreement, incidentally) who fights hard for what he believes. But he is still a man who seeks his objectives within the bounds of normal democratic processes.

"In short, we at times question his politics, his judgment and his choice of candidates, but never yet have we questioned his integrity. Nor do we question it now.

"For 30 years Walter Hall has been a respectable businessman. He has been a faithful civic worker and committeeman seeking to improve conditions in this county, organize school and other districts, finance Boy Scout camps and dozens of other projects. During this period he has worked as a private citizen to help form water districts in Dickinson, League City, La Marque, Hitchcock, Alta Loma and Kemah. He is currently deeply involved in helping to promote the fortunes of Rosenberg Library.

"In 1943 he was appointed to the board of directors of the San Jacinto River Authority and later was elected president. He was to see this agency 'grow up' during his 11-year tenure and become a vital part of our economy.

"After World War II he was named chairman of a county-wide postwar planning committee which started the ball rolling for extension of seawalls of Texas City and Galveston; for the new county courthouse and jail; for the Mainland hospital; for a road and drainage program. Shortly after Hurricane Carla in 1961 he, along with others, urged then Vice President Johnson to come to the county for an inspection trip.

"This trip resulted in setting up certain relief facilities which greatly lessened the loss and suffering. Shortly thereafter Galveston Countians in the bayshore area honored him at an appreciation dinner in recognition of his efforts. The list could go on, but there's no need to document Walter Hall's interest and concern for this county.

"The News had decided several weeks ago to make no specific recommendations to the voters in this race. We have been gratified that both sides have vigorously protested to us that our editorials and-or news coverage on occasion have been unfair to this or that candidate. It leads us to believe we must be approaching that over-all fairness which is our goal.

"For those whose vision has been obscured by the flying mud from all sides this reminder: The election Saturday is between two candidates for county judge, the incumbent seeking a second full elective term who thinks he's been doing a good job and a challenger who thinks the incumbent hasn't and believes he can do it better.

"The News has altered its no-recommendation decision and herewith makes the following recommendation: That the combatants, non-combatants and all others who may have been splattered vote Saturday; that after the polls close, everyone take first a cold shower and then a long, hot soapy tub bath. And Sunday morning together let's start trying to pick up the pieces."

As recorded, Hall's candidate Holbrook won that bitter campaign.

But Hall's candidates did not always win.

An earlier hard-fought campaign was in 1960, when Hall's longtime friend and associate, County Commissioner Johnny Palmer, was challenged by Paul Hopkins.

Hopkins, a former La Marque chief of police, was elected sheriff of Galveston County in 1956 and, after reorganizing the department, decided to seek the more responsible county job on the Commissioners Court.

Hopkins defeated the older candidate; but the political conflicts which might have been expected between Hopkins and Hall did not develop.

Hall and Hopkins became good friends and worked together on a regular and productive basis for many years on Galveston County civic projects.

Hopkins left Galveston County to become a member and chairman of the Texas Water Commission.

Hall later sponsored the creation of—and contributed the land and construction costs for—the Paul Hopkins Community Park in Dickinson.

Hall gave the county 6.54 acres of land for the park—land with about 1,200 feet of frontage on Farm Road 517 and about 275 feet of frontage on Dickinson Bayou. The property was appraised at about $200,000.

Galveston County Judge Ray Holbrook, left, joined Walter Hall in breaking ground for the new building of the Citizens State Bank at 2401 Termini at Pine Drive. The ceremonies were held in July, 1972, and the new building was opened on Sept. 24, 1973.

Hopkins was one of the sponsors of the "Man of Vision" dinner honoring Hall in 1993.

Hall remembers with amusement another fight he lost at a county Democratic convention at the end of FDR's first presidential term.

"Some of the more conservative Democrats in the county wanted to back John Nance Garner for the presidency rather than back the re-election of Roosevelt," Hall said.

"The convention was being conducted by Ben Insulman, the county Democratic chairman. He had agreed with me, in advance, that the convention would be operated under the mandates of Robert's Rules of Order. Included was the provision that in the event a resolution was submitted to the resolutions committee, and was not reported either for or against, then it could be brought up for action on the floor of the convention. But, again, first it had to be submitted to the committee. I wanted that clear, because I figured that what could happen would happen.

"Mart Royston was chairman of the resolutions committee. Maco Stewart was another member and there were a couple of others whose names I don't recall.

"I appeared before the resolutions committee, planning to present a motion favoring the re-election of FDR.

"Royston told me, 'Well, Mr. Hall, you are late. We have already had our meeting, and we have decided to urge the nomination of that great, great Texan, John Nance Garner.'

"I said, 'Well, Judge Royston, if we can't get my report out of here, I am entitled to bring the subject out on the floor, according to Robert's Rules of Order, which Ben has agreed to follow.'

"Royston replied, 'Please, Mr. Hall, let's don't get into a nasty row; let's just have a nice, quiet convention.'

"I said, 'We can't do that. We're strong in behalf of the re-election of President Roosevelt.'

"So in due course he presented his resolution favoring Garner; and inasmuch as I was entitled to present a substitute, I presented a substitute favoring the nomination of FDR.

"A one-armed man got up to second my motion to substitute our motion for the first one.

"I remember very clearly what he said: 'I'm one of those men under the WPA (Works Progress Administration). I'm a timekeeper on a leaf-raking job. And I want to tell you before FDR became president, I didn't have any place to stay except with my neighbors or my relatives. And we didn't have any money to buy anything for our little girls. But now that

I'm a timekeeper on a leaf-raking job, last Christmas we were able to buy a doll for each of our little girls.'

"This was pretty powerful political rhetoric," Hall said, "and at this point Royston had as much as he wanted, so he moved to table my motion.

"I went around to my friends urging them to 'Vote no; vote no; vote no!'

"I didn't go to the man who seconded my motion, because I knew he was on my side and surely knew that a 'No' vote was a vote to kill Royston's motion.

"I insisted on a roll-call vote. When the roll call came, this man, who was chairman of a rather large precinct delegation, voted 'Yes.'

"We lost by a very slim vote.

"After the convention was over, I thanked the man for seconding my motion, and told him I was sorry he couldn't control his delegation.

"He said, 'I did control them! You have to lay the motion on the table to get action on it, don't you?'"

Hall Eyes the Governorship

Walter Hall was approached in 1956 by some of his friends and political allies and asked if he would consider a race for the Texas governorship.

This group, from Houston and Austin, told Hall at a meeting in Glenn McCarthy's Shamrock Hotel that they had $50,000 to support him initially, and could raise more, if he would run.

Hall, of course, was flattered. But:

"I didn't think the suggestion made any sense," Hall said, "because I supported—and still support—the idea of an excess corporate profit tax.

"I think the opposition from the so-called 'establishment' would have been fierce. And as a banker, I realized that $50,000, even then, was not a consequential amount of money to make a run for governor. I think I would have wound up selling a bank or two and still gotten licked."

Steven Long, writing in the Houston Chronicle, interviewed former U.S. Sen. Ralph Yarborough concerning what he calls "Hall's brief flirtation with elective politics."

Long wrote:

"'He made one speech in West Texas, got disgusted and went home,' Yarborough says, chuckling. 'But he really should have been governor of Texas. He is a longtime, front-line fighter for the people. He's a businessman who hasn't forgotten the people.'"

Apparently, Long concluded, "Hall's brief foray into the limelight convinced him that his place in politics was in the background, not on a stump."

A short time after the Shamrock Hotel meeting, Hall said he was in Austin and ran into Ed Clark, the Austin attorney-lobbyist who later was appointed by President Lyndon Johnson as ambassador to Australia.

"Ed said," Hall related, "'One of my spies tells me that you had a little meeting down at the Shamrock about your running for governor.'

"'Yes,' I told him, "'but I have better sense. I'm not going to run.' He said, 'Well, it would sure be interesting to have a liberal with some sense run for governor, and it would be more interesting if he became governor. And I'll tell you what I'll do if you'll run—I'll raise you $50,000—and publicly, I will be for you or against you, whichever will help you the most.'"

Hall remembers many of his encounters with Clark with unbridled pleasure, most of them when the two politically active citizens were sniping at each other.

Once, Hall recalled, he and Clark were conducting a fund-raising event in Houston at the Houston Club, and were greeting guests at the meeting room door. Hall would introduce his guests to Clark, and Clark would introduce his guests to Hall. During a break in the activity, Clark sidled up to Hall and said, "Walter, if you'll stop calling me 'the fixer,' I'll stop calling you the 'little loan shark.'"

During the time Hall was considering the race for the governorship, he received at least one communique worthy of note, from a financial friend but a political adversary. The Houston banking executive wrote:

"...you have been urged to run for that high office. If you ever do, I am going to have quite a struggle with my conscience, for I do not believe I could bring myself to vote for someone who still believes that Franklin D. Roosevelt was a great man and a great president. Except for that misguided thinking, I am sure I could go along with you. I think you would make a fine governor."

Hall's Strategy Alters a State Race

When Walter Hall was a member of the State Democratic Executive Committee, his strategy was credited to a great degree with the election in 1950 of John C. White of Wichita Falls as agriculture commissioner of Texas.

Briefly, Hall said, "We voted to 'kick off' the incumbent (from the ballot) as he was not a Democrat and would make no pledges to support the Democratic Party.

"If my memory is accurate," Hall reported, "It was up to the SDEC to approve the names on the Democratic ballot. I raised the issue on John White's opposition, J.E. McDonald. Immediately some lawyers made the point that 'We could not do it.' I recognized, of course, it might bring about a lawsuit, but if so it would also bring the type of publicity I wanted that would show this man (McDonald) was not a Democrat but was running on the Democratic ticket.

"We postponed the necessary vote until after lunch, and during that time I explained to the other members of the committee my objective could only be good either way it went. Then after lunch we voted almost unanimously to 'kick off' John White's opponent."

White recalls the incident vividly and said that Hall, with the support of Stuart Long, the Austin newsman, had raised the possibility of eliminating McDonald's name from the ballot "because McDonald had not supported Democratic nominees in the past presidential election—Harry Truman, specifically."

"Of course the lawyers all said, 'You can't do that—it's illegal.' But Walter Hall said if we listened to the lawyers we never could get anything done. The committee then did vote to do it."

The move obviously was questionable, White said, and McDonald successfully challenged the action in court and his name subsequently was included on the ballot.

"But meanwhile," White explained, "McDonald got a week or maybe a little more of unfavorable publicity about his voting record—his disloyalty to the Democratic Party. My campaign accordingly gained strength. This was the major incident in getting me elected."

In the 1950 runoff election on Aug. 26, White defeated McDonald by a vote of 352,000 to 342,000.

White thus ended McDonald's reign as agriculture commissioner that began in 1931.

White served as Texas agriculture commissioner through 1979. He then became chairman of the National Democratic Executive Committee and later was a lobbyist in Washington, D.C., heading the firm of John White Consulting.

"John White and I have been friends for many years, and I have great admiration for him," Hall said.

(White died in January, 1995.)

Hall, Allred, Stevenson and Johnson

Walter Hall's involvement with the San Jacinto River Authority (related in Chapter 3) led him into a relationship with former Texas Gov.

James V. Allred and, through him, into an interest in the political life of Lyndon B. Johnson.

Along the way Hall met Gov. Coke Stevenson, and that encounter also created another interesting chapter of Hall's political life.

Those instances were related by Hall in his interview with David G. McComb for the LBJ Library:

"...Jimmy Allred is the person who first caused me to have an interest in Lyndon Johnson," Hall told McComb. "Of course, I was aware of the lack of interest in water development by what I call the business 'establishment' in Texas. Like practically every major issue in Texas, they give great lip service to dealing with the problem, whether it's education, mass transportation, better highways, air pollution, water pollution, or whatever. You get great speeches by the leaders of the industry, whatever part of the 'establishment' it may be, but when the chips are down and the legislation is introduced into the Legislature, of course it soon dies or is amended to be meaningless.

"I had had an encounter with Gov. Coke Stevenson as a member of an executive committee made up of members of the various river authorities and others who had tax remissions from the state. Under the law that prevailed, during the war (World War II) the state had not been able to spend money and, accordingly, had a surplus and therefore there was no legal basis for a tax to be levied. The tax from which our remissions came could not be levied in the usual manner. We were faced with a dire problem. There were some 25 or 30 of us who organized ourselves, all public bodies, all holding jobs at the hands of the governor or of the State Board of Water Engineers or whomever. We were trying to get the governor to call a special session to deal with the problems by special measures.

"Our executive committee met with the governor; and when he declined to call a special session to deal with this problem, many of us—not the San Jacinto River Authority, but some of the others—were faced with the failure to meet their bond issues that they had authorized, depending upon the taxes that were to be remitted by the state.

"It was clear to me and to all of us that the governor was not going to call a special session. I asked him if he had any advice or counsel that he could give me to take back to my board of directors about how to plan for the coming year in the absence of money—how to plan to proceed with things we desperately needed to do such as the acquisition of rights of way, the enlargement of canals, small pumping plants, and things of that nature.

"I remember so vividly Governor Stevenson, who was personable in many ways...sucked on a pipe...and...had a very cold, calculating—some would say mean—steely eye. He did not like to be asked the questions for which there were apparently no good answers. And when I asked him that question, he cocked his eye over at me and he sucked on that pipe a time or two, and, believe it or not, he said to me, 'Oh, Hall, those questions usually take care of themselves.'

"This was such an utterly absurd comment coming from a governor of a great state that I immediately arose from my seat and told the attorney and the others who were there (the attorney was not Jimmy Allred—it was the attorney of this association group that we had formed) that I felt we had imposed upon the governor long enough and ought to be leaving, so we promptly left.

"...I didn't think that (Coke Stevenson) really understood the problems of Texas, and that he was so conservative that he was not willing to do anything consequential about the problems, no matter how dire they might be."

At one time, Hall said, he thought he should divorce himself from statewide political efforts if he were going to continue as president of the San Jacinto River Authority.

"But my encounter with Governor Stevenson caused me to re-examine that," he told McComb.

When the race started between Stevenson and Johnson for the U.S. Senate seat in 1948, Hall asked Allred for his opinion of LBJ and received a very positive reaction.

"I said," Hall told Allred, "'Well, we've got hell in our county to do much for him because our county is still pretty conservative and they think Coke Stevenson is a great man, but we'll do what we can.'

"I was able to start a little effort in Galveston County. It's very interesting now to recall that only two businessmen of prominence and willing to be actively identified with the Lyndon Johnson effort came forward to help...There was Maco Stewart (of Stewart Title Co.), who had served on the State School Board under an appointment from (Gov.) W. Lee O'Daniel. Maco and I had never agreed on anything much politically. But when he found that I was going to do what I could for LBJ, he called me and asked if he could come up to see me...He came in with utter candor (and) said:

"'I want you to know right now that I want to help you in any way I can to beat that (censored) Coke Stevenson. It's not because I love Lyndon Johnson, but you know I wanted to be reappointed to the State

School Board, and Coke wouldn't do it. I'm going to try to help you beat him if I can. I'll be either with him or against him publicly...'

"I said, 'Maco, I don't want you for him publicly because that wouldn't help. But I'll tell you what you can do. We'll need some money.'

"He said, 'I'll pay one-half of every dime that's spent to beat Coke Stevenson in Galveston County.'

"I said, 'OK, we'll leave it that way. I may call on you for some advice and counsel,' which I did during the campaign...

"The other man was Jim Bradner, who was the owner of Radio Station KGBC in Galveston...Jim had organized the radio station, he was an engineer, a very progressive, liberal-minded man, and he held Coke Stevenson in utter contempt because he'd had some contacts with him and found that he was, according to Jim, not only unconcerned but uninformed about some very basic Texas problems.

"So LBJ came into Galveston County and Jim Bradner and I were the only two men who met him...We took him around in Galveston without much enthusiasm on the part of those he called on, but he was received courteously by some of the folks because I had business contacts there with the men who were gentlemen even if they didn't go along with the man I happened to be supporting at the moment.

"We brought him over to Texas City, and LBJ made a very effective campaign—very brief, but he went up one side of the main street and down the other, shook hundreds and hundreds of hands, showed what a great campaigner he was, and that evening—this is a very significant thing to me—we had a rally at La Marque. They have pretty well gone by the board now, rallies have, but they were of some consequence at that time. Nearly every community would have one at least in every campaign. They would usually start off with the candidates for minor offices making their speeches, and then you'd come to the major office-seekers last.

"So LBJ made his speech there. I really hadn't had a chance to talk to the man—to use a country-town, oil-field expression, to 'swab him out,' on how he felt, until going back from La Marque to Galveston that night. And so I felt that before I could really go all-out for a man like I felt I should do, before I could properly explain my position to folks that I was identified with who felt keenly about certain things, that I ought to have it straight from him how he felt.

"So I raised a number of very basic questions. I then felt that our treatment of the Negro was vile and that it should be changed. I felt that the old people were getting a raw deal from the standpoint of what medical care was costing. I ran into that, being just a country banker, when the old people would come in, and sons and daughters who were taking care of their parents, and would tell me of the high cost of hospitals, of medicine, doctors, etc. In many cases it was a terrible problem for these people to receive reasonably good medical care. I felt that our educational system, particularly in Texas, was lousy. I knew what difficulties our graduates were having in staying in the better universities. (I wanted to know his thoughts) on various things like water development...

"So I had become aware of these things, and I wanted to know how a man who is seeking to be a senator from Texas really felt. I asked as piercing questions as I knew how. I remember Lyndon (saying), 'Jimmy Allred has told me something about you, Hall. He said that I could depend upon your treating in confidence anything I tell you.'

"I said, 'Well, Jimmy's right about that. Just what do you mean?'

"He said, 'Well, you've asked me what my basic philosophy is about the pressing things.' He proceeded then to tell me. I think Lyndon Johnson was telling me the truth. I think he had a burning compassion for unfortunate people, irrespective of their color. I think that he wanted to do something about it. He was confronted with the problem of how he could go about that. He dealt with this very frankly. How could he go about that, coming from a state that as yet had shown no signs of being as liberal or progressive as he would like to see it?...He made no specific commitments to me about what he was going to do if he became senator. He convinced me, though, that if he ever got in a position of real power to where his own political life would not be sacrificed on the altar of liberal legislation, he would act. I am too pragmatic to expect any politician to sacrifice himself—I've known too many of them. After all, you can't do anything unless you are in office. I was convinced that once that man got in real power, that he would bring into reality legislation that would deal with the problems that I felt were so basic to the welfare of the nation.

"Now there (were) times when his conduct...caused me to wonder, but never more than wonder. I always felt that he was doing what he felt was absolutely necessary to, shall we say, stay alive politically, or at least stay alive from the standpoint of any influence."

Hall and LBJ

Walter Hall has never publicly expressed his feelings concerning Lyndon B. Johnson in such a manner; but through his interviews, correspondence and some personal discussions, it is obvious that frequently he had mixed emotions about the Texas Democrat who held the nation's highest office.

As reported, Hall first started supporting Johnson when the Austin congressman made his successful race for the U.S. Senate against Coke Stevenson in 1948.

Walter Hall greeted Lady Bird and Lyndon Johnson at an area airport, probably during LBJ's political career before he became vice president. The occasion is unknown.

This probably was the most famous election in the history of Texas. Johnson won his Senate seat by a controversial 87-vote majority out of almost 1 million votes cast. It earned for Johnson the title of "Landslide Lyndon."

Hall liked the way Lyndon Johnson "talked and got things done."

Johnson, Hall said, was one of the finest campaigners he ever knew.

"He could shake more hands inside of five minutes than any man I ever saw," Hall said.

The relationship of the two men was tested early in Johnson's life in the Senate.

"Lyndon sent me a copy of his maiden speech in the Senate," Hall related. "The title of it was 'The Right of Unlimited Debate,' but it was nothing but a defense of the filibuster. He sent me a note attached to the speech that said, 'I thought you might be interested in my maiden speech in the Senate.' On the bottom of that little piece of paper I wrote, 'Thank you for sending me a copy of your speech. I am sorry to see that you think more of your right to speak without limit than another man's right to vote' and sent it back to him. That hurt his feelings, and he told me so the next time I saw him. But I always supported him, and he knew that. I always did everything I could for him."

The most bitter controversy between Hall and Johnson was the result of the September, 1956, State Democratic Convention when the liberal Democrats were defeated by the Allan Shivers forces. The incident, called the "Cow Barn" incident, and events leading up to it are related in more detail in the segment of this chapter titled "The Democrats' Fight in the 1950s."

Later, after the ashes from that fire had cooled, Hall was visiting Sam Rayburn, then speaker of the U.S. House of Representatives, during a trip to Washington. Rayburn asked Hall if he would be interested in talking to Johnson, who had become the majority leader of the Senate.

Hall indicated that he had "nothing else to do" that afternoon, but said, "Mr. Sam, I don't think Lyndon cares to see me now after the controversy we had over the Cow Barn.

"Mr. Sam said, 'Oh, you've got Lyndon wrong; you know Lyndon is not vindictive.' That brought a laugh; it was funny, of course, because vindictiveness was one of Lyndon's characteristics. But that didn't keep him from being a great man and in many respects a great president.

"So Rayburn," Hall said, "called LBJ and said, 'Lyndon, there is one of the great Democrats of Texas here at my desk. I wonder if you would like to see Walter Hall.'

"Lyndon obviously said 'Yes,' so I asked Rayburn's aide, John Holton, if he would let one of his pages take me over to Lyndon's office. I was up there so rarely that I felt I might get on the wrong underground railway.

"When I got to Johnson's office, I told the young lady, his receptionist, my name. There were some eight or 10 people in the reception room. I took my seat, expecting to wait my turn.

"Pretty soon, Lyndon came to the door of his private office, ushering out a man, and Lyndon waved me in ahead of all those other people.

"Well, it was a bit embarrassing, but I went. And that's when and how I got the Johnson treatment.

"Lyndon was about a foot taller than I, and he put his arm around my shoulder and said, 'Lady Bird and I often think that if it wasn't for you and a few like you, I'd never be here.'

"I said, 'Well, Lyndon, I've always been there to support you and I'm proud of what you have done up here, but I want to make it clear now that my position on the Cow Barn hasn't changed a damn bit.' And he said, 'Oh, let's don't talk about the unpleasant things; let's just talk about the good things.' I said, 'OK, let's consider it closed.' "

Hall recalled a later meeting with Johnson, in Houston's Rice Hotel. Johnson at the time was vice president. A few days earlier presidential aide Cliff Carter had called Hall to check on an economist who was being considered for a post on an economic delegation President Kennedy planned to send to India.

Hall gave the vice president the information he needed after Johnson had made a speech in the hotel. Later, after Johnson invited Hall to his room, the vice president gave him what Hall called a "penetrating stare" and asked, "Walter, why don't you ever ask me for anything?"

"And I said," Hall continued, 'Well, I guess because I don't need anything; but you have done some things.' I mentioned that he had, at my request, obtained a discharge from the Army for a young man who was desperately needed to come back to take care of his family; his daddy was dying of cancer. And I mentioned that he had done something for some friends of mine in Mexico.

"The vice president said, 'Oh, that's just customary. That's not doing it for you.'

"And I said, 'Well, I guess if I needed anything I'd ask you.'

"He looked at me and said, 'Hall, you're unique.' Well, I didn't know then, and I don't know now, how to reply to such a thing as that."

Despite the differences Hall and Johnson had throughout Johnson's career in Washington, Hall always supported Johnson.

This was not true of many of Hall's political friends. An insight into such differences was recalled by Ronnie Dugger. Dugger, the social-policy writer now living in New York, and owner and former editor of the Texas Observer, wrote:

"Walter believed in Lyndon Johnson more than I did or could and sometimes—putt-putting around the bayous in his yacht, for example—we had a number of direct, but always civil, discussions about that. It's characteristic of Walter that, finding me unpersuadable, instead of becoming a foe of the Observer, as most powerful men would have done, he continued to support us and accepted my invitation to write a comprehensive appreciation of Lyndon, which I published with pride in our 'journal of free voices.' Johnson must have had mixed feelings when he saw it because by that time he would have buried us 'Observer boys' alive or dead if he could have."

Hall remembers that Johnson would goad or "needle" a friend or associate as well as a political enemy if he considered the occasion appropriate.

He said one weekend the president had a group of guests at his ranch, including John Connally.

Hall said another guest told him he overheard this conversation between the president and Connally:

Connally: "Mr. President, since you have no great regard for Senator Yarborough and the other senator, John Tower, is a Republican, why don't you consult with me when you have a judicial appointment or some other appointment to make in Texas?"

Johnson: "Well, John, any time you have an idea for an appointment just let me know, and I'll run it by Ralph for his consideration."

Hall praises the social reforms that Johnson directed during his presidency and said that in his opinion, they stand "right alongside the Emancipation Proclamation and New Deal efforts."

"We did not always agree, but we shared the belief that an important objective of government is to help those who need it most," Hall re-emphasized.

Hall said on a visit to Johnson's ranch after he retired, LBJ was sitting by himself for the moment by the side of his swimming pool. Hall approached him and said, "Honest Injun, Mr. President, how do you feel since getting out of the White House?" And LBJ replied, "Honest Injun, Hall, I am bored stiff."

After Johnson's death from a heart attack in 1973, the family friendship continued with Lady Bird Johnson, whose ranch at Stonewall is a short distance from Hall's Clear Rock Ranch near Johnson City.

Although Hall's association with Johnson was more personal than with other presidents he knew, Hall also was a friend, though not a close friend, of John F. Kennedy and Jimmy Carter.

Hall and Texas Governors

Democrats of Texas, famed for their interparty fights, lived through some of their most bitter days in the 1950s. Walter Hall was one of the most intense battlers of that time.

Many of the fights involved the politicians who have held the governorship, and Hall is very opinionated concerning them and is not hesitant to express his opinion.

Most of the fighting involved the politics of Allan Shivers. Shivers had been lieutenant governor of Texas, elected with Gov. Beauford H. Jester in 1947. When Jester died in July, 1949, Shivers became governor. He was elected to a full term in 1950 and was re-elected in 1952 and 1954—but not without a lot of movement and static within the Democratic Party.

During his interview for the oral history project for the College of the Mainland library, Hall explained some of his views.

He said that after Shivers became governor in 1949, he (Hall) was convinced that Shivers "was damaging the party that elected him and more important, was also hurting Texas."

"He was elected from Beaumont as a senator and later as lieutenant governor," Hall said. "He had been a reasonable, progressive, liberal-minded man. But on becoming governor, he became quite conservative and a member of what you call 'the establishment.'

"He and another man who became governor of Texas had in common what I consider one great defect. They both, in my judgment, had far too great respect for money and people who had it.

"Allan's money-making ability was demonstrated when he got out of the governor's office," Hall continued. "Many people think he made a tremendous governor because of his intelligence, his powers of leadership, and his power of speaking.

"He could have led Texas down a highly progressive road, and the same could be said for John Connally. But that's not the case, as we all know.

"Texas, under their leadership and those who came before and after them, has continued to worship at the shrine of the dollar mark. 'The establishment' has been in control."

Discussing Connally later, Hall said, "John Connally did one thing that was of genuine benefit. He made a real contribution to the public education system in Texas. That's about all he did that I approve of."

Hall also said, "It is a pity that our state did not have men with vision and desire running the state during the time the vast fortunes of oil and gas were being taken from it. Had Texas had such leadership it could have set aside a far greater amount of those resources through taxes for use either for current needs or an endowment, the incomes of which would be used for future needs and Texas would be far, far ahead in basic human resources. By that I mean an educated people."

Hall explained in more detail his criticism of Texas leaders:

"My long activity in statewide politics, and particularly concerning the governorship, was because I felt, ever since I was an adult, that the tremendous wealth that was in Texas, due principally to oil and gas, was being misused. Texas was not benefiting from it properly. Most Texans seemed to think that many Texans were getting the major part of that great wealth. The major part of the wealth was going out of state to the big oil companies, and Texans were usually getting a sixth or an eighth of the royalty. This, of course, was except for the independent oilmen, some of whom were majors from the standpoint of personal wealth; but they were minor compared to the overall production of oil and gas in Texas.

"I resented the fact that our leadership would not deal with the major factors of a good road system, with education and with crime.

"I was opposed to the people who did not believe that Texas was worth paying taxes to develop; and therefore we never had adequate taxes, we never had adequate education, we did not deal with crime, and we did not deal with social services, which of course includes education."

The Democrats' Fight in the 1950s

Walter Hall had told Sam Rayburn in 1952 to be prepared for Texas Gov. Allan Shivers to bolt the Democratic Party.

"I am not going to say that Allan is a liar," Hall said he told Rayburn during a Washington visit, "but I cannot believe that a man would spend two years going all over the State of Texas and elsewhere denouncing the Democratic Party from top to bottom and then, when the opportunity came to hit it a hard lick, he would fail to do so. I believe he is going to bolt the party.

"Mr. Sam said that he was convinced that inasmuch as Allan Shivers had given him his word he would not bolt the party, that he would simply not do it. He said, 'Walter, I can't believe that the governor of Texas would lie to me. He sat in that chair you are sitting in and told me that he would not bolt the party.'"

Hall's belief was based on facts later recorded in the book, "Allan Shivers: The Pied Piper of Texas Politics," written by Sam Kinch and Stuart Long, veteran Texas newsmen.

In 1951, Kinch and Long wrote, Allan Shivers first gave public indication that he might defect from the Democratic Party if the Democrats nominated President Harry Truman for a second term—or nominated any other candidate who had similar views.

Following some interparty political jockeying, which aroused the suspicions of the Roosevelt-Truman Democrats, a meeting of the liberal group was scheduled for Austin in October, 1951, in the name of the Volunteer Democratic Committee.

The 300 who attended condemned a Republican-Democratic "cross-filing" plan, and organized the Loyal Democrats of Texas, with Walter Hall as chairman.

Kinch and Long wrote:

"The loyalist band was not originated to fight Shivers, but when he began to get more outspoken against Truman, it turned in that direction. Hall said the governor was being used as a stalking horse by the forces which had taken over the 1944 delegation to the national convention. The break became clean on Dec. 7, when Shivers met in his office with third-party leaders...After the meeting, Shivers made clear his views.

"'If we say we're going to support the nominees—no matter who they are—we might as well send a letter to the convention instead of a delegation,' he snorted.

"That brought the Loyal Democrats of Texas into fast action."

Hall said that Fagan Dickson of Austin, a former legislator and first assistant attorney general, was named president; Creekmore Fath was named executive director; and Hall was designated as the chairman.

They maintained that the loyalty pledge imposed by the 1948 convention still was in effect.

After that initial meeting, words flew across Texas for the next few months.

Then in April, 1952, the State Democratic Executive Committee met in New Braunfels, Kinch and Long wrote, "to perfect plans for the May 27 convention in San Antonio and specifically to act on the pledge requirements at precinct conventions..."

"Walter Hall of Dickinson, who held his wife's proxy on the committee, had carried the Loyalists' cause at the New Braunfels meeting," Kinch and Long wrote. "He pledged that if Shivers would pledge to support the party nominees, he and Dickson would withdraw from convention opposition to Shivers. But Shivers' speech was so strongly against the idea of supporting the nominee without reservations, that there was no ground for compromise."

Hall recalls a more detailed and dramatic version: "A very able lawyer from Midland, Tom Sealy, was presiding as chairman, and he finally recognized me. Allan, of course, was there, and a half dozen or so newspapers were represented inasmuch as they knew I was going to have something to say.

"So I took the podium and delivered this challenge: 'You come and take my time here, Governor; you, who have received the highest honors as a Democrat at the hands of the people of Texas, come and tell us whether or not you will support the Democratic nominee for president.

If you do, I will recommend to the Loyal Democrats that it disband and stand behind you to carry this state for the Democrats.'

"Well, Allan was as mad as a hornet; his face flushed a little and he didn't move. Tom Sealy got back to the mike and said, 'I don't think the governor needs to respond to such an emotional appeal or request.'

"I know of no major newspaper that carried the fact that I had challenged Allan," Hall said.

Hall said years later he asked Allen Duckworth, a reporter for The Dallas Morning News, and Sam Kinch, a reporter for the Fort Worth Star-Telegram, why the story wasn't printed.

"They both told me," Hall said, "they had sent the story in, but that portion had been cut at the desk."

Hall and his friends have never understood why such an important challenge to the governor would be chopped from the story of the convention.

The brawling continued at the May state convention in San Antonio, and the liberal faction, led by Maury Maverick Sr. of San Antonio, walked out of the convention. The liberal group held its own convention at nearby La Villita.

Both Texas conventions named delegates to the national convention scheduled in Chicago.

At the 1952 national convention, Hall said, "We had our delegation that did not get seated. We were not seated because the senator from Georgia, Richard Russell, who was running for the presidency, had told the high powers who ran the convention that if they kicked out the Shivers delegation of Texas he would bolt the convention. And Adlai Stevenson had, at that time, agreed to be a nominee. Stevenson said he didn't want to be the nominee of a split party. Harry Truman had given to Maury Maverick his commitment that he would support us and see that we got seated. But Harry Truman was not at that convention and we were not seated. So, therefore, the Shivers group was seated."

At one point during the convention Shivers was asked a question about whether his delegation had signed the assurance that it would support the party nominees to be designated at the convention.

"It did that..." Shivers replied, as a nationwide TV and radio audience listened.

"Without any reservations?" Shivers was asked.

"And without any reservations," Shivers answered. In August of that year, Shivers met with Stevenson in Illinois. He was told that Stevenson planned to veto, as Truman had done on two occasions, a bill which would restore Texas' title to the tidelands.

(Hall said Shivers' trip to talk to Stevenson was an attempt to "blackjack" Stevenson into a position on the tidelands issue.)

After Shivers returned from Illinois, he gave a radio report on his conversation with Stevenson.

He announced he would not support Stevenson in the 1952 election.

Sam Rayburn, in his radio response, declared that if Shivers and Price Daniel, the state attorney general, had gone along with the tidelands compromise that he (Rayburn) and Truman had agreed on in 1949, Texas would have shared the revenues from the entire 18 million acres of the outer Continental Shelf instead of just the 3 million acres inside the three-league limit of Texas.

"Under Allan's leadership," Hall said, "the State Democratic Convention in Amarillo endorsed the Republican nominee, and Shivers actively campaigned for Dwight Eisenhower."

During the campaign, when Adlai Stevenson got off his plane at Houston to make a campaign speech, he saw Hall and said, "You are the one that cautioned us about Allan Shivers."

"He had quite a memory," Hall said, "because I had met him only once.

"Later, when Mr. Rayburn called a few of us to Dallas to do what we could in that campaign, we went to the home of his sister. Pretty soon Rayburn came into the room. After shaking hands with all of us, he pointed at me and said, 'Fellows, Governor Shivers damn sure did not have that country banker fooled; he called the shots on him six months before he did it.'"

...

The most caustic disagreement involving Walter Hall and Lyndon Johnson, when they were on opposite sides, resulted from the State Democratic Convention in Fort Worth in September, 1956.

It was the incident they called the "Cow Barn." It gained that name simply because it was held at the Fort Worth Stockyards, said delegate J. Edwin Smith of Houston, a close personal and political friend of Hall.

Earlier, at the May state convention, Hall said, "Lyndon told me that if I would join him and let him control the May convention (which appointed delegates to the national convention) and assure his election as the chairman of the delegation, that he would use his influence in my behalf at the September convention. That was the one where members of the State Democratic Executive Committee were named.

"We—the liberal Democrats—wanted to get control of that State Democratic Executive Committee," Hall said. "But we couldn't do it by ourselves.

"So I used a lot of my 'shot and powder' to call a meeting of my liberal friends and asked them to line up with Lyndon to beat Allan. They wanted to extract something else, I guess, because they were reluctant. But I explained to them that our votes, with the votes Lyndon controlled, could whip the hell out of Allan in September.

"Finally they agreed to stay with me. Remember, now, if we had stayed aloof, Allan would have beaten Lyndon for the chairmanship of the Texas delegation to the national convention. The liberals were the swing votes.

"So we did help Lyndon beat Allan Shivers at the May convention.

"And then, after we had put Lyndon in charge of the delegation to the National Democratic Convention, he, in the September convention in Fort Worth, lined up voters in North Texas with the Shivers conservatives (we called them 'Shivercrats') and cut our throats. They provided votes to give Allan's crowd continued control of the State Democratic Executive Committee."

So Johnson, apparently with the help of some forces from counties in Sam Rayburn's congressional district, had joined Shivers' forces to beat Hall's liberal Democrats at the convention.

Hall, although reluctant to point a finger at Sam Rayburn, said that "Anybody who was politically informed could tell the way those counties came in that they were the way Lyndon wanted them, and they wouldn't vote that way if Mr. Sam wanted them to vote some other way."

Nevertheless, Hall said he was never able to denounce Sam Rayburn to the extent that he did Lyndon Johnson for the defeat of the Texas liberal Democrats.

Another repercussion of the fight at Fort Worth was that the delegates voted to eject from the convention the Houston delegation, headed by Frankie Randolph, powerful liberal leader. (See next segment.)

Recalling the fights of the 1950s, Hall said, with a tinge of regret in his voice, "We never did beat the Shivercrats."

Hall and Dueling Democrats

Walter Hall, during the bitter political fights within the Democratic Party of the 1950s, was able to retain—or regain—personal friendships with most of the dueling Democrats who had differing viewpoints at different times.

These included Lyndon Johnson, Ralph Yarborough, Sam Rayburn and Frankie Randolph. Excluded, of course, was the leader of the Shivercrats, Allan Shivers.

Hall even tried to serve as a peacemaker at times, and at least one time his effort failed miserably.

"When it was clear to me that Lyndon was going to seek the nomination of his party for the presidency in 1960, I sent word to him through his aide, Cliff Carter, that I thought he should make the announcement in Texas, and that we could sponsor a dinner for him in Galveston, inviting leading Democrats from throughout the state.

"Carter reported back that Johnson thought it would be a good idea, but that he wanted it to be a 'Gulf Coast Hamburger Party' instead of a big dinner. So we held a hamburger party for him in Galveston—the kickoff point for his campaign.

"Lyndon made a good speech, and it was a successful affair. After the party we went back to his room at the Galvez Hotel, where we could have more privacy.

"I told Lyndon, 'Unless we can make some arrangements here with Frankie Randolph, there are going to be a few Texans under her leadership who will not be for you, and it would be better to have a unified state.'

"Lyndon agreed, and asked, 'What do you have in mind?'

"Would you agree to a deal like this: Frankie Randolph would make a public statement that although it was known all around the state that she had major differences with Senator Johnson, she knew he was favored by the great majority of Texans for the Democratic nomination for president; and that, speaking as Democratic committeewoman from Texas, she was therefore going to support Senator Johnson in his efforts.

"Now," Hall asked Johnson, "if she would say that, would you then come back and say something like this: 'I deeply appreciate Frankie Randolph's pledge of support. She has been an outstanding and devoted servant of the Democratic Party and the people of Texas, and I praise her for this. Furthermore, if she so chooses, I will do everything in my power to see that she is re-elected as national committeewoman.' Now, Lyndon, this is the gut."

Frankie Randolph, both Hall and LBJ knew, was a very strong, opinionated leader. "She wanted much more liberal conduct out of the public officials of Texas than we were getting from Lyndon," Hall said. "She was not a woman to compromise—she wanted 100%. She had a big impact in Houston on local candidates. Frankie Randolph was an inspiring woman and she had money, time and intelligence."

LBJ had been thinking about Hall's suggestion, and "When he was thinking, he looked straight at you," Hall explained. "Then he said, 'I'll go for that. See if you can put it over.'

"So in a few days I went to Frankie and ran this scenario by her. Her answer was, 'Hell, no; I'm not going to make a deal with that SOB on any issue.'"

Hall tells another story about the Randolph-Johnson feud which he says he cannot verify, but it is part of his repertoire of political stories.

"Frankie didn't tell me this, but one of her friends did.

"One day Johnson, when he was president, called Randolph and said, 'Hello, Frankie, how are you?' And she replied, 'Who in the hell authorized you to call me by my first name?'"

Mrs. Randolph continued to work for the liberal movement until her death in 1972.

Hall Avoids a Democratic Convention

Walter Hall was not among those present at the 1960 Democratic National Convention in Los Angeles—the convention at which John F. Kennedy was selected as the party's nominee.

Although Hall and Lyndon Johnson had violently disagreed at times during the 1950s, as related elsewhere in this chapter, for the sake of Democratic harmony on the national level they had buried their hatchets.

Hall had been scheduled to attend the Los Angeles convention as a delegate; but because of an unusual series of events he declined to make the journey.

Johnson, who had decided to challenge Kennedy for the nomination, had entrusted his efforts to the hands of John Connally, who later would become governor of Texas. Connally headed the Texas delegation, both in its formation and its activities for Johnson.

Connally was no political friend of Hall. "I knew his record and his beliefs," Hall explained. "I did not trust him, and felt he sought power for the benefit of the 'upper crust.' He did not know the meaning of the word loyalty. This was demonstrated when he switched to the Republican Party. While seeking the Republican nomination for president, he reportedly spent $7 million and got one vote."

Connally exercised the power Johnson gave him to change Hall's status from a delegate from Clark Thompson's congressional district to an alternate delegate, which was meaningless. So Hall decided he was not needed or wanted in Los Angeles.

Others had a different opinion about Hall's necessity at the convention.

Jake Pickle, another member of Johnson's convention brain trust, was one of those. Although Hall and Pickle had earlier differences (Pickle had been a stalwart on Allan Shivers' team), they had become good friends.

Walter Hall, right, greets former North Carolina Gov. Terry Sanford in Hall's Citizens State Bank office. Sanford was his state's governor from 1960 to 1965 and U.S. senator from North Carolina from 1986 to 1993. He also was president of Duke University from 1969 to 1982. Sanford was brought to Texas in 1975 by Weyman Walker of Houston, chairman of the Texans for Sanford Committee, when Sanford was seeking the Democratic nomination for the U.S. presidency.

(Photo courtesy of Weyman Walker)

Hall reported that at one point when the liberal Democrats were fighting the Shivers crowd, Pickle was campaigning for a congressional seat from LBJ's former Austin district. Hall's liberal group, seeking financial support to fight Pickle, adopted the slogan, "Dollars for Democrats but not a nickel for Pickle." Pickle won, and as a congressman, Hall said, "Jake proved to be a good Democrat and proved he had not given his political soul to Allan Shivers."

When Johnson discovered that Hall was not in Los Angeles—and that he needed Hall's counsel and help in wooing delegates from some states such as North Carolina—he asked Pickle to call Hall at his home in League City to try to get him to come to the convention.

Pickle's call to Hall came the day before the convention opened.

"Jake said Lyndon had asked me to please fly to L.A. so I could meet with the North Carolina delegates. Lyndon had no one to caucus with them; and the North Carolina people were all asking why Hall was not a delegate."

Terry Sanford, the newly elected governor of North Carolina, was head of his state's delegation. He was a close friend of Hall; Hall described him as "a highly intellectual liberal and a Jack Kennedy man." Hall said he knew that "Terry Sanford was not going to be swayed by anything I would say, despite our friendship."

Hall said he asked Pickle if he thought it would really be of any help if he (Hall) were at the convention.

Pickle's reply was negative.

"Jake said that there would be a dozen Kennedy men to go in and do whatever needed to be done (to get Kennedy nominated) and that 'we were going to get the hell beat out of us.' That is, of course, exactly what happened." So Hall's political experience and Pickle's political insight kept Hall from being part of that particular political defeat.

"You may be assured," Hall later reminisced, "that when Lyndon found out exactly what happened, he was a 'bit upset' with John Connally."

The Kennedy Assassination

Walter and Helen Hall were in Houston the night of Nov. 21, 1963, and heard President John F. Kennedy speak at a public testimonial dinner honoring U.S. Rep. Albert Thomas of Houston.

They were joined at the affair in the old Sam Houston Coliseum by Houston banker Melvin Rouff; and while waiting for the program to start, Rouff observed that, despite all the Secret Service presence and other protection provided, it probably still was not enough. He noted the many ushers and others scurrying up and down the aisles and said, "If someone wanted to assassinate the president, he could probably do it."

The following day, Nov. 22, 1963, Walter and Helen Hall drove to Austin.

Kennedy was scheduled to make a statewide telecast speech that night in the state capital, following appearances in Fort Worth and Dallas, and the Halls planned to attend the Austin event.

While eating lunch at a Mexican restaurant, the Halls were told by a waiter that the president had been shot and, a few minutes later, that he was dead.

"Looking back," Hall remarked, "I think that his death was the greatest tragedy that our nation has suffered since the assassination of Abraham Lincoln."

Hall believes that the Vietnam War, which he called "a tragedy in every sense of the word," might not have escalated if Kennedy had lived.

Ignored Advice for Humphrey; Hall Is 'Dismissed' from White House

Two incidents concerning the Vietnam War had unusual conclusions for Walter Hall. One was a serving of political advice that the banker gave which was not followed; the other was an incident some of Hall's friends call the time Walter Hall was "kicked out of the White House."

Vice President Hubert H. Humphrey, left, greeted Walter Hall at the vice president's office in Washington, D.C. Hall backed Humphrey in the campaign for the Democratic presidential nomination a short time later. The effort was unsuccessful.

Hall is credited by many friends—including Texas City attorney Jim Simpson—with giving advice to a presidential candidate who, had he followed it, probably would have been elected to succeed Lyndon B. Johnson in 1968.

Hubert Humphrey failed to follow that advice, and Simpson firmly believes that his failure to follow Hall's suggestions cost Humphrey the election.

Hall recalls that Humphrey was to visit Houston in 1967 to make a television speech.

Humphrey called Hall and told him he'd like to see him during his visit to Houston to get Hall's ideas about the campaign. Hall had become supporter No. 22 in the Citizens for Humphrey organization after he found out that Johnson was not going to run for re-election.

Only a day or so earlier, Hall said, Humphrey had made a speech in Salt Lake City in which he appeared to move a step away from Johnson's position on the Vietnam War—which gratified Hall.

Hall was very blunt in the meeting with Humphrey about his feelings concerning the war and the role he thought it would have in the election.

Hall reported the occasion:

"Humphrey; a member of his staff; Congressman Bob Eckhardt (and I believe Congressman Albert Thomas); Eckhardt's driver, and I were in the car together riding to the TV station for Humphrey's appearance there. When we arrived Humphrey asked me to wait a minute, and the others went into the station. Humphrey told me he was concerned about how the campaign was going, and asked what I would suggest.

"I told him, 'Hubert, you're a good man and a progressive man and you should be the next president of the United States.

"'But, you cannot be elected president so long as you're tied to Lyndon Johnson. Lyndon is a good friend of mine, but I now know that the Vietnam War is absolutely divisive and grossly wrong.

"'What you have got to do is disavow the Vietnam War.'"

Humphrey told Hall that Lyndon Johnson objected to him taking any position other than support of his, and was sharply critical of the mild stand Humphrey took in his Salt Lake City speech.

"Then," Hall said, "you have got to go before the public and say, in effect, 'I have been a loyal vice president, I have done everything I could to be of help to the president and make his path a little less rugged.

"'But I am announcing today that I am resigning as vice president of the United States so that my position on the Vietnam War will not hamper him in his own efforts.'

"In that way," Hall told Humphrey, "nobody can accuse you of stabbing your president in the back—coming out in the open and saying that you respect your president and respect his views, but that those views are not your views. And that you do not think it's best for the country to continue a war that is devouring so many young Americans—that we do not have enough at stake in that part of the world. You are asking the people of our country to make you president and accordingly they are entitled to know how you stand on all major issues.

"Otherwise, you are going to get your — beat."

(Hall later learned that George Meany, national president of the AFL-CIO, had given Humphrey the same advice.)

"Would you," Hall said Humphrey asked him, "write and send me a copy of what you think I should say? Send it to my vice-presidential office."

Hall said he would and did. "It was a very brief speech following the lines we discussed," Hall said.

Humphrey obviously did not follow Hall's advice.

Simpson said he believes that if Hubert Humphrey had followed Hall's advice, "This country may never have been saddled with Richard Nixon."

Hall explained that he became a supporter of Humphrey when even some of Hall's fellow Democrats disliked Humphrey and his views. And that explanation reveals another philosophical characteristic of the Dickinson banker.

Sam Rayburn verified the fact to Hall that the House speaker at one time was bitter about Humphrey, but told Hall he had changed his position. Rayburn, Hall said, became angry at Humphrey at a Democratic convention in Philadelphia when Humphrey, at that time a Minnesota mayor leading his state's delegation, was speaking on behalf of a civil rights bill.

Rayburn reported that Humphrey said, in effect, "We've been hearing here in this convention, and for many years before, speeches from our friends in the South who will not vote for civil rights legislation. They constantly refer to states rights. It is time for the people of America to start referring to 'human rights.'"

"That guy," Hall said Rayburn told him at the time, "is going to ruin the Democratic Party."

Hall had a different opinion.

"That speech," Hall said, "impressed me. I applauded it when I heard about it."

. . .

Hall laughs that the interpretation of the event at the White House was considered by some an ejection of the banker by President Johnson.

But he does admit that he and his wife, Helen, were guests in the White House several times and his treatment on this particular occasion was somewhat different.

"I had written two articles for the Texas Observer concerning the Vietnam War," Hall said. "Lyndon Johnson had sent a lot of troops to Vietnam; and I wrote that because he knew a lot more than I did about the situation I would not join those who criticized him. As time went on it looked like there was a lack of direction of the war, and I wrote another article that simply said the president should tell the American people exactly what were the objectives and how he intended to achieve them.

"Then he invited Helen and me to the White House to stay overnight. The next morning, a secretary called me and said the president would like to see me at 9:30.

"I walked into his office and Lyndon asked, 'Walter, what's the deal on Vietnam?'

"I said, 'Mr. President, you either ought to win or get out.'

"He slapped his desk and said, 'You don't understand, and besides I'm busy!'" Hall said he decided he was "dismissed."

LBJ did accept Hall's thanks for his hospitality, Hall said.

Later, friendly relationships were renewed, and after LBJ and Lady Bird left Washington, Hall was invited several times to the Johnsons' ranch at Stonewall.

Hall and Yarborough

Walter Hall and former U.S. Sen. Ralph Yarborough are two politically active Texans who greatly admire each other.

The two men first became political allies; then almost immediately a bond of friendship was formed which has existed until this day.

"I helped in Yarborough's campaign for governor right from the start," Hall said, "because I was opposed to the 'establishment' which was personified best by Allan Shivers. Yarborough had run unsuccessfully for attorney general—but I didn't know him at that time and wasn't interested in that race. But I felt that Allan Shivers was not good for Texas and I supported Ralph right from the first time he ran for governor."

Yarborough lost to Shivers in the Democratic primary in 1952 and in the runoff primary in 1954.

Then Yarborough ran against Price Daniel and was defeated in the second Democratic primary in 1956 by 3,171 votes in a vote count that Hall considered "questionable."

Yarborough was elected to the U.S. Senate in a special election in April, 1957, and was elected to a full term in 1958. He was re-elected in 1964, and served in the Senate until 1971.

"Some of the things I remember about Ralph," Hall said, "are his vigor and his willingness to work 12 or 14 hours a day. We were able to generate tremendous racial-wise support for him in Texas and Galveston County and, to a degree, in Harris County.

"One of the things I remember that reveals the man's understanding of campaign strategy was an event in Texas City. He was running for re-election as U.S. senator. We had a big campaign event planned for him at the biggest hall in that city.

"Ralph had asked me to please send to his office a list of the things I thought he should emphasize in his speech. And I did.

"When you're going to speak in Galveston County, there are two things you want to say: 'I am amazed, as so many people are, at the way Galveston showed its courage and fortitude after suffering the great calamity of the 1900 hurricane; then, again, Galveston County came back from the great explosion of Texas City.' And then I continued to list the things I knew Galveston County residents were for, both statewide and local issues."

Hall said at almost the last minute he had a chance to look at the speech Yarborough was going to give.

"One of those geniuses that the campaigners without much money always get in their campaign headquarters thought he knew more about writing an appropriate speech for delivery in Galveston County than I did," Hall recalled.

"He had started off Ralph's speech by praising the Houston Ship Channel."

Hall convinced Yarborough that this would be a disaster, and that he must trash the speech and speak extemporaneously.

"As a U.S. senator, you can discuss foreign affairs in a skillful manner," Hall told Yarborough.

Meantime, trashing the speech also meant trashing a radio schedule already arranged for Yarborough's original speech.

Hall said that with the help of Steve Cowan, a radio executive, they were able to remedy the situation.

Cowan, head of Galveston's Radio Station KGBC, had arranged for a network of three stations to cover Yarborough's speech—his station and two in Houston.

"Hall was devastated when he read Yarborough's speech just a few minutes before air time," Cowan said. "I believe it was the angriest I've ever seen him."

By hiding in a small closet at the side of the stage, where Yarborough could see him but the audience could not, Cowan was able to signal Yarborough when to follow Hall's instructions.

Yarborough was to begin his introductory remarks, keeping an eye on Cowan. Cowan would give him a three-minute signal—by holding up three fingers—before his network time was to begin. At the appropriate moment, Cowan held up his three fingers, Yarborough concluded his introductory remarks to the audience and, at the precise time, started his address on foreign affairs which was broadcast.

"It worked like clockwork," Hall said. "And Ralph gave one of the best speeches I've ever heard him give."

Hall was a front-row observer of the political disharmony between Yarborough, Lyndon Johnson and Sam Rayburn.

"It would really be very odd for Ralph to have the same affection and respect for Mr. Rayburn as LBJ had," Hall told Dr. Anthony Champagne of the University of Texas at Dallas in a 1980 interview.

"Lyndon and Ralph were almost at sword-point on occasions, even though they usually voted pretty much alike. But anybody as close to LBJ as was Mr. Rayburn wouldn't be too close to Ralph Yarborough. If Lyndon ever did anything to help Ralph in a political campaign other than on a ticket basis, like when he, John Connally and Ralph were all on it together, I don't know about it...

"I think Ralph's independence of Lyndon Johnson and Mr. Rayburn's connection with Lyndon was the problem, even though on major issues their interests were pretty close together, if not identical. Ralph was determined not to be known as a rubber stamp for Johnson."

Hall said Yarborough sponsored many outstanding bills that were passed by the Senate.

"To give one example," Hall said " he finally, over the opposition of two or three presidents...and others, got through the bill extending GI rights to the veterans of Korea.

"There is no question of Ralph's importance as senator," Hall said. "He probably has as much legislation to his credit on education and veterans' benefits as any man who has served in the U.S. Senate."

Yarborough, still practicing law from his office in Austin, remembered Hall's great help—and his opinion of the Dickinson banker—in this tribute:

Walter Hall and Ralph Yarborough were pictured during a happy moment when Yarborough visited Dickinson in 1964.

"When I announced for the governorship of Texas the first time, in early May of 1952, I had not alerted the people of Texas to the fact that I was about to enter the gubernatorial campaign. It was just a few days before the filing deadline, and I announced without any preliminary speech or campaign manager or fund-raisers.

"A few days after my announcement, there came a great voice, like a massive thunder from the skies: Walter Hall calling to congratulate me and to say that he would put his best efforts into my campaign. He did give his best efforts through three partly lost and partly stolen campaigns against us for the Texas governorship. Then in April of 1957 came the winning race, and I was elected to the U.S. Senate, followed by more winning races for the U.S. Senate.

"Walter Hall was the most unusual of all my supporters I had helping me in those races. He was one of my three largest contributors. Most large contributors think that they don't need to do more if they give large amounts of money to a campaign, but Walter Hall made continuous contributions of all kinds, helping me to...finally be elected. He organized rallies in the Gulf Coast area, financing those rallies, and speaking at them, introducing me to the people. He worked constantly on my behalf, organizing supporters, using his vast influence with his banks and other businesses, his contacts with people.

"Walter Hall enlisted every aspect he could draw on throughout his network of people and business to further my campaigns. My support in that Gulf Coast area remained steady, race after race, because of Walter Hall. He contributed money, ideals and energy to my campaigns for progressive government, one that would be amenable to all of the people. Not only in campaign years, but year after year, Walter Hall continued to make actions that advanced our cause for better government for the people."

Yarborough exhibits two programs from his political memorabilia collection to illustrate Hall's importance in his political life:

"One (is) a statewide Texas Salute to me on Oct. 19, 1963. That was mainly a tribute to my success on my first major bill, the Padre Island National Seashore Bill. Note the importance of Walter Hall, who was toastmaster at this big statewide program, the biggest and most impressive we ever had to raise money to pay off my campaign debts...On the list of 'Friends of Ralph Yarborough,' toward the middle of the program, Walter G. Hall is listed as Chairman of the Steering Committee that raised the money to pay off my campaign debts...

"The second program for a Texas Appreciation Dinner held July 27, 1972, in Houston lists Walter Hall as a member of the 'Patrons Committee' who were the biggest contributors to that meeting. Walter Hall was one of those five.

"These programs show the importance of Walter Hall in my political career for which I have received credit from political scientists and history professors as having passed more national legislation than any other Texas U.S. senator in this century."

Yarborough also remembers Hall's political acumen in times not so happy.

He said that Hall warned him in 1970, just a month or two before the primaries, that he was in danger of losing the election.

Yarborough continued:

"That was the only warning I had, Walter Hall's knowledgeable attempt to aid me in my race for re-election in 1970 when Lloyd Bentsen was running against me with all his money and falsehoods.

"With my re-election in 1964, I had such prestige that I was passing more bills in my last six years in the Senate than I had at any other time, and I presume that maybe I got too egotistical, thinking I could win again in 1970.

"In the November, 1958, general election, I led in 249 out of the 254 counties of Texas, and in the first Democratic primary against the 'Thrifty Old Scotchman' Gordon McClendon of Dallas, 1964, I led in 213 counties. In the general election of 1964 against George Bush (later president), I led in 220 counties with 1,463,938 votes for me. My leads were going up constantly.

"My efforts to push that Big Thicket Bill through to form the Big Thicket National Preserve, my War on Cancer Bill which I worked on for 12 years, my effort to amend my Cold War GI Bill, and though I had pushed through my Bilingual Education Bill in one year in 1968, the administration had locked the appropriations for it, and I was working to get appropriations for it, all of that was going on in 1970 when I should have been home campaigning.

"Walter Hall had warned me to be careful when everyone else was telling me I had it won and not to worry about the election...Walter Hall (told me) that I had better wake up and do something. He said, 'They have prepared a mighty package for you, Ralph...'

"I do not think my supporters turned against me, but they just fell apart and failed to go to the polls. The Texas establishment saw to it that Preston Smith (generally a Democratic governor who always had opposition) had no opposition that year to pull people to the polls. They did the same to other statewide candidates—they were practically unopposed.

"Had Smith had opposition, I would have been re-elected. The point of this is that Walter Hall had gotten information and knew what was going to happen and he tried to warn me; but I did not respond quick enough nor ably enough to save the election. I lost it for the people of Texas, but Walter Hall was the one person in Texas who warned me that I was in danger."

(Despite the rancor of the Yarborough-Bentsen campaign, after

Bentsen's election Hall said the new senator's policies surprised him. Senator Bentsen, Hall said, vigorously supported many programs the banker applauded and had long supported; and as a result Hall became a Bentsen advocate.)

Ralph Yarborough paid a tremendous tribute to Walter Hall with this statement:

"Walter Hall was one of the most unusual men I have ever known in my political life, and one of the few great men you will find in any political activity. I would like to see a monument erected to Walter Hall and his influence for good in this nation."

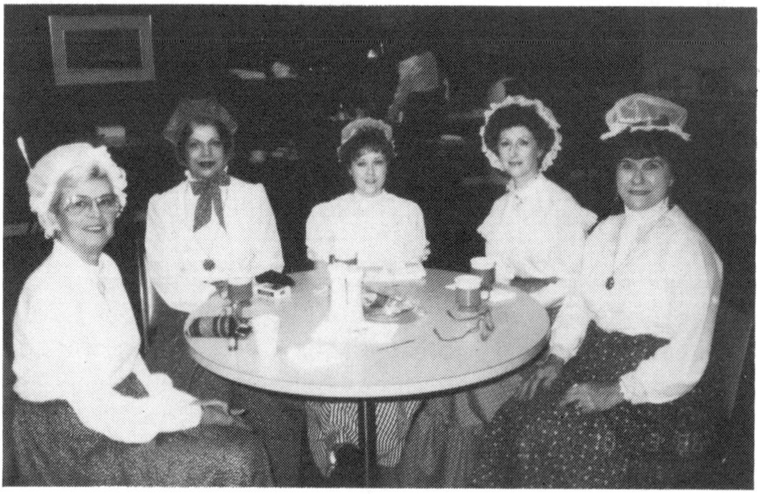

A group of bank employees and friends, dressed for the occasion, relaxed during the 1986 observance of the 80th birthday of the bank. From the left are Alice Saunders, Katherine Phelps, Marsha Thompson, Darlene Whatley and Rene Barta.

Pleasant Remembrances of 'Mr. Sam'

Although Walter Hall considered U.S. House Speaker Sam Rayburn a close personal friend and political ally, Hall did not consider himself to be a member of Rayburn's "inner circle."

"I enjoyed very much my relationship with Mr. Sam," Hall said. "We became good friends, but I was not one of the men really close to him in his political conduct."

Nevertheless, Hall tells some revealing stories about the man he always called "Mr. Sam" at the speaker's request.

Many of those stories were related by Hall in a taped interview with Dr. Anthony Champagne, the associate professor at the University of Texas at Dallas.

Hall said:

"I called him 'Mr. Sam' because he had asked me to when I was referring to him as 'Mr. Speaker.' I took this as quite a compliment as I later learned that he didn't ask people to call him 'Mr. Sam' unless he regarded them with some degree of affection or respect or both."

Hall recalled that once when he was in Rayburn's Washington office an aide, John Holton, came in and said, "Mr. Speaker, Congressman (blank) is here to report to you on those three congressmen you asked him to check with regarding their vote this afternoon."

Hall said he started to get up and leave but Rayburn said, "Keep your seat, keep your seat; this won't take but a minute." Rayburn got up from his desk, went to the door and invited the congressman in. The congressman said, "Mr. Speaker, I talked to Congressman (blank) of (blank state) and he feels the bill is a good one in his judgment; it's good for him politically and he will be there; you can count on his vote. Congressman (blank) from (blank state) said he would have to vote against the bill and you would understand why. Congressman (blank) of (blank state) said that he didn't know whether or not the bill was good for him politically, but that he was going to be there and vote for it on the basis of something you said to him once and that was, 'Now and then you ought to do something just because it's right.'"

On another occasion, Hall was at Rayburn's home in Bonham at a time before they knew whether President Truman was going to run for a second term. Hall became active under Rayburn's leadership in Truman's surprising victory over Tom Dewey in 1948.

"We had a little lunch in front of the fireplace and I was about to leave," Hall said. "My congressman, Clark Thompson, who was extremely close to Mr. Rayburn, had told me a story that Harry Truman told him. I wanted to confirm it."

So Hall confronted him: "Mr. Sam, stories are going around something like this: A day or two after Mr. Truman became president, he was in your office to discuss some legislation. He looked at his watch and said, 'Will you have John call my car? I am late for an appointment back at the White House.'

"You said, 'My car is waiting and I will drive you back, if you like.' He said, 'OK, OK.' The two of you went down to get in the car and you said, 'Now Harry, and I am not going to call you Harry any more after this—you are going to be Mr. President to me—I want to tell you something: You are going to get down in the White House and after awhile the staff is going to start telling you what a good man you are; then these congressmen and senators are going to ask you to appoint this man and that man and do this and do that, and they are going to tell you what a great president you are.

"'Then these foreigners are going to be coming in and want you to do things, and some of them are going to say you are the greatest president we have ever had.

"'But, Harry, don't you believe them—because you ain't!'

"Mr. Sam looked at me and grinned; he neither confirmed it nor denied it, so I am confident it is an accurate story.

"Then I asked, 'Mr. Sam, do you think the president is going to run again?' He answered, 'I don't know.' I said, 'Well, I hope he does; I think he has been right on the great issues. He was right to stop that terrible war with the atomic bomb; he was right to create NATO; and he was right to stop the communist march to the West.' Mr. Sam said, 'Oh, you are right; he was right on all the great issues, but can't he foul up the little ones?'"

Hall said he thinks that was very interesting coming from a man who loved Harry Truman.

Hall also related Rayburn's not-happy reaction to a statement of another president, Richard Nixon, who in a political speech in New Orleans reportedly had called the Democratic Party a "party of treason."

"There had been newspaper reports confirming Nixon had indeed made the speech, and I had read about Mr. Rayburn's anger at the speech," Hall said.

"I was in his home shortly thereafter, and I asked Mr. Sam about it. He said—and his eyes got pretty mean—'I know he made the statement in the speech because five responsible newsmen told me they heard him make it. What he said was that the Democratic Party is a party of treason. No man can say that about my party and I resent it. And furthermore, Walter, this country cannot survive if those in disagreement about political matters start calling each other traitors. There is no place for that in American politics. Nixon said that, and that explains my position.'"

One of the very few bitter moments in the Hall-Rayburn relationship came after the 1956 State Democratic Convention in Fort Worth, when Lyndon Johnson and Allan Shivers defeated Hall's liberal Democrats (detailed in "The Democrats' Fight" segment).

"Even though it appeared that voters from Rayburn's district were helping Lyndon beat us, I could never bring myself to denounce Sam Rayburn," Hall said.

Hall, discussing LBJ's role in the defeat of the liberal forces at the 1956 convention, expressed his deep disappointment to Sam Rayburn.

David G. McComb, in his interview of Hall for the LBJ Library, reported Rayburn's response, as recalled by Hall:

"He said, 'Walter, here's what you've got to keep in mind. No politician can operate both on a state and national level with the exception of Harry Byrd. He runs Virginia and he's also an influential senator. But every other national politician has to look upon his state as a base of operations. He cannot get involved in the local controversies in that state; otherwise, he would so crystallize the opposition that he would probably not be elected. You've got to recognize that Lyndon is a national politician, and he cannot engage in these things down here in Texas on the basis that you people want him to.'

"I differed with Mr. Rayburn then and I still think that Mr. Rayburn was wrong on that score. I feel that had Lyndon Johnson and Mr. Rayburn not prevented a liberal State Democratic Executive Committee in 1956, I think most of the political direction of Texas would have been changed and I think it would have gone along more liberal routes."

Asked about the reason for the breakup of the liberal 1956 coalition, Hall told McComb:

"That is very hard to say. When I later talked to Lyndon about it, and we had very strong differences of opinion, he was vague about it. But I gather that pressures came to him from some of the people who had been very important to him in his campaigns, financially and otherwise, who felt that it was not in their best interest or in the best interest of Texas or in Lyndon Johnson's political career to have 'screeching liberals,' a term that one man applied to us, in the saddle in Texas.

"I think Lyndon, after great mental turmoil and intellectual struggle on the thing, bought that, and I think he was wrong...I think that we could have gone down a much more progressive trail starting then and there."

But, "I never did downgrade Lyndon Johnson the way some people did in the presence of Sam Rayburn. You just couldn't do it."

Hall related another incident concerning Rayburn which reveals some interesting details of the political process as well as Sam Rayburn's high regard for a request from Walter Hall.

"I felt that some people were being gravely mistreated," Hall said. "Monsanto Chemical Co. built a huge plant on Chocolate Bayou—in Brazoria County and near the Alvin State Bank, of which I was then president.

"Under the law at that time, if a private corporation spent money to open up and develop a waterway and then later on tonnage other than that belonging to the developing company moved over the waterway, the company could apply through the Army Corps of Engineers for reimbursement, inasmuch as the investment had become a public asset and was being used by the public.

"As I recall, the Corps of Engineers had to keep a record for three successive years for an applicant to be eligible for reimbursement for the costs of such a project.

"One day the man in charge of legislative liaison from Monsanto's home office in St. Louis visited me in Alvin. He told me his company would like to apply for reimbursement under the law, but that eligibility would be for naught unless an upcoming bill contained an appropriation for $10,000 to permit the Corps of Engineers to continue its record-keeping and investigation of the waterway.

"Do you mean to say," I asked, "that your senators can't get a $10,000 appropriation for a thing like that?"

"He said, 'They can't.'

"I was surprised because Stuart Symington, although a Democrat, was a powerful man and one of the senators from Missouri. He had been the first secretary of the Air Force after World War II and was serving as a senator under another military man—although elected by the Republicans—President Dwight D. Eisenhower.

"Well," I said, "I'll be glad to talk to Clark Thompson."

"'Congressman Thompson,' he said, 'has informed us that he has already done everything that he can do, that the budget committee said the White House wanted to delete that item from the budget.'"

Hall said he asked the Monsanto representative to write him a memorandum, which he did.

"I was in Washington shortly thereafter and took the memorandum with me to Mr. Sam's office," Hall continued. "In the course of our conversation, I told him about the problem and handed him the memorandum.

"He was concerned that there was a problem when only a $10,000 appropriation was needed. After all, Monsanto had spent its money, the waterway proved to be sound, other people had used it, and the Corps of Engineers was able to testify as to tonnage.

"In due course the Monsanto man called me from St. Louis and said he understood my congressman was going to call me and give me the details; but he wanted me to know that Monsanto had been informed by the Corps of Engineers that the $10,000 had been included in the budget."

Hall said Clark Thompson called him in a few days and said, "Yes, that appropriation was put in the bill; I went over to the budget committee and talked to several of the staff about it and how it got in after what they had told me and Symington.

"One of them said, 'Looking at the file, there is a man by the name of Walter Hall whose footprints are all over the page.'

"So I know exactly what happened: It is logical that neither Eisenhower nor any other knowledgeable man was going to turn down Sam Rayburn on a $10,000 item. It was just that way, and it was only fair this was done.

"It was a case of Mr. Rayburn's vast influence, his quick understanding of the situation as to what was right and fair and his moving in to do something that, certainly, I felt, ought to be done."

Hall Is Honored by Democrats

Because he has many friends with the same political beliefs he has and because of his untiring work for the Democratic Party and its candidates, probably no award has pleased Walter Hall more than the one he received in 1974.

He was named Mr. Democrat of Galveston County.

A dinner honoring Hall was held on Saturday, Oct. 19, at the Moody Civic Center in Galveston. Some of the stalwarts of the party—local, statewide and national—gathered to pay tribute to the banker.

A.R. (Babe) Schwartz, state senator, was toastmaster, and the invocation was given by the Rev. Victor Stevens.

Writer Joel Kirkpatrick, at that time a reporter for The Galveston Daily News, described the stage setting for the night with this introductory paragraph of his story:

"Democrats of all persuasions rolled out a golden carpet of words of praise for Walter G. Hall..."

"County AFL-CIO President Al G. Goodson called Hall a friend of labor, said he had probably lent more money for the construction of union halls than any banker in Texas—and never lost a penny doing it," Kirkpatrick wrote.

"Clark Thompson, formerly congressman from the 9th Congressional District, and elder statesman for the event, noted he has been friends with Hall for a long time, and he urged those present to stick with the Democrats..."

State Rep. Neil Caldwell of Alvin, (now a state district judge living in Angleton), said all those present were indebted to Hall in many ways.

Caldwell noted that Hall was characterized in the program as a "country banker."

"He's a country banker in about the same way that Sam Irwin is a country lawyer," Caldwell said, referring to the attorney prominent on television during the Watergate hearings.

Kirkpatrick's story continued:

"Caldwell said what he appreciates most about Hall is his 'concern and appreciation for the dignity of people.'

"Former U.S. Sen. Ralph Yarborough noted Hall had been in there with the Democratic Party all the way, and said 'two presidents had begged Hall to come to Washington to accept some high post—and Hall chose to stay in the area he loves.'

"U.S. Rep. Bob Eckhardt noted that Hall had built some of the biggest fires under politicians he had ever seen. He said that perhaps Hall could have been governor of Texas, but he chose to stay in Galveston County because of a belief that 'the action is where you are.'

"U.S. Rep. Charles Wilson of Lufkin called Hall '...one of the greatest Americans it has ever been my privilege to know.'

"U.S. Rep. (Jack) Brooks said Hall was for '...good citizenship, good government, and human brotherhood and represents the very best the nation has to offer.'

"U.S. Sen. Lloyd Bentsen said he had had Walter Hall against him and he had had Walter Hall for him, 'and it's sure a lot better when he's with me.'

"Bentsen called him a 'unifier—a man who brings people in the party together.'

"In his response to all the accolades, Hall characteristically didn't dwell on himself but called for a program of work for the Democrats present.

"He urged the election of a 'veto proof' Congress, establishment of a state utility commission, a look to a strong excess profits tax for corporations instead of thinking up new taxes for individuals.

"He noted that the failure of courts to provide speedy trials in cases before them was giving truth to the old saw, 'Justice delayed is justice denied.'

"And he called for a great awakening of simple national pride. He noted that after all, it was America that put a man on the moon, and that the space program was a great investment for the nation. And in the end, because Hall has a roomful of plaques, he was given another bank.

"This one was a small silver ceramic Democratic donkey, one made by Charlotte Mattingley. It bore the legend, 'Mr. Democrat—Walter G. Hall.'"

The printed program for the night's events included tributes not usually found in such testimonial affairs.

Portions from it follow:

"Walter Hall is indeed a prosperous country banker, insuranceman, trader in this and that. Yet he has lived by a simple creed: Citizen first; banker, businessman second. To the amazement of many, his fights and interests associated with being a Liberal Democrat have been pursued while he was achieving more than average material success.

"He's a friend to those who want to be his friend. He is like fire—warm to those seeking aid, comforting to those who share his beliefs, cheering to the depressed, yet blistering and caustic to his adversaries. Those who know him best describe him as a wire scouring pad chasing grime.

"Walter Hall has served as Democratic precinct chairman, as a member of the State Executive Committee and as delegate to state and national Democratic conventions. An avowed supporter of liberalism, he has waded into many frays. He is a proven crafty fighter during the contest, yet a conciliator with no grudges after, and always sports a hearty smile and an invitation to all: 'Let's do business.'

"Walter Hall, a self-styled populist, counts among those he has supported with enthusiasm Democratic standard bearers Franklin Roosevelt, Harry Truman, Adlai Stevenson, Lyndon Johnson, Hubert Humphrey and Ralph Yarborough.

"A longtime friend of the late president from Texas, he called Johnson in 1961 when the terrible Hurricane Carla hit the area. Urging the then-vice president to come to the area, Hall joined Johnson and Congressman Clark Thompson for a sobering tour. Immediately following, every federal aid program was set in motion.

"His political efforts are entwined with his civic work . . .

"He is a contradiction of the banking stereotype—favoring and fostering the interests of the many and fighting the intrigues of those (with) whom he disagrees...He is financial counselor to little people with big aspirations everywhere in the country, and he is a hardnosed realist to big people.

"...Of civic work generally, he now says, 'Call me only if you REALLY need me. I don't want to be deadwood on any committees.' He is an activist, pure and simple...

"His wit is well known, and he has practiced it upon some of the giants of his time. He can also ease through tough truths with jests; a favorite saying is proof: 'Aw, it's no disgrace to be poor. Damned inconvenient, but no disgrace!'

"He advises cold showers for hot heads, and he often takes his own advice. He has a simple philosophy: toleration, generosity, and respect for the dignity of his fellow men. And, what's more, he is unashamed to tell all who will listen that he is unalterably convinced that the Democratic Party is THE vehicle through which these things are best sought.

"Undoubtedly, Walter G. Hall is Mr. Democrat of Galveston County."

Dugger Evaluates Hall's Philosophy

Ronnie Dugger, a social-policy reporter and writer, founded, edited and became publisher of the Texas Observer, a biweekly "journal of free voices" published in Austin. Dugger offered this insight into the manner in which Hall is willing to support financially his political philosophy:

"From the first days late in 1954 when a group of Texas national Democrats were trying to form the Texas Observer I was told about 'the liberal banker down in Dickinson' (sometimes they'd say Galveston), Walter Hall. He was one of the ten or a dozen most important people in the liberal political circle then huddling together in Texas, and in a short time we became good friends the way a wise older man and a comer sometimes will. As an adviser and a financial contributor to the Observer—and from time to time as a writer—Walter was as helpful to the paper as he was hellzapoppin to Allan Shivers. Once when Jim Hightower (later agricultural commissioner of Texas) and I thought the paper might go under because of worse-than-usual money troubles, he just up and wrote out a check for $20,000."

Liz Carpenter's Evaluation

One of the better-known and better-respected voices of the Democratic Party in Texas is that commanded by author Liz Carpenter.

Carpenter, former press secretary to Lady Bird Johnson when LBJ was president, also served as assistant secretary for public affairs in the U.S. Department of Education in the Jimmy Carter administration and later was vice president of Hill and Knowlton, the international public relations firm. After returning to Texas from Washington, she has pursued a relentless career of writing, speaking on public issues and serving as a consultant for the LBJ Library in Austin.

Carpenter raises her voice to a high pitch when discussing Walter Hall. And probably there is no more loquacious and sincere voice in praising him and his politics.

At the Walter and Helen Hall Lectureship at Rice University's Department of Sociology in 1992, Carpenter delineated her personal views of Hall and his politics:

"I am here to speak well of Walter Hall for this lectureship which is named for him and his darling wife, the late Helen Hall. They were partners in politics, representing the best of us—dedicated, honest and courageous. Politically, they were Democrats and liberals and were never timid about saying so. In fact, if Ronald Reagan had asked them, they would have been glad to stand up and claim the dreaded 'L' word and make it popular. They gave the right to conservatives or Texas Dixiecrats or right wingers to be what they wanted to be.

"If you were in the Texas political conventions in the glory days of Franklin Roosevelt and Harry Truman, when Speaker Sam Rayburn and Lyndon Johnson were trying to hold the Democratic Party together as the Texas Dixiecrats were trying to lure it away, you saw the Halls—sturdy, unwavering. It was a time of heavy political shenanigans...a time when the opponents might stall a vote and dispatch two private planes to East Texas and West Texas to get some absent delegates. It was a time of flowery oratory. There was a long tug of war over a civil rights plank in the Democratic platform. State Sen. Joe Hill took the podium, 'I was born of a Democratic mother, nurtured on a Democratic breast. But tonight, like Robert E. Lee, I'm going to saddle old Traveler and ride to Richmond...' You can't find passion like that any more.

"Walter and I are both political veterans of the barbecue and fish fry circuit, of whistle stops through Dixie, and sitting spellbound next to the radio—or was it the crystal set?—waiting for returns. Yes, we are two political artifacts."

Later, when she was asked for a more personal assessment of the banker, Carpenter wrote:

"When I think of Walter, the qualities of compassion, steadfastness, guts, and good humored conviviality spring to mind. Not many successful bankers are caught using phrases like 'what's good for the folks' but that is Walter's top priority and has been for half a century of Texas politics.

"A generous check writer, he has been helping out progressive candidates for public office for half a century.

"He meets the feminist test. When the Equal Rights Amendment battle was on, I wrote Walter asking him for a donation, expecting $100 or $200. But promptly, the check arrived. It was for $1,000.

"Walter loves political stories. He likes to hear them and he likes to tell them. One Saturday evening, he invited a group of friends from Central Texas to come out to his ranch and have some after-dinner political stories around the fireplace. After we all got through, Walter stood up and rattled off one after another, rich in the earth and ballot boxes of Texas. He topped us all.

"The ranch house is spiritual to me. He and Helen had a modest camp on that hill country vista for years, and finally built their dream house, a hospitable, sprawling rock house which embraces the land of rolling hills, live oaks and mesquite brush. A humming bird feeder hangs on the veranda, and below deer feed. Inside the house was filled with the treasures of china, silver, paintings, rugs that the Halls had collected over a lifetime. Then, Helen died. Walter was crushed. And a year or so later, a fire burned the place to the ground. A lesser man would have withdrawn and spent his last years in melancholy. But Walter built it all back—right on the spot.

"Another disaster occurred when the sprinkler system, installed to prevent other fires, went berserk and watered down the new furniture. Walter jutted his jaw and put it back shipshape. It continues to reach its embracing arms to friends and political shapers. It is a monument to a man of undaunted faith in the future."

Miscellaneous Political Notes

Two incidents at a statewide Texas Salute in 1963 for Ralph Yarborough, which the former senator discussed elsewhere in this chapter, reminded Hall of noteworthy footnotes in Texas political history.

Some of the greatest figures in Democratic Party history were in Austin to pay tribute to Senator Yarborough—at which Hall was the chairman and toastmaster. The dinner saluted Senator Yarborough for his sponsorship of the legislation establishing the Padre Island National Seashore Park. Among those national political celebrities scheduled to speak were Jack Brooks and Henry Gonzalez, congressmen from Texas; Olin D. Johnston, senator from South Carolina; Lee Metcalf, senator from Montana; Ernest Gruening, senator from Alaska; Daniel K. Inouye, senator from Hawaii; Frank Church, senator from Idaho; and John A. Gronouski, U.S. postmaster general.

The printed program, an impressive 20-page document with semihard-back cover, had been completed under the direction of liberal Texas Democratic leader Creekmore Fath.

At almost the last moment, Hall said, a "little man physically, but some sort of a 'doctor,' showed up the afternoon of the ceremony and demanded a place on the program because, he said, he had an important award for Senator Yarborough regarding Padre Island.

"He claimed to be president of some sort of group interested in 'saving' Padre Island. We told him, of course, that the program had been completed, with congressmen, senators and the postmaster general scheduled to speak. Despite this, he did talk to Ralph in Ralph's room in the headquarters hotel.

"A few minutes later Ralph said he would like to have the award the man was to give him.

"The man had a speech typewritten, single-spaced, on three sheets of paper. We agreed to give him a brief moment on the program, but not enough time for that sort of speech. Creekmore took his speech, summarized it, gave the man the summary and told the man that would be OK.

"However, the man had his original copy of the speech; and when he was recognized at the dinner, he read every word of that three-page speech.

"My family members, Helen, Sonny, Sam and Charles, were at a table in the front of the room. They knew I had tried to curtail the man, and they just laughed like hell!"

Later, after the dinner, Hall said he, Idaho's Senator Church and others were talking in Hall's hotel room about President Johnson.

"I'll tell you how he works," Church said.

"I had dinner over at the White House a few weeks ago, and the president said, 'I need to talk to you,' and when the two of us were alone together, the president said, 'I believe I will need your vote on that bill coming up.' I said, 'Mr. President, I do not have my mind made up. Did you read the Walter Lippmann column in the Washington Post this morning?'

"The president replied, 'No, Frank, I did not. But you just get Walter Lippmann to sign that bill you want for that damn dam in Idaho!'

"Then I understood exactly what the president meant!"

A Battler for the Corporate Profit Tax

Walter Hall is, always has been and undoubtedly always will be a determined advocate for a corporate profit tax for Texas.

His most vigorous effort to "sell" such a program came in December, 1987, when, under the banner of The Coast Foundation, Inc., of Dickinson, he produced a study called "A Case for the Corporate Profit Tax in the State of Texas."

The study is filled with arguments, facts and figures and reflects the great amount of thought and effort Hall has expended in his fight for what he believes is right for the state and its tax structure.

His foreword, perhaps, best summarizes his tax beliefs. "It has been long recognized," he wrote, "that taxes are the cost of civilization. On an applied basis, it amounts to taxes are the means by which society acquires those benefits it desires or needs."

Hall continued:

"Among the many contentions regarding taxes is one that calls for taxpayers to pay in relation to benefits demanded and received. This idea is interesting, but obviously unworkable. The logical and fair basis for payment is ability to pay.

"The Texas Constitution calls for taxes to be fair and equal. It provides for laws which enable the people of the state and its political subdivisions to tax for public goods and services on a unit basis as well as paying statewide taxes.

"It is generally agreed that taxes should be levied and gathered equitably, utilized for purposes the taxpayers approve, and spent efficiently and honestly.

"It appears clear that among the major things Texans want are better educational opportunities, more and better highways, expanded and better Department of Corrections facilities and programs.

"The question then is, are Texans willing to pay more taxes and, if so, how do they want them raised. Simply stated, 'Is Texas worth paying taxes for?'

"Present Texas state taxes are grossly unfair, and the recently passed tax code increased the unfairness. They not only are unfair, but also are becoming counterproductive. An example is the recently increased franchise tax. While the corporate profit tax, like the franchise tax, applies only to corporations, it differs in that the corporate profit tax applies only to profitable corporations, whereas the heavy franchise tax applies to every corporation.

"It is clear that oil and gas cannot now, nor probably in the foreseeable future, resume carrying such a major portion of Texas' economy and accounting for taxes directly and indirectly anywhere close to the amount they provided in the past. The recent sharp increase in franchise taxes has decreased oil and gas companies' chances of survival just as it has some other corporations.

"Obviously this paper does not provide a comprehensive study of the problem; it is an effort to present some facts, data, and comments on our state tax program. Data used were the most current available.

"It is recognized that the final taxing responsibility rests with elected officials. The complex nature of Texas' rapidly changing economic conditions, along with the realization that our educational system must be improved and the obvious and urgent need for upgrading our highway and prison systems, requires thorough and detailed study of the issues and tax revenue needed to meet them adequately and fairly and with minimum adverse impact on citizens and businesses.

A Republican would not have been welcomed at a Lakewood Yacht Club Party on April 15, 1977. The occasion was a meeting of the NASA Area Democrats honoring U.S. Rep. Bob Gammage and state Sen. A.R. "Babe" Schwartz. Among those present were, from the left, Schwartz; Bob Krueger, a state representative at the time and later U.S. senator and a U.S. ambassador; Walter Hall, Gammage and Hal Coward, president of the NASA Area Democrats.

"It is hoped that there will be set up a commission, or if one now exists, it will be increased to include in addition to elected officials, professionals in the fields of taxes, economics, education, and social needs who can contribute information and thinking to a report that will be recognized as truly professional and politically unbiased so that it will be of value to the public and responsible elected officials.

"Data referred to in this report were gathered from many sources. Various people and institutions were most kind in responding to requests for information. In particular I thank Dean L. Todd Johnson and Dr. Robert F. Hodgin of the School of Business and Public Administration of the University of Houston-Clear Lake, Dr. Francis L. Tuggle of the Jesse H. Jones Graduate School of Administration, and Dr. Chandler Davidson of the Department of Sociology, Rice University...

"In our view the time has come, indeed it is overdue, for those who are sincerely concerned about Texas' problems, and believe Texas is worth 'paying taxes for,' to give serious consideration to the use of a corporate profit tax to help provide for the basic needs now and in the future. As Sam Rayburn said, 'Now and then you ought to do something just because it is right.'"

Probably the most convincing arguments in Walter Hall's Coast Foundation publication for his tax proposals are in what he called "Twelve Tax Myths and Realities."

"In view of the many myths regarding corporate profit tax, it is appropriate to present some and to return reality to them," Hall wrote.

His list follows:

"MYTH NO. 1: Raising the sales tax rate would be the best way to solve the state's budget problems.

"REALITY: Because the sales tax rate has been raised to an extremely high level, one of the highest in the nation, it has been pushed to the limit for all practical purposes. Compared to other states, this sales tax constitutes an especially burdensome tax on business and exacerbates the inequities inherent in the sales tax wherein lower and middle income people pay a larger proportion of their incomes in sales taxes than do wealthier people.

"MYTH NO. 2: If raising the sales tax rate would not be a good solution, then perhaps instead the sales tax base should be broadened.

"REALITY: Broadening the base might be less inequitable than raising the rate, especially if certain essentials such as food and medicine were excluded from the base and items such as professional services included in it. However, the fundamental inequities inherent in a sales tax (as opposed to certain other kinds of taxes) would still be present. The conduct of the Legislature during the passage of the present tax bill clearly proved that broadening the tax base to include professional fees—attorneys, doctors, and similar professionals—could be passed only after basic changes in the Legislature.

"MYTH NO. 3: If raising the sales tax rate and/or broadening the base are unsatisfactory, then cutting state services must be the answer to Texas' fiscal problems.

"REALITY: Whatever is done should not impede the state on its road to economic recovery. That means the state will need to provide as many enticements as possible to the business sector, which means providing the level of state services required by business. As noted in The Wall Street Journal (6-22-87), chief executives surveyed regarding what factors are 'absolutely essential' in considering new office locations for employees indicated that good public schools, a low crime rate, affordable housing and efficient highway system all were rated more highly than what was termed 'reasonable state and local taxes.' That is to say, high quality state services are more important than low taxes to business decision-makers.

Officers and other staff members of the Citizens State Bank posed for a victory photograph in 1965 after going "over the top" in the United Fund drive that year.

"MYTH NO. 4: Preserving state services by raising additional revenues through taxes would place a heavy burden on Texas taxpayers.

"REALITY: Not necessarily. Texas is already a 'low tax/low service state,' hence there exists a significant degree of additional capacity for taxes relative to most other states, most of which have income taxes that are deductible for federal income tax purposes.

"MYTH NO. 5: Texans cannot afford the burden of maintaining state services if it means new taxes would have to be paid out of their own pockets.

"REALITY: Texans cannot afford not to. If the new tax were carefully chosen, Texas could end up with 100% of the services while paying for considerably less than 100% of the tax cost by using taxes that are deductible for federal income tax purposes. By relying on the sales tax (which is not deductible by individuals for federal income tax purposes) rather than some form of income tax, such as a corporate profit tax (which is deductible), Texans in effect are subsidizing the taxpayers of other states. The payment for many state services, certainly education, is recognized by most Texans as an investment, not an expense. Thinking people realize investment in education of youth is the soundest investment a society can make.

"MYTH NO. 6: An income tax is not politically feasible at this time.

"REALITY: Many of the general population oppose a corporate profit tax on the basis of opposing all taxes or because they have been led to believe that a corporate profit tax is anti-business. Detailed information on this tax has not been widely spread, but opposition to it has been used politically by some who apparently have not carefully considered the whole tax picture, and by some who apparently believe it is good politics to oppose a corporate profit tax. An increasing number of Texas leaders in the business community recognize the need for additional revenues, and accordingly believe the time has come for consideration of including a corporate profit tax.

"MYTH NO. 7: A corporate profit tax would still be a tax on Texans.

"REALITY: Only part of such a tax would be paid by Texans, for several reasons. First, any corporate profit tax paid by corporations to the state of Texas would be deductible for federal income tax purposes; thus, assuming a federal income tax rate of 34%, for every $100 in corporate profit tax paid to Texas, corporations would save $34 on their federal taxes, leaving a net cost of only $66. Second, the net corporate profit tax (federal and state) would be a cost factor virtually the same as any other cost except that they, unlike most costs, would be imposed only in the event of profit.

"Like all costs, the corporate profit tax is usually passed on to customers or, in cases of high competition, absorbed by stockholders through decreased earnings and dividends. That means some of this tax would be paid by out-of-state customers and stockholders of Texas corporations. Thus, out-of-state customers and stockholders of Texas corporations would be in the same position as Texans who do business with or own stock in corporations in states where a corporate profit tax is levied.

"MYTH NO. 8: To generate significant amounts of revenue, a high corporate profit tax rate would be necessary.

"REALITY: A corporate profit tax rate that approximates the average rate imposed by other states (between 7% and 8%) would generate at least $1.6 billion annually for Texas. Thus, a corporate profit tax similar to those in other states would replace a significant part of the shortfall caused by the decline in oil prices.

"MYTH NO. 9: A corporate profit tax would be costly to administer and audit.

"REALITY: Compared to many other kinds of taxes, a corporate profit tax is relatively easy to administer for the following reasons:

"1. Few collection points are involved.

"2. Compliance would be less of a problem because corporate federal tax returns that are already prepared, usually by professionals, could be used as the basis for a state tax.

"3. The state agency infrastructure to administer, collect, and audit a corporate profit tax would be relatively small. Thus, the cost to collect a dollar of corporate profit tax would be less than for other taxes.

"MYTH NO. 10: Texas would be placed at an economic disadvantage because most states do not have a corporate profit tax.

"REALITY: Of the 50 states in the union, the vast majority already have a corporate profit tax. Texas is one of only four that have no form of corporate or business tax, the others being Wyoming, Nevada and Washington. (South Dakota has a corporate tax on banks only and Michigan has a single business tax levied on all forms of enterprise.)

"MYTH NO. ll: Having a corporate profit tax would stifle economic growth in Texas.

"REALITY: The facts do not support this contention...Of the 10 states that have experienced the greatest value and growth of manufacturing shipment rates for the period 1977 to 1982, seven have the corporate profit tax.

"MYTH NO. 12: A corporate profit tax would be unfair to the business community.

"REALITY: A corporate profit tax would embody the 'ability to pay' principle, which is widely regarded as a cornerstone of an equitable tax. Corporations would pay only if they earned profits. By comparison, the present franchise tax requires corporations to pay the tax whether or not they earn a profit."

. . .

Hall later updated and emphasized his thoughts: "In support of a corporate excess income tax, I was simply urging that Texas be on an even basis with nearly all the other states. (I think now all but three have income taxes.) I have always supported the income tax process because there is no tax unless you make profits, whereas the ad valorem, sales and franchise tax (except for a small amount) are not based on profits. We know it will not be easy to do away with ad valorem tax because bonds have been sold against them; but as our needs go up we will need to do something to generate money. We are subsidizing the other states by their keeping part of their income tax, while we send all of ours to Washington. I know I have said this before, but before long reality is going to cause us to look for additional revenues, and I think we should be on an even basis with the other states."

Chapter 6

Some of the Honors Accorded Walter Hall

Clear Lake Area Chamber of Commerce

A special event which meant a great deal to Walter Hall was a roast and toast event on March 24, 1983, sponsored by the Clear Lake Area Chamber of Commerce at Hobby Hilton Hotel in Houston.

"More than 700 people gathered Thursday night to honor a cabinet-maker, a duck-hunter, a fisherman, a banker, a politician and a humanitarian," reported a Bay Area newspaper, The Citizen.

"This man was one and the same and his name is Walter G. Hall Sr., who has come to be beloved and respected in the country towns like Dickinson, Alvin, Bay City, Webster and League City, and to be respected in the state Capitol in Austin and the halls of Congress and in the White House."

The Citizen report continued:

"Walter Hall Sr. was roasted and toasted by a series of comedians, politicians and academicians...

"Hall's activities have become legend as he has helped financially strapped individuals, companies and obscure political entities in the Galveston, Brazoria and lower South Texas counties.

"But as a hard-headed practical banker, along the way he managed to keep a banking empire solvent, and growing...

"After having darts shot in his direction for most of the evening along with accolades from old acquaintances, Hall turned out to be the most amusing comedian of the evening.

"Richard Cole kicked off this...roast-toast affair in his role as chairman of the board of the Clear Lake Area Chamber of Commerce.

Television personality John Henry Faulk took over from there and a series of admirers carried the hilarious evening from there.

"A.R. 'Babe' Schwartz, former Texas senator and long-time friend of Hall's, recalled various encounters he had with Hall through the years. But, before closing, Schwartz described Hall as the most deserving person in the area whose hundreds and thousands of good deeds would be remembered.

"Schwartz said many people were healthier and better educated because of the contributions that Hall had made in these areas. The former senator paid respect to the late Helen Hall, Walter Hall's wife and inspiration, as did other speakers who followed.

"Dr. Robert Gilruth, former director of the Johnson Space Center, described Hall's contribution to the space program and praised his closeness to people in the Clear Lake area.

"Dr. Frank Vandiver, president of Texas A&M University and former provost at Rice University, was the next speaker. He lauded Hall as a person who loved the great and the poor alike, and brought applause from the audience when he told Hall, 'You love us all, you love people.'

"Hall's contributions to Rice University have been many, and Rice was where Hall earned his higher education long before Vandiver became associated with that school.

"Next came Jim Mattox, Texas attorney general, who noted that every single thing and person that Walter Hall backed on the last state ballot won.

"Mattox turned toward Hall and said, 'You can walk with kings and not lose the common touch.'

"Others who had high praise for Hall included E. Hagan McMahon Jr., executive director of the Independent Bankers Association of Texas; W.0. 'Bill' Cooper, who is retired from the foreign service; and Ralph Yarborough, an Austin lawyer and former United States senator.

"Hall's response to all the praise and sarcasm was taken in high good humor and his punch lines brought applause and laughter from the audience.

"'All this is damn well overdue. My humility has held me down all my life.'

"This remark brought down the house because they knew Walter said this in jest. They rose in resounding applause when he called for the end of hunger and pestilence among all mankind.

"Walter G. Hall probably shook more hands Thursday night than during any other occasion in his 75 years. He was at his best—warm, sincere, jovial, appreciative, humble and lovable."

Bayou City Club

Walter Hall, a champion of human rights in Galveston County for many years before the movement became a front-page item, received an emotional boost when he was honored by the Bayou City Club of Dickinson.

At its 8th annual banquet on March 16, 1983, the Bayou City Club, which provides a location for Dickinson social events and recognizes outstanding civic achievement, recognized Hall as its humanitarian of the year.

"We want to recognize one of the greatest citizens we know," said club Treasurer Pino Burns. "We are so appreciative of the many services he has rendered to the community. His ears are sensitive to the needs of the community, and if there is a way for him to help, he listens and responds," said Burns as he presented Hall with a plaque which is on Hall's office wall today.

Oscar Woods, president of the Bayou City Club at the time, also was president of the local chapter of the National Association for the Advancement of Colored People.

Hall was introduced at the banquet by County Judge Ray Holbrook.

"If ever there has been a man with his heart in the community, it is Walter Hall," Holbrook said. "He's been there with elbow grease, with advice and with a pitchfork in the rear of the elected officials to do what is needed, do it right and do it now. And I know."

Remembering the War and the Bank

The Citizens State Bank, as the financial "good citizen" of its community, has aided scores of organizations through times good and bad.

One of the more poignant reminders of its role as a good citizen came in March, 1986, at a meeting of the Dickinson Veterans of Foreign Wars Memorial Post No. 6378. The occasion was to burn the mortgage on the post home.

Zero Residori, the six-time commander of the VFW post, reminded the audience that Dickinson had progressed greatly since he became its first commander in 1946, and that the community's population was only about 4,500 at that time.

Then, reported a story written by Beverly Miller in The Citizen, "The person who had lent $104,000 on the strength of 3 signatures so that the VFW could build its home was in the audience.

"Walter Hall not only accepted thanks of the members of Post 6378, he thanked them," The Citizen continued.

"'I thank you,' Hall said, 'for being there when our country needed you, and for giving to your country fully and freely.'"

Galveston County Park/Walter Hall Park

The site of the Galveston County Park in League City has been of interest to Walter Hall since he was a youth.

As a small boy, he had visited there when the county poor farm was on the edge of League City, near his father's home. Hall recalls that he discussed with an "inmate" of the poor farm the art of growing tomatoes.

"I remember very vividly when two black boys and I were playing and decided to have a look at the poor farm," Hall said. "While we were exploring we came upon an inmate working in a garden. My playmates were brothers, L.V. and Eldridge Winfield, and both became ministers when they grew up. The day after our adventure I was at the store with my mother when the clerk told her they had just gotten in some exceedingly nice poor farm tomatoes."

The history of the poor farm is traced to 1886, when the Galveston County Commissioners Court purchased a 200-acre tract, part of the one-league grant patented to Stephen F. Austin in 1832 by the government of Coahuila y Texas.

The county wanted the tract to be used as a poor farm to house the sick and elderly residents who had no relatives to care for them and had no money to care for themselves. Small cottages were built to house the "inmates." Lack of funds forced the county to close the farm in 1913.

In 1928, the present park was created by the county Commissioners Court on 70 of the 200 acres which had not been sold. It was the county's first park. A new pavilion was dedicated in 1929.

Hall recalls attending basketball games at the park and even playing in a few. And he and his wife, Helen, won third place in a dance contest held at the park's pavilion. Later they took their three sons to picnics in the park.

Hall also once barbecued chickens for the Chamber of Commerce at the park and said he was "overwhelmed" by the number of people who came from miles around to have a free dinner in the 1930s, during the heart of the Great Depression.

So Hall considered it a great honor when the Galveston County Commissioners Court in 1985 decided to formally change the name of the Galveston County Park to Walter Hall Park, and the dedication ceremonies were among the most memorable of the countless honors Hall has received.

Hall said he thought it was "highly logical" that a banker should have a former poor farm named for him.

Walter Hall Park

◆

Dedication Ceremonies

October 18, 1985

An artist's conception of the entrance to Walter Hall Park in League City was used on the cover for the dedication ceremonies of the renamed park on Oct. 18, 1985.

Kathleen Mayse, editor of the League City News, in 1985 wrote that "throughout the...years that he has called this county his home, he has lived in the shadow of the great oaks of the park and fished along the banks of the creek that winds its way toward Clear Lake."

"The picnics and the festivals, the fairs and the celebrations are a part of this man's history as they are a part of the history of the almost 100 acres of land that comprise the park," she wrote.

"This week, the two will become linked together indelibly for future generations—in the presence of his friends, his family and his hometown, Galveston County Park will cease to exist and that tract of land will become Walter Hall Park.

"It can be said that they belong together, this land and the man whose name it will carry—in a sense, they grew up together and contributed to the well-being of those whose lives they touched."

The Galveston County Commissioners Court at the time was composed of Ray Holbrook, county judge; and Commissioners Earl Llewellyn Jr. of Precinct 1; Frank Carmona of Precinct 2; Ron Crowder of Precinct 3; and Billy J. Pegues of Precinct 4.

Those on the Galveston County Beach & Parks board of trustees were Joe K. Tombrella, chairman; John Schmidt, vice chairman; Charles Delgado, secretary; and Tom Manison, B.T. Sears, Pete Fredriksen; Frank Carmona, county commissioner; and Pat Hallisey, department director.

Included on the program at the dedication ceremony on Oct. 18, 1985, was music by the Clear Creek High School Chorale; welcome by League City Mayor Joe Lamb; invocation by Msgr. Eugene Cargill; introduction of guests by Judge Holbrook; comments by Dr. John Ward, superintendent of schools for the Clear Creek Independent School District; comments by Paul Hopkins, former county commissioner and at that time chairman of the Texas Water Commission; keynote address by U.S. Rep. Jack Brooks; introduction of Walter Hall by former state Sen. A.R. "Babe" Schwartz; and comments by Walter Hall. Hallisey served as master of ceremonies.

The printed program that day, an elaborate 12-page affair, was, Hall said, "very kind" to him. In a short biography, the program said Hall "might be termed a pragmatic visionary," and called him a "Galveston County citizen at large."

The program material undoubtedly was written or ordered written by elected officials, and it duly reported: "Elected officials have been heard to say, 'It is easier to comply with Walter Hall's suggestions for community improvements than to explain to his satisfaction why it could not be done.'"

Hall, the program said, has been "a prime mover and driving force behind the growth and development of Galveston County and the Bay Area. His leadership style is subtle."

"Some of those elected officials," Hall said later, "may not agree with that last statement."

Among the praises of Hall which were expressed that day:

Congressman Brooks: Hall "has an uncommon ability to get things done."

Ex-Senator Schwartz: "He started worrying about us long ago, when we didn't have enough sense to worry about ourselves." Schwartz also said that while he was in the state Legislature, for 23 years, Hall never once asked him to do something for Walter Hall. "He was always asking me to do something for others. As far as his own business was concerned, he could take care of that himself," Schwartz said.

Hopkins told Hallisey that Walter Hall Park looked "perfect," and advised that Walter Hall himself would see to it that it stayed that way by coming out every morning to check on it.

A Distinguished Alumnus

When Walter Hall was recalled to Rice University in Houston on May 1, 1992, surely it was one of the greatest moments of his life.

The reception of the Association of Rice Alumni was part of the 79th commencement, and Hall was recognized as a Distinguished Alumnus of the famous school.

Other distinguished alumni recognized at the same time were Charles M. Blair (1931), a chemist and business leader who holds more than 100 patents in the chemical and pharmaceutical fields; Robert L. Clarke (1963), former comptroller of the currency, heading the agency that supervised 4,000 federally chartered banks; and Robert B. Morin (1959), scientist whose work at Eli Lilly led to three major patents significant in the field of human medicine.

Following the presentation of the Distinguished Alumnus Award to Hall, and his introduction by Dr. William Martin, chair of the Sociology Department, Hall explained some of his philosophy in the acceptance remarks he was asked to make.

Those remarks follow:

"Thank you, Dr. Martin, for that kind introduction, and let me add that my appreciation for receiving this honor is matched only by my amazement.

"This is an appropriate time for me to answer some questions I have been asked about why I, in founding the Tsanoff Chair, stipulated that it be Tsanoff Chair of Public Affairs when Dr. (Radoslav A.) Tsanoff was a noted philosopher. The answer is very simple. Like many of you here tonight, I owe a great deal to Rice, and a great deal to Dr. Tsanoff because it was through my contacts with him that I gained several benefits, two in particular. One was objectivity, or tolerance, if you please, and the other was an increasing of what perhaps was already an active curiosity, and how to proceed toward satisfying it some, only some.

"My hope was that the occupants of the chair would be people like Covey T. Oliver, a distinguished undersecretary of state; former congressman, ambassador and presently a member of the Texas Railroad Commission, Bob Krueger; former Lieutenant Governor Bill Hobby; and former Mayor Kathy Whitmire. It was my hope that by having such men and women occupy this chair that many of those who teach at Rice and who come to Rice as students would benefit, through contacts with such people and possibly develop a greater interest and understanding in our society and, accordingly, some of them would participate in public affairs where they are needed.

"I was much impressed by the work being done by sociologists Dr. Bill Martin* and Dr. Chandler Davidson* in advancing learning about people.

"And through Dr. (George) Rupp (president of Rice University) meeting Dean Michael Hammond of the Shepherd School of Music, I saw the plans for the grand new music building and like you I felt additional pride.

"As a man whose long life has spanned most of this century and as the television comedian said, 'Having reached an age where I no longer buy green bananas,' I tend to view this century with mixed dismay, exhilaration, and hope.

"During the same period, I have seen fantastic developments by engineers, scientists, chemists, medical researchers, nuclear engineers, and others. I have seen the automobile and airplane become parts of the daily lives of most of us; likewise, I have seen terrible diseases become rare or virtually eliminated, such as yellow fever, polio, smallpox and many others. Many discoveries and inventions of this century have made life better, but along with a great development of 'things,' I have not seen anything comparable improving people.

"In what are regarded as civilized countries, individuals usually use the courts to resolve their differences, but when people act in groups, whether it be tribes, factions, or nations, war is far too often the final instrument.

"I was a small boy during World War I and at no time since has the world been free of war. It boggles the mind when we think if even one-half of the cost of wars in this century could have been used in improving education, from which wisdom stems, and more learning about increasing food production, medical problems, and energy research and man's treatment of man.

"While much has been done thus far this century, it has come slowly compared to need.

"Old men are privileged to dream, and I shall have a dream. I shall come upon a crowd gathering in a courtyard in the shadow of a beautiful building at a university on the coastal plains of Texas. I will see Dr. Rupp* extending a welcome to those present, and I will learn the significance of the gathering when Dr. Rupp states in his remarks that the purpose of the meeting is not only to review some of the great accomplishments of the men and women present, but also to have those outstanding minds exchange ideas as to how further benefits can be brought about.

"I recognized in a huddle Dave Hellums,* Larry McIntyre,* and Antonios Mikos,* and with them I see Dr. Tom James* and Dr. Bill Levin* of the great Texas Medical School in Galveston discussing with Sir Alexander Fleming* and Dr. Norman Shumway* the many developments that will combat cancer and afford far more successful organ transplants.

"In another direction I see Herb Ward* and Phillip Bedient* with my old friend, Herb Allen,* and they are rejoicing because the 'greenhouse effect' is no longer threatening the world. Ken Kennedy* and John Dennis* and Sidney Burrus* are being congratulated for their developments in computer science and electronics technology.

"Another group I approached seemed to be enjoying very much the topic of their discussion, and I recognized Dr. Bill Martin* and Dr. Chandler Davidson* among those discussing the great benefit that was coming from the desalting of sea water and the fact that a breakthrough had finally been made for low-cost energy, which together permitted the irrigation of hundreds of thousands of acres of arid land resulting in a tremendous increase in the food supply of the world. The group's discussion moved into great satisfaction that for years there had been no wars and that all nations had discarded war as an instrument of foreign policy. And the group commented on what a great step this was toward meeting the needs of the world and how, indeed, this revealed real progress in the development of people as well as 'things.'

"This dream will reveal that Rice, as would be expected, would be playing a major role in these continuing efforts, and makes clear that it and other institutions of learning and research, and hopefully the wisdom related thereto, will justify some hope that together with many great 'things,' there will also eventually be comparable improvements in the people's ongoing struggle for human dignity.

"I cannot be sure if the dream will be of an era of five years, 50 years, 500 years, or more, but as old men will dream, I will have that dream and it shall be good."

One of those present for Hall's speech wrote a dramatically penetrating critique of Hall's remarks.

Arthur C. Goforth of League City, a retired educator (longtime principal in the Clear Creek schools and assistant curriculum director of the school district) and a personal friend of the banker, said:

"The two hundred or so friends of his present were amazed and delighted with his remarks. Walter, who is in his mid-eighties, spoke as though he were a 25-year-old banker, just beginning his career. He spoke of (life) not of today or tomorrow, but 20 or 30 years into the future. I wouldn't bet against Walter's being there to see his predictions happen."

The Distinguished Alumnus honor is not the first major honor bestowed on Walter Hall by Rice University. He received the Founders Club Award for 1973-74.

*Dr. George Rupp: At the time, president of Rice University.

Dr. David Hellums: Longtime professor of chemical engineering at Rice, former dean of engineering.

Dr. Larry McIntyre: Professor of chemical engineering at Rice.

Dr. Antonio Mikos: Rice University professor of chemical engineering.

Dr. Tom James: Professor at the University of Texas Medical Branch at Galveston.

Dr. Bill Levin: Professor at the University of Texas Medical Branch at Galveston.

Sir Alexander Fleming: English bacteriologist who discovered penicillin.

Dr. Norman Shumway: Renowned surgeon based in California.

Dr. Herb Ward: Rice University professor of environmental science and engineering.

Dr. Phillip Bedient: Rice University professor of environmental science and engineering.

Herb Allen: Research engineer, graduate of Rice University, former member of board of governors, former chairman of the board of Cameron Iron Works of Houston.

Dr. Ken Kennedy: Rice University professor of computer science.

John Dennis: Rice University professor of mathematical science.

Sidney Burris: Rice University professor of electrical engineering.

Dr. William Martin: Rice University sociologist of religion, specializing in "electronic evangelism"—radio and TV preachers; author of "A Prophet With Honor," about Billy Graham; chair of the Sociology Department.

Dr. Chandler Davidson: Rice University sociologist whose specialty is politics and race. Chair of Sociology Department for several years. Best-known book: "Race and Class in Texas Politics."

1993 'Man of Vision'

For what probably are obvious reasons, during the 1980s and 1990s, when Walter Hall had reached what most people agree is senior citizen status, Hall became somewhat weary and leery of presentations of awards and testimonial dinners tossed in his honor.

However, in 1993 he was met with a barrage of sincere friends and also bearers of influence to accept at least one more: His friends wanted him to receive the honor as the 1993 "Man of Vision" of the Gulf Coast Branch of the Texas Society to Prevent Blindness.

It was truly an honor which Hall appreciated, and he agreed to participate in the ceremony.

As a result, surely what was one of the most gala fund-raising events of its kind was held on May 18, 1993, in the Crystal Ballroom of the South Shore Harbour Resort & Conference Center in League City.

Dinner chairmen were Charles T. "Chuck" Doyle and Harris L. "Shrub" Kempner Jr.; treasurer was Mrs. Marilyn Schwartz; master of ceremonies was Vandy V. Anderson.

The dinner committee was composed of scores of leaders of Galveston and Brazoria counties and the dinner sponsors represented a cross-section of Texas leaders and organizations.

State Rep. Mike Martin made the official presentation to Walter Hall after many verbal tributes were offered by Pat Hallisey, director of the Galveston County Beach & Parks Department; County Judge Ray Holbrook; Texas City banker and Mayor Charles T. "Chuck" Doyle;

H.L. "Shrub" Kempner, Galveston banker; Wayne March, M.D.; and Charles F. "Chuck" Hall Jr., Dickinson banker.

IBAA
INDEPENDENT BANKERS
ASSOCIATION OF AMERICA

James R. Lauffer
President

John Shivers
President-Elect

Richard L. Mount
Vice President

David L. Stone
Treasurer

Robert W. Hawkins
Chairman

Kenneth A. Guenther
Executive Vice President

Ode to Walter Hall -- A Man of Vision

For a northern, Yankee Republican, associating a yellow dog Texas Democrat with the concept of vision was a very difficult challenge. But then I met Walter Hall.

The opening conversation was remarkably blunt. Walter said, "I am a country banker, but the Speaker of the House will return my phone calls. I assume that President Reagan will return yours." After my coughing fit subsided, Sir Walter graciously accepted my explanation of political impotence at that level.

This conversation opened the door to a man of very strong causes--one of which is the importance of community banking. When the battle was joined, Walter was there. And over the past decade, the battle was frequently joined. He had a very different vision for the future of the financial services industry than did Presidents Ronald Reagan and George Bush. None of this massive consolidation crap at the expense of community banks for Walter Hall. His vision was more about what is good for America's Main Street--and it is obviously the true vision.

Vision, energy, commitment, persistence--this is part of Walter Hall. And for these virtues, even a yellow dog Democrat must be forgiven.

Affectionately,

K

Kenneth A. Guenther
Executive Vice President

WASHINGTON OFFICE, ONE THOMAS CIRCLE NW, SUITE 950, WASHINGTON, D.C. 20005-5802 • 202 659-8111

An indication of the regard Walter G. Hall is held, even by traditionally conservative bankers, is revealed in this letter from Kenneth A. Guenther, executive vice president of the Independent Bankers Association of America. Guenther sent the letter to sponsors of the "Man of Vision Dinner" honoring Hall in 1993.

Dr. March, chairman of the Department of Ophthalmology of the niversity of Texas Medical Branch at Galveston, revealed publicly for the first time that Walter Hall himself has a visual impairment: He is blind in one eye and has had cataract surgery on the other.

After the disclosure, Dr. March said: "Walter Hall is not a complainer. He's a fighter. He's an inspiration to us all."

But the star of the night was not a member of the dinner committee or even Walter Hall himself. The star was Walter Hall's grandson, banker Charles F. (Chuck) Hall Jr., who told the guests about some of his adventures with his grandfather.

Grandson Hall's remarks follow:

"You may recognize the man being honored here tonight by one or more of the following: Mr. Hall, Mr. Banker, Mr. Chairman, or Mr. Democrat. But to me he is Papa Bear.

"My dad tells me that I pinned that name to him when I was young. I must have been young because I don't remember. He has always been Papa Bear to me, and the stories I am going to share with you tonight are between me and him.

"My dad tells a story about the two of us. He was on the telephone at my grandfather's house one summer day and looked out the window. What he saw was my grandfather, in a white suit, running through the lawn sprinkler with me chasing him. Dad says I was 2 or 3. He figures Papa Bear was showing me how much fun it was to run through the sprinkler.

"My grandfather and I have always been very close. We have hunted together, fished together, built projects in his woodshop together, and a multitude of other things too numerous to mention. But in addition to all of the many fun things we have done, growing up with my grandfather has always been an educational process as well. We have had many 'discussions' through the years, as I am sure many of you in this room have experienced as well, where you sit and listen, and are mighty glad when the so-called 'discussion' is over.

"The reasons for most of those 'discussions' were because my grandfather has always looked out for my best interest. When I was young, Papa Bear and I were going to go for a walk around his pond. When he asked where my shoes were, I told him I was tough and that I didn't need shoes. He thought I should wear shoes but I insisted I was tough and didn't need them so off we went. Several minutes later I wandered into a fire-ant bed. Needless to say I started to cry. Papa Bear picked me up, brushed off all of the ants, and asked why I was crying. I told him I was crying because it hurt. But you said you were tough, he said. I told him tough, Papa Bear, just not tough enough.

"Growing up, I never really realized just who Papa Bear was, and the importance of the things he did. When my grandmother took me to the bank to see him, I would run into his office and jump into his lap, regardless of who was there or what he was doing. Rep. Jack Brooks could have been in an important meeting with him, and I would fly into his office and onto his lap.

"I graduated from Southwest Texas (State University) two years ago and immediately went to work for my grandfather in his three banks. Working for him these past two years, my respect and admiration for him have increased tenfold. For the first time I saw the other side of Papa Bear. Not the hunter, fisherman, or grandfather, but the banker and the community-oriented businessman. One of the things I have learned about and am still amazed at is his schedule. My grandfather arrives at work at 7:30 in the morning, works all day until 4 or 5 in the afternoon, goes home and reads, has dinner, and then reads for several more hours so that he can stay abreast of everything.

"I can remember that every time I went to my grandparents' house, I would go into Papa Bear's bedroom after dinner where he would be on his bed reading as he has always done. As soon as I came in, he would set aside all of his work and tell me hunting and fishing stories about a fictitious young boy named Jonathan. At that time he owned five banks. I see how busy he is now with three banks and can only imagine how busy he was with five then. Every time I came to his room, he would put aside his work and tell me one of his stories. He never once said I'm busy, please come back later; he always found time to tell me that story.

"I was introduced to banking at age 8. You might think this is a bit young but let me tell you the story. Sears had a go-kart in their mail order catalog that I just had to have. The only problem was I didn't have the money to buy it. I asked my dad for the money and got turned down. So I went to my grandmother and she recommended I go to Papa Bear. I thought all right, an easy target. So I went to him and hit him up for the $200 go-kart cost. After hearing my story, he told me he would give me the $200. I thought great, a new go-kart, that sure was easy.

"Then the stipulations hit. He explained the $200 was a loan. No problem, I thought, a loan from Papa Bear. Then he explained that when I paid him back, I would owe him $250. I was puzzled and asked him why I had to pay back more than I borrowed. Interest, he said. Needless to say, I never got that go-kart.

"My grandfather and I have always been very close and have done many things together. He was there on my first hunting trip, he was there on my first fishing trip, he was there the first time I ran through the sprinkler, and he was there on my first day at work.

"I look forward to him being there on many more occurrences. The only thing that exceeds my love and admiration for him is my respect for him."

Some of Many Other Honors

In addition to the many major honors Walter Hall has received locally in his life, he has been cited by other groups in his community, state and nation, for his civic, business and humanitarian achievements and activities. He also has been active in many other organizations that reflect—and have recognized—his variety of interests.

Politically, he has served as chairman of the Galveston County Democratic Executive Committee; he has served as precinct and county chairman and as a member of the State Democratic Executive Committee; he has been a delegate to both state and national Democratic conventions.

He has served as a director of the Texas Bill of Rights Foundation.

He received in 1979 the National Citizenship Award from the national Oil, Chemical and Atomic Workers Union at its national convention in Hollywood, Florida.

He received the Howard O. Payne Award presented by the First State Bank of Hitchcock in 1974.

He served for several years as president of the Mainland Chamber of Commerce.

He has served as a trustee of the Rosenberg Library of Galveston, and when he resigned, in the late 1960s, he was replaced by Mary Moody Northen.

He has served as a member of the governing board of the Lakewood Yacht Club of Seabrook, and was named honorary commodore in recognition of the work he did in organizing the club.

He served from 1975 to 1979 as chairman of the Special Gifts Division of the Bay Area Boy Scouts of America.

He is a member of the Philosophical Society of Texas.

He is a member of the Conference of State Bank Supervisors.

He was a founding director of the Independent Bankers Association of Texas, and the association named him "Banker of the Year" in 1980.

He is a member of the Independent Bankers Association of America.

He is a member of several organizations associated with Rice University, including the Rice Associates.

To recognize the work Walter and Helen Hall completed for the county and benefits in the health field gained by their accomplishments, the county's Environmental Health Center in La Marque was dedicated to the banking couple in 1978.

Walter Hall received the first Lifetime Achievement Award at the North Galveston County Chamber of Commerce banquet at Dickinson in February, 1993. Hall was described as "the true benchmark for future recipients." The award was presented by Bob Holley of Dickinson, former chamber president and the first mayor of Dickinson.

Hall was honored by the Bay Area Museum Guild at its Annual Christmas Open House on Dec. 13, 1992, at Clear Lake Park.

The Bay Area community's Clear Lake Symphony at a pre-concert reception in May, 1990, honored Walter G. Hall, Lynn Wingate and Bob McShane for service to the orchestra.

He received the Red Apple Award of the Clear Creek Teachers Association for 1969-70.

He received a certificate of appreciation from the Gulf Coast Science Foundation in 1965.

Walter and Helen Hall Day was observed in League City on March 10, 1974.

Walter Hall Day was observed by Galveston County on May 18, 1987.

Hall had been a member of the Houston Club for 30 years—and is believed to have been its oldest member at the time—when he resigned in 1993 because of his inability to participate more frequently.

Chapter 7
The Personal Life of Walter Hall

'The Right Place at the Right Time'

While good luck and remarkable timing of course are not responsible for Walter Hall's incredible ability, certainly, as he is the first to recognize, he has been fortunate in an amazing number of situations.

Hall himself—as his friends laugh—frequently attributes his fortune to being in "the right place at the right time."

His friends and associates insist that Hall somehow knows when that right time is coming and positions himself at the right place.

Hall mentions as examples of his timing that after the Citizens State Bank was moved to Dickinson, the oil fields of the surrounding area—Dickinson, League City and Hastings near Friendswood—were developed, and the chemical plants at Texas City began their mushrooming growth. Then came Camp Wallace and other military developments in the area.

Hall insists that he had no premonition of Alvin's great growth when he purchased controlling interest in the Alvin State Bank in 1953.

However, Hall said he did have a "hunch" that prospects for the oil potential of Alvin were far greater than generally realized.

"I had information from a friend with a major oil company—as well as information available to anyone from the Texas Railroad Commission—that oil and gas reserves within a 15- or 20-mile radius of Alvin were tremendous," he said. "In addition, rice was the major agricultural crop. For many years there were more tons of long-grain rice, or table rice, shipped from Alvin than from any other spot in the country. And there was a substantial and important cattle industry in the Alvin area.

"I had wanted to buy the Alvin State Bank for quite some time," Hall continued, "but I was always told that the owner said it wasn't for sale.

"Then during the 1950s, a fine Angleton attorney, Cleveland Davis, told me that the new owner, Verna Browning, who had inherited the bank when her father died, might be interested in selling."

Hall said he studied two or three reports from state bank examiners, made an offer to Miss Browning and it was accepted.

Hall said that he quickly observed that only about 10% of the bank's assets were in loans, and asked why the bank did not have many of the big farmers, ranchers or oil recipients among its customers.

"I was told," Hall said, "that the bank's policy had been based on the philosophy that the rich farmers, ranchers and oilmen could get their loans anywhere they wanted, but if the Alvin bank didn't lend money to the little ones, they couldn't get loans at all."

That policy quickly changed, Hall said, and the bank started lending to big customers as well as those smaller.

Hall said he had no advance information that Monsanto would build its plant at Chocolate Bayou, near Alvin.

"The decision (to buy the bank) was based on the premise that oil in the area would cause other industry to grow," Hall told a reporter. "It did. But they were primarily of a diversified nature—rice farming and dairy and beef cattle ranching. I had no idea that Monsanto would build at Chocolate Bayou."

Hall said he could have made money on the purchase of the Alvin State Bank one day after he bought it. A friend, an official of a Houston bank, called him, Hall said, and told him he wanted to buy the bank.

"I just bought the bank," Hall said.

"I know," explained his friend. "But I was supposed to have bought it, and I'm about to be fired because I didn't. I was trying to be cagey and buy it at a bargain price." Hall, of course, rejected his offer. Whether Hall's friend was fired is not known.

The following day, Hall said, he received a call from Dallas "from a man I had never met."

"Mr. Hall, I'd like to make you an offer—I'll give you $50,000 more than you paid for the Alvin State Bank," Hall said the man told him.

"How can you offer me that?" Hall said he asked the man. "You don't know how much I paid for the bank."

And the man replied, "My boss told me that anything Walter Hall bought would be worth more than $50,000 more than he paid for it." Hall, of course, also rejected that offer.

Hall opened the Webster State Bank—now the Bay Area Bank & Trust—in 1963.

Development of the huge Bayshore area, spurred by the Johnson Space Center and the recreational frenzy of the area, quickly followed.

Hall's probable role—which he denies—in the location of the Johnson Space Center and his foresight in financing waterfront area business establishments have been chronicled earlier in this book.

There is no doubt: Walter Hall has managed to "stay ahead of the band" if indeed he wasn't the drum major.

One other example the banker likes to relate as an example of his ability to take advantage of a situation—or at least gain credit for it—came during the time Friendswood was seeking to expand its Water Control and Improvement District.

The application of the Friendswood officials apparently was pigeonholed somewhere in a Washington office, and after a wait of several months the local officials were growing more concerned that their application would fail.

They approached the man who undoubtedly was the No. 1 citizen of Friendswood, Cecil Brown, a son of the Quaker community founder, Frank Brown. Cecil Brown was a stockholder of the Citizens State Bank.

Cecil Brown telephoned Walter Hall, with the local WCID officials listening to the conversation, and explained their concerns.

"You know," Hall told Brown, "those things take weeks to process—you can't untangle Washington's red tape in a few hours."

Nevertheless, Hall immediately called U.S. Rep. Clark Thompson and sought his advice.

Through what Hall insists was a coincidence, within 24 hours the Friendswood officials were notified that their WCID application for funds had been approved. And to them Hall was a hero, despite his insistence that the quick action truthfully was a coincidence.

Hall later told Thompson that he appreciated the congressman's efforts, but that he knew actually that the time was just exactly right for the Friendswood application.

"That's all right," Thompson said, laughing. "You let 'em think that you and I unwound the string to make this thing happen. Take all the credit you can get."

The Hall Sense of Humor

Walter Hall has what has been called a "self-deprecating" sense of humor.

Bankers Monthly magazine has called him direct and folksy, warm and disarming.

The magazine called his favorite oath, made against those who don't stop by to visit him, the "Hall Hex": "Your chickens won't lay. Your fireplace will smoke. And your roof will leak."

Hall attributes one of his favorite quotes to a comedian—but Hall has been saying it for so many years that his friends think the comedian might have stolen the idea from Hall:

"At my advancing age, I don't even buy green bananas any more."

At one time Hall referred to himself as a "boll weevil country banker."

Hall has said that he "took to politics" and became "more voluble than effective."

Hall believes that the best lubricant in the world is humor; his wit is recognized by his friends and enemies, and it has been practiced on some of the giants of the area—both present and past.

The manner in which Hall can intermingle his humor, politics and political finances is possibly best illustrated by a story told by Dr. Frank E. Vandiver, distinguished university professor and president emeritus of Texas A&M University. Dr. Vandiver is former provost, vice president and acting president of Rice University, and also former president of North Texas University as well as Texas A&M University.

"Back in 1964," Vandiver related, "I put together an organization called 'Texas Professors for Johnson, Yarborough and Connally,' and got over a thousand Texas academics to sign an ad advocating the election of the whole ticket. Getting the ad published cost a whole lot more than I had guessed. A full page in The Houston Post and Chronicle came to $1,800 then; so, too, with the big dailies in most big Texas towns.

"Those professors who signed made such contributions as they could, but none of us had much money.

"My surest ally, the best source of funds, was Walter Hall. I'd call and tell him we needed a bit to run an eighth of a page ad somewhere, or more in another place. Each time he'd come back in that dry voice, 'Well, lessee, there's another gas station down the road apiece I haven't robbed yet. Come on, we'll get it.' And he always came through."

Another of Hall's personal friends, attorney Stanley C. Woods of Houston, related a few of the conversational "gems" Hall has tossed his way:

"He had said, 'Woods, if you won't tell the truth on me, I won't tell a lie on you.'

"He has also made it clear to me that when we were engaged in a discussion of issues confronting the country that he granted me the RIGHT to be WRONG.

"One day he and I were talking about problems that beset all of us in life, and he said, 'Let's make a pact that if either one of us gets to feeling sorry for himself, we grant the other one the right to hit him between the eyes with a 2" by 4".'

"One of the most comical ones he gave me is, 'Woods, I never tell a lie unless it helps me.'"

Pirate Jean Lafitte, as portrayed by John Crowley, a bank staff member, surprised Walter Hall at a party celebrating Hall's 80th birthday on May 30, 1987, in the Citizens State Bank Building in Dickinson. Hall previously had joked that the early Galveston pirate still owed him money. Behind the pirate, obviously enjoying the confrontation, is Stanley C. Woods, Houston attorney and a close friend of Hall. Others in the photo, behind Hall, are, from the left, Madeleine Rogers, bank staff member; Frances Jamison, Friendswood fig producer; Stella Coffman, bank staff member; Barbara Liefert, bank staff member; and (partially hidden) Bert Jamison, Friendswood fig producer. Behind the "pirate," from the left, are Woods; John T. Creden, bank staff member; Charles L. Hutchins, bank director; H.C. Lewis, bank staff member; and Charles F. Hall, Walter Hall's son and head of Hall's Insurance Agency. The teddy bear in the chair at the left was a gift for "Papa Bear" Hall, his grandson's nickname for his grandfather.

When Hall was involved in work with the Post-War Planning Committee of Galveston County, he was asked why he was working so hard for a sea wall for Texas City when the industries of Texas City were bitterly fighting the tax reform measures Hall wanted. Hall replied, "Hell, I just want to see them paying the proper amount of taxes they owe—I don't want to drown them!"

Hall likes to remember, with humorous sarcasm, the days in Texas when wealthy oilmen were considered experts on any subject and every subject.

"When a man with enough oil wells started to speak," Hall said, "everything got quiet, because oily pearls of wisdom were going to flow.

"Once, immediately after a Republican administration was installed in the White House after several years of Democratic reign, I was eating in a Houston club. My companion, Gordon Turrentine, a Houston Chamber of Commerce official, introduced me to Hugh Roy Cullen, the oil millionaire and University of Houston benefactor. Gordon told Cullen I was a leader of the loyal Democrats.

"Cullen said, 'Well, I wonder what you Democrats are saying now?'"

And Hall replied, "Mr. Cullen, I hope we Democrats get along as well under you Republicans as you Republicans did under us Democrats."

The comment was overhead by a Houston Chronicle reporter and his report was republished in "Post Election Quips" on Page 1 of the New York Times.

Hall once reviewed his various sporting activities, such as offshore fishing near Galveston, hunting royal elk in New Mexico, big game in Alaska, pheasants in North Dakota, and also said he liked to "protect the local area from flying ducks."

One of the early "celebrities" of Galveston County, Jean Lafitte, has been linked with Walter Hall by the banker himself, always when joking about his advancing age.

One such occasion was at the dedication of the Walter Hall Park at League City in 1985.

Hall said he wanted to dispel the rumor that he was old enough to have met the famous pirate when Lafitte landed in Galveston.

He then added that he actually had met the pirate in Kemah and the two still had business to settle.

Hall said he loaned the pirate money and Lafitte defaulted on the note. The banker said he would forgive the interest if the old pirate would just pay up.

Knights of the Oblong Table

Walter Hall is demonstrating his sense of humor in a more than vocal manner through meetings of his "Knights of the Oblong Table."

Hall "organized" the Knights in 1991 by "demanding" that about a dozen of his friends, whom he considered "highly intelligent, informed and tolerant," meet him for lunch at the Lakewood Yacht Club in Seabrook.

Hall assured his friends that his new organization would have "no dues, no officers, no consequential responsibilities, no viable issues (I can think of) and no records or minutes."

"It is recognized," Hall wrote, "that historically knights of various types of tables have been men of high honor, great courage, and dedication to all that is good and holy, vowing to meet all challenges. Accordingly, 100 percent acceptance (of this invitation to join) is not only requested, but demanded!" Hall designated himself "Sir" Walter in Charge of Chambers, the organization's only office.

"In recognition of the great character, mental and otherwise, of the members," Hall said, "one of the original members, County Judge Ray Holbrook, presented to the Sir Knight the sword that his grandfather carried in the Civil War. That is the sword that is used to knight new members, few as they are, by hitting them on the posteriors as they stoop over."

Hall revealed the type of "meetings" he holds with these sample "agendas" sent to "members" with his invitations to meetings:

"...The length of time since our last meeting explains to a degree why things, international, national and local, have deteriorated. However, I am convinced we should not let these matters go much longer, and accordingly we are having a meeting of the Knights of the Oblong Table on Thursday..."

"The long delay since the last meeting has allowed important issues to increase, and they are now of such a serious nature they cannot be ignored any longer. Accordingly, you are expected to be present, and your absence will be a matter of discussion by those who are present in order that suitable punishment/penalty can be levied against those who are absent, and as I recall from past actions, the penalty will be very serious!"

"Due to rapidly deteriorating national and worldwide conditions, and with the conviction that things can only be 'saved' through the genius, proven strategic expertise, contemplative thought, and superb (but chivalrous) action of the Knights of the Oblong Table, I hereby summon said Knights to a meeting...Let me add that the delay in calling this meeting has been due to the conviction that things being as bad as they are, they couldn't get any worse, and change would only mean they would get better. They continue to get worse! The responsibility now lies with us so please give thought to what you, personally, and our group as a whole, can do to save the world, even the perpetrators of the crimes (most of whom are REPUBLICANS) that have brought the sad state of affairs to us in such a devastating degree."

"Now that the election is over and our nation is again in the hands of those dominated by character, righteousness and dedication, it is time for us to again meet and review the unsolved problems that remain and prepare advice and counsel to forward to the powers who have been selected by this nation on the basis of their unqualified abilities. The world awaits hearing from us."

There is very little evidence that members of the Knights of the Oblong Table have slain many dragons or accomplished great deeds, other than conversation, but those members who are honored by Walter Hall's invitations rarely fail to attend his meetings.

Hall the Citrus 'Farmer' and Woodworker

Walter Hall's home in League City in earlier years was the site of many barbecues and other festive affairs that Walter and Helen Hall sponsored for their friends.

Some of the barbecues on the spacious grounds of the home honored members of volunteer fire departments in the communities served by Hall's banks as a measure of appreciation from his financial institutions and insurance agencies.

Many other groups, including area teachers and coaches, also have been honored at such barbecues.

Many of those who attended the parties failed to realize that they were also visiting the home of a successful citrus "farmer."

On the grounds of Hall's home are many huge live oak, Spanish oak, pecan and camphor trees, and a relatively good stand of orange trees and also some grapefruit and some lemon trees. Hall himself planted all of those trees on the impressive grounds at his home.

Hall's philosophy extends to his farming as well as his banking.

"When you're growing grapefruit," he told Brad Messer, at that time managing editor of The Galveston Daily News, "you have to remember to grow enough for the birds, relatives, friends and for yourself."

"Hall is generous with the fruit he grows," Messer wrote in 1974, "but he gets a little out of sorts with people who get the fruit and don't bother to let him know they appreciate it."

Messer said that two or three people on The Galveston Daily News in the 1970s received nice packages of oranges and grapefruit from Hall and apparently overlooked thanking him.

"I don't mind it when you fellows disagree with me on political issues, or when you have some comment about my banking business or capabilities," Hall told Messer, "but when you just totally ignore my talents as a citrus grower, that does it."

A bountiful fruit crop claimed the interest of Walter Hall at his residence in League City. This scene was an event of Oct. 24, 1974, but was duplicated many times over many years.

(Brad Messer photograph courtesy of The Galveston Daily News)

Hall explained to Messer that "banking" in his citrus orchard meant something not related to his primary business.

A citrus tree is "banked," he said, by piling dirt up around the trunk a couple of feet all around the tree to protect it from freezing weather.

"If a hard freeze comes, only the exposed branches of the trees are killed," he added. "We trim them back and then the next spring the trees start growing again."

Citrus trees have not been the only type of trees befriended by Walter Hall.

His interest many years earlier, in the 1930s, led to positive action when a Works Project Administration group, known as a "leaf-raking" group, was assigned by County Commissioner Earl Noble to League

City to work under Hall's direction. In that program, oak trees in the League City Park were trimmed, thinned and beautified.

Hall said he resents the failure of the city park personnel of League City to properly treat and care for the beautiful live oaks and other trees in the city, including the "Butler Oaks" along Highway 518 through League City.

Hall's home in League City also reflects the interest of a man with many talents.

Hall has a workshop behind his house with many types of saws, drills, woodworking tools, a bandsaw and other "handyman" equipment. Another room is packed with stored materials and the kind of "junk just too good to throw away," Hall said.

One part of the Hall workshop is reserved for fishing tackle repairs and includes all kinds of parts for rods, reels and fishing gear.

And, Messer added, Hall had enough decoys to make "any flock of ducks jealous."

The Halls bought the house on Coryell Street in 1935. It was built in 1905, two years before Hall was born in Houston. The house has been remodeled and expanded several times and at one point was raised 10 1/2 feet above any high water threat.

Hall's hobbies, in addition to "farming" and woodworking, include hunting and fishing. Many friends and associates have enjoyed visits to his Gulf-side Galveston cabin; on his boat, the Helen B Good; at his cabin in East Texas, where he fishes for bass; and to his cattle ranch in the Texas Hill Country, where he says he watches the "deer and turkeys play."

Hall the Engineer

Walter Hall's talents as a citrus farmer and woodworker are not secret to his friends, but possibly his genius as an engineer will surprise many of those who know him.

And the story of what has become known to bank directors as the "infamous antique can opener" is told by the same friend who explains Hall's accomplishments as an engineer.

Charles L. Hutchins of La Marque is a partner in A & A Machine of La Marque and a director of the Citizens State Bank. He claims that "Mr. Hall is a mechanical engineer and architectural engineer at heart and a banker by trade."

"A & A Machine has been involved in several of Mr. Hall's engineering projects," Hutchins related. "Mr. Hall designed the time vault in the foyer of the bank to be opened in the year 2000. We fabricated this watertight vault to his specifications.

"Mr. Hall designed a 32-foot span sign for the Clear Rock Ranch and asked us to build the sign. It is quite a structure and Mr. Hall said he would give us the measurements for the existing bolt pattern where this sign would fit on top of the rock wall he had built. I was very concerned about these measurements and he assured me he would handle the task. One day he came in with two plywood boards with a hole pattern drilled. He laid them on the floor and measured the exact distance between and gave us a drawing and said, 'If you make it fit this pattern it will fit at the ranch.' We did and it did!

"So over the years A & A Machine has built Walter Hall-designed flagpoles, bearing mounts for eagle wind indicators and various other products. The only project that A & A Machine has failed on is the infamous antique can opener. This can opener is still in review but not forgotten."

Pressed for details, Hutchins explained:

"When the ranch house burned down Mr. Hall lost a can opener. One day when I was at the bank he asked me to look at making a can opener. He had taken a 3-cornered file and a handle and showed me the basic design of this can opener.

"I started trying to make this opener and make it exactly as he had described. We made the basic unit but could not get the cutter blade to work right. I finally decided that we should find one somewhere and copy it. I found a picture in an antique kitchen utensils book but so far have not found one exactly as he described and like the one in the book.

"Now we have several and we are still looking. I have a trader in New York called 'The Primitive Man' who has sent me about four of these that are close but not quite...

"Meantime," Hutchins continued, "a couple of years ago when this first started Mr. Hall announced to the board that we were forming an antique can opener company and if anyone of the board wanted to buy stock we might sell some stock. So every meeting for several months I had to give a report on the can opener. Finally I had a fairly good working model and we opened a can of pork and beans at the beginning of the board meeting."

"However," Hall emphasized, "it still does not meet my specifications!"

Hall added that he persuaded Frans Gillebaard, a director of the League City Bank & Trust and owner of three restaurants in Kemah, to buy him one of those huge can openers that are used in hotels and restaurants.

Hall the Gladiator

Although the banker is not too proud of the fact, Walter Hall at one time carried the title as a "gladiator." It was bestowed on him after one of the few physical fights he ever had in his life, and the only one since he has been an adult. And probably the only fight ever allowed on the premises of the Citizens State Bank. This incident was in the early days of the bank, when it was at League City.

"It typifies my personality then, which is far from what it is now," Hall claimed.

"A local man who was quite large was known as 'Bull.' He had borrowed some money from the bank before I got there in 1931, and of course I was trying to collect. But he had been very uncooperative and would not respond to our notices.

"Finally one day he came by the bank, came in to see me about his note and obviously was short-tempered. He became very upset and began to use a lot of profanity.

"Remember, now, that was 'way back, when women didn't use much profanity that I knew anything about; and I was offended because my young wife, Helen, was there helping me and Bull was using all those cuss words in her presence. I asked him to stop.

"It didn't slow him up at all, and I walked around from my side of the desk to where he was, on the other side. I had no intention of hitting the man. But I got around there and he continued his cursing. So I hit him in the chin. It didn't faze him in the least. He had a huge belly, and outweighed me about 100 pounds. He started flailing, his big old fists were whizzing by my ears and I knew that pretty soon he was going to connect and knock me through the wall.

"I was hitting him in his belly right above his belt and sinking my fists 6 inches into his stomach. I couldn't even make him grunt. So I knew the situation was in bad shape. But I had a smattering knowledge of wrestling, and I knew something had to be done. Our building had a concrete floor, so I stooped down and put my arms around one of his knees, raised it as high as I could and flipped him. I was fortunate because his head fell in a corner and I had a toehold so he couldn't get up.

"My wife ran out of the bank shouting, 'Help! Help! Fight!'

"I was trying to break his leg, and was pouring it on him to such a degree that he was screaming like a wildcat.

"Two or three people came in, including Emil Schenk, who had a bakery down the street, and Dr. Orlando Patton, a physician. Emil told me to turn Bull loose. Then he grabbed my hand and tore it loose, and we both then went outside. I was mad as a hornet, but I figured that I could run if needed while outside.

"The others told Bull to leave, and of course I was glad because I wasn't any match for him. So that was the end of the fight.

"But it was amazing how fast news travels. That very afternoon I had to go to Galveston, and I was driving my car. Near the causeway I passed a car and the driver waved frantically at me, so I stopped. The driver was our county commissioner, Earl Noble, who was president of the Texas City National Bank.

"He had already heard about the fight, was laughing about it and said, 'I thought you had more sense than to take on a man that size.'

"I gained the nickname 'Gladiator,' and some of the men would laugh and say, 'You mustn't cuss around him or you'll have a fight on your hands.'

"Of course I was embarrassed that I would be led into such a thing."

A short time after the fight, Hall said, he and his brother Emory were riding horses and Walter Hall's horse pitched him off and Walter's head hit the ground.

"I suffered a slight concussion," Hall said, "and the next morning I was completely normal. One of my sons, however, says I've never fully recovered."

At any rate, the doctor told Helen Hall to keep cold packs on Hall's head for at least a day.

"So one of her brothers brought a tub and some ice, and an ice pick," Hall said. "My sister came over to help, and after she had chopped ice for the ice pack she hid the ice pick. She thought I was belligerent enough that I was going to kill someone with that ice pick."

Bull finally paid his debt to the Citizens State Bank after about three years and he and the banker became friends, Hall said.

Hall Forestalls a Possible Race Riot

Few people today realize that Walter Hall, almost single-handedly, may have saved Dickinson from a race riot.

It was after the U.S. Supreme Court in 1954 had unanimously ruled segregation in public schools unconstitutional and President Eisenhower had sent federal troops to Little Rock, Ark., in 1957 to enforce integration there.

Integration of the Dickinson schools was scheduled to begin in the mid-1960s. The integration plan was approved in November, 1963, to be effective in September, 1964.

But not all Dickinson residents were ready to accept the decision.

"One morning the superintendent of the Dickinson school district, O.J. Baker, rushed into my office, all upset," Hall recalled.

"He had received word that a new redneck in town had talked to a lot of his redneck friends, and they decided they were not going to have any integration in Dickinson.

"Other citizens had expressed another view, Baker told me, and he feared there would be violence."

Hall told Baker he'd find out what he could. He called the newcomer to visit him in Hall's office, and the man did.

"I told the man," Hall said, "that I understood that he was opposed to integration, but that it was provided by law and that there was no alternative. I reminded him that President Eisenhower had used troops in Little Rock to enforce integration.

"The redneck used quite a bit of profanity and said, 'Yeah, we know how to stop those blacks here. They'll have to face our shotguns."

"So I said, 'Let me check around and see what's happening and then I'll get back in touch with you.'

"I did some checking. There was no doubt about it—he and some of his friends planned to stand on the steps of the new school and try to halt integration, with shotguns if needed.

"Then the blacks heard about it, and they also were threatening to have shotguns.

"When I saw the redneck again I tried to talk to him very calmly. 'We mustn't have violence here,' I told him.

"In the meantime I had phoned about 24 people, told them what was happening and asked for their help. I asked them to stand with me, with shotguns, if violence developed, to prevent a real race riot.

"Out of the group I called, about 10 or 12 said they would make the stand if I would. I told them to remember, that this was not play. Among those who have lived here in recent years were Dr. Joe Magliolo; his brother, the late Dr. Amedeo Magliolo; and Ernest Brown.

"Meantime, I had talked to some black preachers, friends of mine, and they were relieved. Some of the hotheads in their group, too, were demanding recognition.

"I sent for this redneck again. He came in and I tried to talk to him, but he said, 'Aw, they're not going to face that hot lead and cold steel.'

"I told him, 'I want you to know it's not going to be blacks you're facing. It's going to be me and some other white folks. And if it's violence you want you're going to get it.'

"Do you know, most men like that are basically cowards. He was shocked. He said, 'Mr. Hall, do you mean you're going to protect this business of mixing these kids?'

"'I told you we were going to observe the law, that we are not going to have any racial violence in Dickinson,'" Hall said he told the trouble-maker.

Hall added:

"He wilted like an Easter lily in the hot sun. That was the end of it, and we never did have a race riot."

Willie Matthews of Dickinson recalls that while there was a great amount of talk at the time in the black community, because of Hall's action no violence developed.

"Mr. Hall nipped that situation in the bud" and became quite a hero, Matthews said.

Hall recalled the conversation when he asked Dr. Amedeo Magliolo to join him and the others with their shotguns. Magliolo said to let him think about it overnight.

"The next day," Hall reported, "he called me and said, 'I've been hearing these stories about old Walter Hall not being very strong mentally. Now that you want to get down there and start fighting with a bunch of rednecks, I know the stories are accurate. But if you're crazy enough to do it, I'll be with you.'"

Relative to the early days of the civil rights movement, Hall likes to repeat an incident as reported to him by the late U.S. Rep. Clark Thompson of Galveston.

A black congressman from Chicago, believed to have been Rep. William Dawson, was defending a bill before the House of Representatives.

He concluded his argument in this way (possibly paraphrased): "If you hold it against me because I am unclean, I can take a bath; if you hold it against me because I am ignorant, I can go to school; but if you hold it against me because of my color, I can only refer you to the God who gave it to me."

Hall the Thinker

Walter Hall, at the age of 88, undoubtedly is far more concerned than most of his fellow citizens about the many problems facing the nation—such as schools and education, crime and violence, the deteriorating highway system and world diplomacy.

And he is constantly thinking of ways some of the problems might be solved, and discusses proposed solutions daily with friends and associates.

Two examples will illustrate his concern for the nation and the world.

The United States has institutions of higher learning for studying the military problems of fighting wars—such as the U.S. Military Academy and other service schools—but has none for studying or solving the problems of peace or attempting to maintain peace.

Hall wants some university or other organization to sponsor an academy for diplomacy, where students can study the people, the customs, the languages of foreign nations and other aspects of diplomatic relations.

Graduates of that academy would be far-better equipped to serve in the nation's diplomatic corps than those citizens who are selected merely because of large sums of money donated to political campaigns, Hall argues.

He believes that one project he envisions might help solve two major problems, crime and the nation's deteriorating transportation system.

"We have thousands of prisoners overcrowding our jails," he explained, "and we're paying millions of dollars to keep them there with little thought of rehabilitation. Why not establish a system, comparable to that of the Citizens Conservation Corps of the 1930s, to subsidize their work on the highways and substandard bridges?"

Hall suggests that commercial contractors would not only use the labor of the prisoners, paying them a minimum wage, but also would teach the prisoners trades which would be useful when they are released from supervision.

Walter Hall's Religion

Walter Hall is reluctant to discuss religion.

"A person's religion is the most personal thing in his life," he said, "and I prefer not to discuss my beliefs."

He did, however, discuss a class he took in Rice University from his favorite professor of philosophy, Dr. Radoslav Tsanoff, which might give some indication of his thoughts or why he declines to discuss religion:

"In the philosophy of religion, we studied most of the major religions and some of the minor ones. He (Dr. Tsanoff) was so objective in his teaching and so tolerant of all ideas in the various schools of religion and philosophy that I don't know to this day which ones he thinks had the most merit...That made a lasting impression on me."

Hall also had said: "I respect greatly the Ten Commandments and the Sermon on the Mount. Unfortunately, we do not practice those to a great degree in this country."

Walter and Helen Hall posed for a photo at the 50th anniversary celebration of the Citizens State Bank in 1956.

The Ability to Adapt: Helen's Problems

Former state Sen. A.R. "Babe" Schwartz, a close political ally and personal friend of Walter Hall, marvels at the banker's ability to adapt to new and possibly unusual ideas when it becomes necessary.

Schwartz said that at one time Hall's wife, Helen, was so physically incapacitated she was unable to work.

"Despite the fact that Walter was surrounded by traditional doctors," Schwartz said, "to try to give her some relief he agreed to let her try acupuncture; and as I recall she was able to return to work later."

One of the Halls' sons, Charles F. Hall, said that although his mother was in constant pain with her knee for at least the last 10 years of her life, "I was unaware that mother had acupuncture.

"She did everything in her power to hide her pain and physical problems from the family," Charles Hall said. "If a person did not have the ability to solve a problem of any type, she would shield that person from the results of the failure.

"She was a remarkable woman in many ways and I thoroughly believe that dad would not have met the success he has without her.

"She kept all of us in our places and was very quick to deflate our egos when they became too large."

Walter Hall's Family

Walter and Helen Hall had been married for 54 years when she died in 1981.

An ex-student of the University of Texas, Helen Hall was active in her community's civic and business affairs. For eight years, beginning in 1935, she was postmaster of League City and after post office hours worked with her husband in many phases of the banking business.

The Halls had three sons: Walter G. (Sonny) Hall Jr., Charles F. Hall and Samuel Hall.

Hall additionally has eight grandchildren and five great-grandchildren.

Charlie Hall has assumed management of Hall's Insurance Agency; Sammy Hall, stationed in Washington, D.C., is chief of the Recreation Grants Division of the U.S. Interior Department's National Park Service; Sonny Hall, when he returned from service in the Korean War as a captain in the Marine Corps, decided to leave the banking business. He organized a savings and loan association in Dickinson, and was indicted in 1991 and convicted for making some illegal transactions. He declared personal bankruptcy and in 1995 was serving time in a federal penal institution.

Walter G. Hall was not involved in any way with the ownership or operation of his son's savings and loan business.

Charlie Hall, in addition to his management of Hall's Insurance Agency, is a director and vice chairman of the boards of directors of the Citizens State Bank, League City Bank & Trust and Bay Area Bank & Trust.

Hall's Insurance Agency, founded by Walter G. Hall in 1931, was incorporated in 1988, with control assumed by Charles F. Hall.

One of Hall's grandsons, Charles F. (Chuck) Hall Jr., is assistant secretary of the board of all three of Hall's banks.

In an early tragedy in the Hall family, one of Hall's grandchildren—W.G. (Skipper) Hall III, 2 years old, the son of Sonny Hall—drowned in a pond at the Walter Hall home in League City.

Helen Hall's father, W.E. Lewis, was a tax assessor-collector of Galveston County. An uncle of Helen Hall, M.M. Cox, was the first editor of the Texas Coast Promoter, the first newspaper on the Galveston County Mainland, published in League City in the early part of this century.

Helen Hall, a member of the library board, had expressed the wish that if anyone desired to remember her at the time of her death, she preferred that they do so with a gift to the League City Library rather than sending flowers. Hall, of course, relayed that wish to the media when she died.

Within the next few weeks, more than $50,000 was given to the League City Library in her honor.

The remarkable fact was that only two gifts were for more than $50; the others were contributions of $1, $5 or other smaller gifts.

This indicated the tremendous love and admiration the citizens of the community held for her, and shortly thereafter the library was renamed to honor her.

As an additional indication of the respect with which Helen Hall was held in the community, a tax bond issue for $2 1/4 million was passed overwhelmingly by the voters for an expansion of the library and its services.

As a result, the Helen Hall Library in League City is one of the most outstanding libraries of the state for a community the size of League City.

Helen Hall served as president of the League City Parent-Teacher Association and was the recipient of an honorary life membership from the National Congress of Parents and Teachers Association.

She had served as director and member of the home service committee of the American Red Cross for 30 years and had been a member of the Crippled Children's Society and the American Cancer Society. She had served as a director of the United Fund organization in Galveston County.

During the hectic days after Carla devastated the area in 1961, she often worked 16 hours daily in Red Cross volunteer relief work.

Helen Hall had worked side by side with her husband in political and civic endeavors as well as in banking.

Hall once told an associate, "Strictly from a selfish point of view, I can say that Helen's most important contribution is that people like her so much it tends to offset their antagonism toward me. Over the years, believe me, this is important."

Because of Hall's political activities, frequent harassing telephone calls were made to the Hall residence, often accusing him of being a communist. The calls did not bother him, Hall said, but did trouble Helen.

9TH DISTRICT, TEXAS

COUNTIES:
CHAMBERS
GALVESTON
HARRIS (S.E. SECTOR)
JEFFERSON

JUDICIARY
CHAIRMAN
ECONOMIC AND COMMERCIAL
LAW SUBCOMMITTEE
CHAIRMAN

SELECT COMMITTEE
ON NARCOTICS

Congress of the United States
House of Representatives
Washington, DC 20515

May 18, 1993

Dr. Thomas Mackey
Texas Society to Prevent Blindness
P.O. Drawer 2050
Galveston, Texas 77553

Dear Tom:

Regret that the press of business in Washington prevents my attending your 1993 Man of Vision Award banquet. This year's honoree, Walter Hall, is one of my closest friends. I know Walter as a man of uncommon ability and enormous energy...someone who has contributed immeasurably to the quality of our life here on the Texas Gulf Coast.

He has always felt that he could make a difference and he has always sought to address the very best in every one of us. Whenever he sets out to accomplish a community goal, you know that he will be successful because people sense that Walter Hall is in fact a Man of Vision.

The people of the Texas Gulf Coast are indeed fortunate to have Walter Hall as a friend, neighbor, and community leader. As a close friend, I've always been able to count on Walter to offer both good advice and the hand of friendship in difficult situations.

His work on behalf of the people in all of Galveston County and the Texas Gulf Coast has set a high standard of excellence for others to follow, so, Walter, please accept my heartfelt congratulations for your 1993 Man of Vision Award.

Sincerely,

Jack Brooks

cc: Mr. Walter Hall

A letter Walter Hall prizes highly is this from U.S. Rep. Jack Brooks, sent to the sponsors of the "Man of Vision Dinner" honoring Hall in 1993.

Chapter 8

Walter Hall Is 'Graded' By a Few of His Many Friends

Many of Walter Hall's friends were solicited and each was asked for a "nugget"—a bit of information about the banker—for inclusion in these pages. The response was overwhelming.

Some of the information received in response to the requests is included in the main section of this book. Most of the others are included here, in full or in part.

All of the responses indicate the great regard which Walter Hall's friends have for him (and his late wife, Helen), whether concerning his banking principles, his political beliefs or his personal life. Unfortunately, it was impossible to solicit information from all of his friends and acquaintances, just as it is impossible to reproduce all of the letters in their entirety.

A sampling of those responses not included in the main section of the book follows:

Caroline A. (Mrs. Charles B.) d'Etchegoyen, Houston:

"(Walter Hall) always was attached to the worst-looking old hats. If I saw it today I would recognize the one he wore as a teen-ager. About the time he and Helen bought Clear Rock Ranch he insisted that she take the current old hat and get it renewed. She asked me to go with her on what she felt was a hopeless errand. Sure enough, the hat shop said they were sorry but the hat was beyond anything they could do. She persisted. Nobody could turn Helen down, and they consented to do their best with the hat but warned her not to expect much. Apparently that hat had nine lives because Walter was happy with its improved appearance and immediately started wearing it again. The hat was immortalized; Walter commissioned a large painting to be hung in the dining room at Clear Rock, and there in the foreground of the painting was that hat. Sad to say, the house and all its contents burned to the ground. I have never dared to ask if the hat went with it.

"Walter got a kick out of a successful practical joke he played on several of his friends who had mentioned accounts of valuable paintings and other treasure turning up in people's attics or being bought for pennies and found to be worth huge sums. He was shopping for antiques for the Clear Rock house and came across a big copper pot with a long spout. He composed a letter about this rather ordinary pot, stating that it was one of a rare and historic pair and was of great value. He got the antiques dealer, an old friend, to have the letter typed on his stationery. and as far as I know it fooled everybody Walter showed it to. We all thought he had made the find of the century."

(Caroline d'Etchegoyen was one of nine children who entered the first grade at the League City school in 1914. Others were Walter and Helen Hall. Only d'Etchegoyen and Hall were known to be alive in 1995.)

Walter Gaetjens, Austin:

"His total philosophy is that in any relationship the other person must benefit as much or more than he does—and I have never known anyone who practiced this so thoroughly."

Avo Izmirlian, Nice, France:

"The most striking characteristic in Walter is his genuine sincerity which blurts out very naturally and spontaneously whenever he has something to say about anybody or any subject. In all my conversations with him on America's and the world's problems, I could not help to observe his genuine sense of concern for other people. Rich or poor, his concern and consideration for others is one of the outstanding features of his marvelous personality."

Thomas M. Stauffer, president, Golden Gate University, San Francisco, California:

"I spent ten years in the Clear Lake area. Walter G. Hall was the most interesting personality I met during that decade, and it had nothing to do with his longevity or business success. He is a man to emulate because he stuck to his long-held convictions. Whether you agreed with him or not—and I agreed with him many times—most everyone admired his articulate, indeed forceful, defense of his beliefs. And he lived long enough to cite proofs from the past that few of us are old enough to dispute.

"I recall the visit of a hapless bank examiner a few years ago in a meeting with the board of Bay Area Bank and Trust. The examiner was not very impressive, and around Mr. Hall, she became even less so. While Mr. Hall abided by all courtesies, the examiner gave her findings and raised several technical points. Most bank chairmen fear examiners, especially in recent years; not Mr. Hall. He gave a dazzling display of his own technical knowledge, citing examples of cases before the examiner's birth, and then moved in for the kill. Finally, the examiner conceded Mr. Hall's points and said that she would have to check with her superiors. When the results came in writing several weeks later, Mr. Hall had won on every issue."

Pauline Redman, Conroe:

"He was never too busy to listen and give his opinion or advice regardless of how insignificant it really was. If it was important to you he had time to listen. He always made you feel important and welcome...I remember when we first bought out (a business) we had quite a struggle at first. He came to our rescue with a loan that had to be renewed several times—it was during a real recession. There was never a big hassle or embarrassment; he always worked with you to help but to also see that you did not get in over your head."

Charles F. Wiebusch, Sarasota, Florida:

"His procedure seemed to be to...promote some activity which would give him a ' one-up' on the competition. For instance, he arranged for his bank to stay open late on Fridays to serve the check-cashing needs of workers from surrounding areas. By the time other bankers woke up he was not only cashing checks, he was getting new accounts."

John and Lorraine Peterson, Lothian, Maryland:

"...Then there was the bank's 'social center.' Going to the bank was never just an act of business. It was to be invited into the back room for soup and snacks, coffee and cold drinks and mingling with the employees. Hosting the activity was either Helen (Hall) or her most gracious sister, Grace Lewis...There was an air about Walter's bank that set it aside from all others."

Elaine Mantooth Fleming, M.D., League City:

"After completing my internship in 1958, I wanted to open my office in Dickinson, but I had no money...I did not know Mr. Hall at that time, but knew that a bank was where you got money. I went to see Walter and told him my problem...I got my loan...No collateral, of course. Walter and I have made many business arrangements since that date. Now he's even helping the second generation get started. We have become friends, and I...learned to love him and Helen. I wouldn't take a million for the friendship. He's a great guy!"

George M. Fleming, Ed.D., Houston:

"As administrator of the county hospital, I received a call from Mr. Walter Hall in 1966 advising that the bank had met with a doctor from Louisiana who wanted to build a clinic in Dickinson. The doctor would need privileges at the hospital...I had a rush credit report done on the doctor and found that he had a poor reputation, loss of privileges at several hospitals and lawsuits...I called Mr. Hall and told him the doctor was not likely to receive any privileges and why...Mr. Hall appreciated the information...The clinic was not built and the doctor did not move to Dickinson."

Cecil J. Palmer, Austin:

"In August, 1939, Helen, Walter and I were on vacation in Mexico City. Hitler was stirring up things in Europe. When we could find an English-language newspaper it was out of date. There was plenty of radio news, but none of us could understand enough of it to keep up with what was going on. Among the three of us we were able to read newspapers well enough to know what was happening. When England declared war on September 1, we all knew that World War II had started. Walter said his bank had foreign securities, the status of which was hard to determine in a war situation. So we cut our vacation short and headed for Dickinson."

J. Edwin Smith, Houston:

"Jimmy Allred (the former Texas governor) in 1946 was in private practice, having been denied confirmation for the 5th Circuit (Court) by 'Pappy' O'Daniel. He (Allred) was actively supporting Homer Rainey for governor.

"One afternoon Jimmy had a group of Rainey's supporters to his office for a conference and out of the blue sky announced he was bringing up from Dickinson, Texas, a banker to confer with us. We all were shocked and vociferously protested that the bankers were all against our candidate...Jimmy explained that this one, Walter G. Hall, was a rare species, a loyal, liberal Democratic banker, and to our amazement that proved to be true.

"To demonstrate that Walter's charitable instincts extended to the personal as well as the public, these two examples I experienced: (1) Wanting to live near to the coast before Carla I bought a lot fronting on Swan Lagoon. Walter cautioned, 'Rent a place down here first, before you build; you must be sure you can survive the strain of residing here and working in Houston.' This I did and learned I couldn't handle the daily driving back and forth. (2) When Carla came the lot was inundated; had a home already been built it would have been ruined. Walter volunteered to buy the lot for the (amount) I paid for it. We closed the deal and then he sold it for what he paid me."

Margery Norris, Austin:

"When I think of Walter Hall, I think of a man dedicated to his profession and his community, to his political beliefs and to the pursuit of excellence.

"At the time I was employed as his secretary in 1950, Walter, at age 43, was the youngest bank president in Texas (maybe in the U.S.). Today...he is probably the oldest. His job has been his whole life, and he has worked with enthusiasm, good humor, diligence and uncanny acumen. He is a good judge of character and would sometimes lend money to people based solely on his faith in their integrity. I am sure the bank examiners frowned on this practice, but during the time I was associated with the bank, I think his confidence was always justified, and the bank never lost any money on these loans. Many a rice farmer has Walter to thank for saving him from financial disaster...

"I remember one occasion when Helen came hurrying into the bank holding a pair of shoes. She signaled to Walter that she needed to see him right away, so he excused himself from the customer in his office and went out to see what the problem was. It seems that son Sammy either had to have his picture taken or was in a play or something, but he needed the black shoes Walter was wearing. So Walter obligingly took off his shoes, gave them to Helen, and put on the brown shoes she had brought him.

"...his approach to life: He trusted people (until they proved they were not trustworthy), he treated people fairly, he allowed people the freedom to disagree with him without letting this affect their friendship, he had the courage of his convictions, and he had the ability to take criticism without rancor. He was a hard taskmaster, but I agreed with his philosophy that if anything was worth doing it was worth doing well. In short, I admired the man very much."

Emma J. Long, Austin (former City Council member, widow of newsman and author Stuart Long):

"When I think of Helen and Walter I do so with love and appreciation. They give of themselves and their resources when a friend is in trouble. My trouble came when Stuart, my late husband, was diagnosed as having lung cancer. We tried every treatment in the books at the time. Helen had had great results from a well-known acupuncturist in Houston.

They invited us to stay in their home and travel back and forth to the clinic for weeks at a time. We were just family and occupied the most elegant suite in the Hall home. Their concern and encouragement was very healing and soothed our emotions...

"We shared the same thoughts and ideals about what government is all about and fought many battles trying to keep the conservatives from ruling the Democratic Party in the days before the Republicans 'came out of the closet.' Stuart and Helen were both on the State Democratic Executive Committee for several years. We met in caucuses, conventions and once the executive committee even met under a tree in Congressman (Mr. Speaker) Sam Rayburn's back yard and won a victory over the conservative faction. We four were together.

"Walter never let his banking business hold him back from expressing his views which were 'liberal' for the time—they are all old hat now because we prevailed in the end (in many of the issues)...in my books Walter Hall is a great, wonderful and generous man."

Wilson and Phraulene Deats, Dickinson:

"We have known Walter Hall for 50 plus years, both as friend and as an advisor. In 1943 I worked for him as his secretary. Working for him, I really saw how fairly he treated all who came to him and also how he helped many people who really needed help. One experience we would like to share with you:

"In December 1944 our home burned to the ground and we lost practically everything we owned. We had a 6-month-old son and a 4-year-old daughter. It was during the war and everything was scarce, and many things were impossible to replace. In the spring of 1945, Walter called us and said the bank had had to repossess some furniture and, if we wanted it, we could just pick up the payments and it was ours. What a generous offer! Let me say, the refrigerator (now in our garage) is still working! This thoughtful act by Walter will always be remembered and has been shared with many throughout the years. Thanks, Walter."

Bernard Perlmutter of Perlmutter & Associates, Realtors, Houston:

"In several instances...Mr. Hall wanted to purchase a site upon which to open a bank. It is obvious that if a property owner got wind of a bank being interested in a parcel, the price would go through the roof. So, I would purchase the property in my name or on occasion, I used my father-in-law as a straw party. We would pay the going price. I do not know for sure where Mr. Hall received the information as to where the logical place for a new bank should be, but he always knew more about what was going to happen in an area than anyone else. He was clairvoyant, or perhaps well-connected."

Elizabeth Faulk (widow of John Henry Faulk), Austin:

"It is gratifying indeed that you are writing about good Walter Hall...my late husband was close to him—especially in political matters. John Henry always said that Walter was the ultimate 'Yellow-Dog Democrat.' I have known him on a social level—always a generous and sympathetic friend."

Jane K. Hime, Dickinson:

"(One of the things) that stands out in my mind (when I came to Citizens State Bank in 1952 from Galveston) is the reminder of Helen and Walter Hall's benevolent ways.

"When moving to Dickinson, I had two small children and one on the way. We purchased our first new home in the then-first small subdivision. A housewarming party descended upon us as a surprise, bringing a load of folding chairs, large array of food and housewarming gifts by the Halls and employees of the bank. I had never experienced anything quite like this welcoming us to this small community and the bank.

"The other thing I will never forget are the Christmas parties at the Hall home in League City with Frances Gates playing Christmas carols on the piano and employees with their families gathered around singing. We had previously drawn names for exchanging gifts with a purchase limit of $2.50. Such nice and needful presents were passed around. We then had a delicious meal and everyone really had a marvelous time. These kind of parties continued each Christmas until the number of employees increased and then they were held at Lakewood Yacht Club."

Monsignor Eugene Cargill, Pastor, St. Mary Community, League City:

"While I was the pastor of the Catholic Church in Dickinson, I purchased an old historical house that was to be used as a rectory or parsonage for the church. The house is a beautiful old, wooden structure on Dickinson Bayou. I knew Mr. Hall would love this house, if for no other reason, because of all the wood. I had kept him informed of the progress of the restoration, and when it was completed, had him over for lunch.

"After lunch he told me that he wanted to give me a gift for the house, and that he would get back with me. Without me knowing it, he began to shop for an antique wooden, roll-top desk. On his way to the ranch on weekends, he would stop in small towns and antique shops looking for my desk. He had one shipped to his house in League City, and began to do what he does best: He began to restore the wooden desk in his workshop behind his home. As you can imagine, the desk is a treasured gift from a good friend that I will treasure all of my life...

"...the real 'nugget': I am a priest; Mr. Hall is not Catholic. I am not political or in business, and yet we are very good friends. Does this say something about him?"

Lenore C. Bradner (widow of Jim Bradner, owner of Radio Station KGBC, Galveston):.

"What fun it was to spend a weekend with the Halls while our children were growing up and then to spend days with them after we moved to Galveston...

"Perhaps my keenest memory was the borrowing of money from the Citizens State Bank. Jim...at Walter's suggestion, decided to build and operate a radio station in Galveston. Never had we borrowed a cent from anyone and I was simply frightened to tears. But all went well and I eventually paid off the debt when I sold the station a few years after Jim died. I have lived comfortably from the profit ever since. I shall always be grateful to Walter Hall."

Charles M. Jordan, Galveston:

"Walter helps more people than most of us know about. He gets a lot of credit and receives a lot of accolades for his work, both in banking and in politics, but for me it is the day-to-day contact with the ordinary citizens in our area that makes me admire him so. I have seen him loan money to a man out of his own pocket rather than turn him down. I have seen him go with men and women, not only the extra mile, but the longest mile in waiting for them to repay him either in money or in kindness when he has bent over backwards for them. And, I have seen some of his so-called friends burn him and he doesn't really get as mad about the loss of the money as he does about the loss of the friendship. His hurt is genuine. His pain is real, and it goes to the very essence of this man."

Lady Bird Johnson, former first lady, Stonewall, Texas:

Walter Hall is a man to be reckoned with both in banking and in politics.

"He and Lyndon shared a kinship in many of the things they believed would benefit the country.

"Back in 1948 when Walter first began supporting Lyndon, they explored mutual concerns about such things as civil rights, medical care, and education—subjects Lyndon cared deeply about—and he found that Walter's heart and thinking were very similarly invested. As a country banker, Walter knew from his customers about the problems they encountered in day to day living.

"I will always be grateful for the friendship Walter has shown to Lyndon and me through the years. I think the Johnsons, the people of

Galveston County, and his 'neighbors' everywhere are fortunate Walter Hall put his beliefs to work on their behalf and that he truly cared."

Dr. Frank E. Vandiver, chairman of the board of advisors of the Mosher Institute for International Policy Studies; distinguished university professor and president emeritus of Texas A&M University; former provost, vice president and acting president of Rice University; and former president of North Texas University as well as Texas A&M University:

"Despite his hating to read this, I want to say that I've never known a more thoroughly, consistently, decent man in my life. His friendship is a special richness my wife and I greatly prize."

R.L. Vanderpool Jr., who joined Citizens State Bank in May, 1946, as assistant cashier and resigned as vice president and a director in 1950:

"When I received your letter regarding Walter Hall I thought of a letter that he had written almost 43 years ago. I did not solicit the letter and was only made aware of its existence by the addressee, Mr. Murray Hudson, a leading board member of the Ouachita National Bank at that time.

"I am now retired and almost 75 years old so this copy of that letter is being sent in no sense of self-serving. It is being mailed only to illustrate vividly how unusually compassionate and unselfish a man is Walter Hall. The typical boss would not only (not) have written such a letter but would have been annoyed and unhappy about someone leaving that had first been given a job and then provided opportunities for advancement." (Hall had written a three-page letter of commendation to Vanderpool's new employer, the bank at Monroe, Louisiana, highly praising Hall's former officer and congratulating the new bank because of its new employee.)

Charles Hutchins, partner in A & A Machine in La Marque and a director in the Citizens State Bank:

"In August of 1981 I came on the board of the Citizens State Bank. This has been a very educational process for me as the owner of a small business. I have always been impressed by the amount of involvement the directors of this bank have. The committees and the board meetings are used to gain the full expertise and opinions of every board member. I am proud to serve at a bank where I can send my friends and associates and know they are going to receive personal and considerate attention. The quality of our officers and personnel is exceptional."

W.H. (Bill) Davis, another director of the Citizens State Bank:

"At my first board meeting about 30 years ago everyone was given coffee and a piece of pie—except for one senior director, who was given a longneck ice cold beer!"

Elizabeth J. Guilbeau, Cotati, California:

"(After I resigned from the League City Bank & Trust) Walter Hall told me he really hated to lose me because I was such a good hand and a real asset to the bank. He wanted to know why I was leaving and I told him I had a chance to work with horses...and get into sales. I...told him if he would pay me more (commission) I could have sold more new accounts. I told him that all the time I worked for him I used to see that money and touch it and feel it but I never got to keep enough of it! He just howled...I've always been grateful to 'Uncle Walter' (as I affectionately called him to myself) for my six years of banking experience because I got my education on the public in banking."

N.E. Dudney, M.D., League City:

"The two most distinguishing characteristics I have observed during a 39-year relationship with this fine gentleman is his sincere concern and his relentless efforts to improve the well being of the entire human race. He concentrates his efforts mostly toward the disadvantaged, the elderly and poor. His adult life has been dedicated largely to these fellow human beings...even once representing a client-friend before a judge in a court of law (and winning hands down).

"The second most distinguishing characteristic is his loyalty. As a director in one of his banks I have observed many times this man nursing troubled loans along, to a conclusion fitting the best interests of the borrower, many times salvaging businesses in trouble...

"As his physician I'm instructed from time to time about how long I'm expected to keep him alive and active so as to give him time to accomplish various do-good objectives. As the years go by the objective list grows longer, thus the time requests stay well ahead of the present. I hope for the good of all of us this just goes on and on and on, for there are lots of people out there who can be led to community service by this man. Certainly this is a better world because of him."

Selma Neumann, Seabrook:

"I cannot think of anyone who has done so much for so many community activities and diverse needs as Walter Hall. I know I reflect the affection and admiration of my late husband, Dr. Alfred R. Neumann, who was founding chancellor of UH-CL. A prophet with honor in his own country is a comfort, reassurance and encouragement to us all!"

Lynn Gripon, League City:

"In the early '50s we were without much cash and needed a certain amount to qualify for a loan—so Walter...loaned us the money on a handshake. Naturally the loan was paid off and we got a new home.

"At Kroger's one evening he had forgotten his billfold and was without money to pay for his groceries. I offered to loan him the money. He declined, saying he would go home and get the money."

Velma Bradshaw Leavell, Galveston:

"He has always been most concerned about being able to provide the money and services his clients needed. I remember riding around with him the day before Carla was nearing and we were looking at the farms and ranches and wondering what havoc it would have. He was already planning on how to get enough assets to provide them with what it might take to rebuild, replant or whatever their problem was."

John W. Able, Exceptional Performance Construction Corp., Sonoma, California:

"Over the last 20 years Mr. Hall has been a major source of advice. I have found that his advice, when followed, has become wisdom. His genius rests in years of excellent experience followed with great common sense. I should ask for his advice more often and benefit from his experience, thus avoiding some hard experiences of my own."

Grace M. Lewis, vice president of the Citizens State Bank and sister of the late Helen Hall:

"Mr. Hall was an excellent boss. When he gave you a job to do he had all the confidence in you and expected 100%. He always stood by you in the decisions you made in your department. Only one time did he step in when he thought I was working too many hours and he hired seven people at one time and sent them to me. Needless to say not any of them lasted too long. They soon found it to be too hard."

Charles F. Hall, Dickinson (One of Walter Hall's three sons):

"Some of the most important things about my father are as follows: A generation gap never existed. If anything I would have to say the normal generation gap was reversed in our case...There were never two sets of standards. He always lived by the same values and rules that he expected you to live by...He did not and does not believe in excuses, which made my life hard sometimes but gave me the tools to succeed...His desire and ability to give credit for his success to my mother, the people we work with and the community is one of the items I respect him for the most."

Stanley C. Woods, attorney, Houston:

"The greatest tribute to Walter as a banker and a man is the fact that he took great pains to have his bank serve the community. He has always felt the local banker had a responsibility to the community, and he certainly held to that premise. Another strong point of Walter's throughout the years to my knowledge was never make a loan to someone where it would hurt him more than help him. He wanted to make certain a loan was made to an individual where the borrower had enough money to do what he wanted to do in his business and not loan just enough to hold him as a customer or get him into trouble. He was also most interested in the character of the borrower and not just a balance sheet."

Martin E. Firestone, attorney, Miami, Florida:

"For myself, a young lawyer at the time (of the Mississippi television proceeding) it was the case of a lifetime and it left me with an undying admiration and affection for Mr. Hall (He always was and always will be Mr. Hall to me)...I cannot tell you how delighted I am that, at long last, Mr. Hall, a most remarkable (and delightful) individual will be given some measure of the recognition he so richly deserves."

Sam A. Rowe, retired banker, Alvin:

"Walter Hall was not always the friendly, personal banker that most of us knew most of the time. Like all of us, he did have a temper. It took an unusual event to get that temper aroused in public, perhaps, but it sometimes showed in private situations.

"Several of us, including Mr. Hall, were hunting on a deer lease in West Texas, before he bought his present ranch near Johnson City.

"Mr. Hall had staked out his claim in a blind on the property, and was waiting for his prey. Finally it appeared, the largest, most outstanding example of a deer he had ever seen, he claimed later. Mr. Hall trained his gun in the direction of the deer, got the animal in his sight and was about to get his trophy.

"Suddenly the handyman on the deer lease, a Mr. Harman, appeared nearby, carrying a bunch of clanging feed buckets for cattle. That deer Mr. Hall had in his sight disappeared.

"Mr. Hall, I believe, was the angriest man I've ever seen. All of us agreed that it must have taken an iron will to keep him from getting a human trophy.

"It is my understanding that Mr. Hall did not allow any cattle or livestock to be brought on his new Johnson City ranch for many years."

Madeleine Rogers, director, vice president and auditor, Citizens State Bank:

"The bank had a program that pays the (school) tuition (for employees). This program is still in existence today. I went to school at night a minimum of two nights a week. I did that for 10 years until I obtained my master's degree in finance. Every day, I applied all I learned to the banking business. Mr. Hall's secretary quickly realized that I knew where everything was and could give Mr. Hall instantaneous information in the form that he designed, and he designed quite a few!...Mr. Hall still requests an awful lot of information but the response is getting slower..."

Ronnie Dugger, the social-policy reporter and writer now living in New York City who founded, edited and became publisher of the Texas Observer, a biweekly "journal of free voices" published in Austin:

"Walter, one night in a restaurant—just the two of us over dinner—took me in hand like a son and taught me what I could learn at one sitting about making enough money for yourself, and land values, and that sort of thing. That hasn't been my strong suit; it may have been the first time in my life I gave the subject serious enough attention. Whatever good it did me, what stays with me from that night is learning for sure that Walter cared about me as a person.

"A few times I've been out to the ranch, where Helen was the gracious hostess who always knew exactly what was what, and Walter presided over the ranch with the same generosity, honestly-exerted authority, and well-thought-out standards that he would have applied, too, had he presided over, say Texas—a lot of us wanted him to run for governor, you know. (Probably we were thinking—anyway I was—'Gee, here on our side is a respectable BANKER, of all things, who runs three banks and makes a lot of money and advises people how to run businesses and makes a hell of a speech—why, we'd win, and he wouldn't sell out! A banker who can THINK!') I believe he gave it a go in his head, but he didn't go. He could have won and probably would have."

Ray Holbrook, former county judge, Galveston County:

"(Walter Hall) has been a personal friend of mine for 30 years...for the past 28 years I have been the beneficiary of his advice and counsel on many different subjects, probably at least 500 different items that have come up in the county or before the Commissioners Court. What is so outstanding about Mr. Hall is #1, nothing he has ever suggested or recommended or asked me to do benefited him personally. #2, in looking back over 28 years, I have not been able to discover anything on which he advised me concerning an important matter in Galveston County where he was wrong. In other words, not only did he advise me in the best interests of my future and in the future of Galveston County, but in every single case his advice proved to be absolutely correct. I don't know of anybody I have known in politics or in government or even personally who has been right all the time, except for Mr. Hall. This has been so significant that I thought it was important enough to bring to your attention. I hasten to add, however, that in some of these cases I did not follow his advice and I was proved wrong in every one of them. So for my money, he is the most perceptive and astute businessman and political prophet that we have had in Texas in the last 50 years and it has made a mediocre person like me, with a reasonably good education, what some believe an outstanding county judge. I certainly could not have done it all myself, but with the advice from my family and other friends, and particularly Mr. Hall, I have made only a hundred mistakes out of a thousand issues that I have handled."

An unidentified Galveston County official who was supported in his campaign by Walter Hall was quoted in The Galveston Daily News: "He's the roughest, toughest, meanest, orneriest and kindest-hearted man I know!"

The Butler Building in League City, erected in 1909, was the second home of the Citizens State Bank. The first was a small frame building (demolished many years ago) at the southwest corner of Second Street and Michigan Avenue. The all-brick Butler Building, across the street on the southeast corner of the same intersection, housed the bank until it moved to Dickinson in 1935. The building is being reconstructed by the owner, League City architect David Hoffman, who bought it in 1994 from G.I. Butler, grandson of George W. Butler, who built the structure.

Chapter 9

A Chronological History Of the Citizens State Bank

Walter G. Hall, in his more serious moments, attributes the success of the Citizens State Bank to "just good luck"—again, being in the right place at the right time. Even more seriously, he credits the success of his banks to the vibrant local economy, the petrochemical industry, the Johnson Space Center, tourism and—in particular—his superior officers, directors and employees and ever-increasing numbers of good friends and customers.

"Without those employees and friends—and, through the years, the cooperation and help of my wife, Helen; her sister, Grace Lewis; Lorena Harbison; Dave Gates; and Bob Holcomb—none of this would be possible," Hall said.

"I can never say enough kind words about our employees. They have made it all possible and are still making it possible.

"And again, without our many friends and customers, it would not have been possible."

. . .

Hall always has divided his work week among his banks and other interests. At one time, for example, when he had banks in Dickinson, League City and Alvin, his schedule called for him to be in Dickinson on Monday and Friday; in Alvin on Tuesday and Thursday; and in League City every morning and all day Wednesday.

And for many years he was president of the San Jacinto River Authority, spending many hours and days in Conroe and Houston.

But his staff members did not depend on any schedule to relax in their efforts, because Walter Hall might show up at any moment at any of his banks or insurance agencies.

. . .

The following chronological "map" was conceived as a guide to track personnel changes of officers and directors of the Citizens State Bank.

The "map" includes additions of most officers and directors after Walter G. Hall obtained control of the Citizens State Bank in 1943, but does not include names and dates of most departing staff members.

Additionally, many of the highlights in the life of Walter Hall are included to give the reader a "where in time" many of the changes occurred.

Other dates, facts and figures which may be of interest to some observers of the Citizens State Bank and Dickinson are included.

The abbreviation CSB obviously stands for Citizens State Bank and WGH stands for Walter G. Hall in the "map," and are used as space-saving devices.

The writer does not promise that the "map" is infallible but has tried to make it as accurate as possible.

1906

The Citizens State Bank of League City, Texas, received Charter No. 62 from the State of Texas. Official date on the charter is Feb. 12, 1906. Records in the Texas Department of Banking in Austin indicate that the bank opened for business March 1, 1906. Total assets: $10,000.

Initial officers were Sealy Hutchings, president, and Robert Ingram, cashier.

1907

Walter G. Hall was born in the Houston Heights section of Houston on May 30. He was the youngest of seven children.

1911

The Galveston-Houston Electric Co. began operating an interurban line between Galveston and Houston.

1918

Earliest-known existing minutes of the board of directors of CSB, still in vault of CSB in Dickinson, lists the following as directors: George W. Butler, E.R. Girardeau, Sealy Hutchings, C. Harper Anderson and E.D. Singeltary.

1923

WGH was graduated from the three-grade high school at League City.

1924

WGH was graduated from Central High School (now Sam Houston High School) in Houston. The same year he entered Rice University.

1925

First available statement of condition, dated June 19, from state examiner's report, in CSB vault: Demand deposits, $103,389; total assets, $123,562.

Dec. 31: CSB of League City deposits were $83,833 (from newspaper advertisement).

1926

Dec. 31: CSB deposits were $77,944.

1927

July 4: Walter Hall and Helen Lewis were married.

Dec. 31: CSB deposits were $79,724.

1928

WGH was graduated from Rice Institute (later Rice University) with a bachelor of arts degree. Almost immediately he was employed by the Texas Company at the Lena Clay Mine in Fayette County.

Dec. 31: CSB deposits were $75,681.

1930

WGH was transferred to the Houston office of the Texas Company. A short time later he resigned in anger.

Dickinson's population was an estimated 760.

1931

WGH began work for CSB in League City as cashier. The same year he organized Hall's Insurance Agency.

First "call" statement of condition of CSB after WGH became cashier was dated July 10, and signed by WGH as cashier. Total assets were $57,219; deposits were $38,201.

Dec. 31: CSB deposits were $30,980.

1932

The First National Bank in Dickinson paid off its depositors in full and closed its doors. Dickinson was without a bank for three years.

1933

In the depth of the Great Depression, President Franklin D. Roosevelt declared a "bank holiday," closing all of the nation's banks for four days.

WGH continued to open the back door of CSB in League City so his depositors could buy medicine and food.

CSB deposits on Dec. 31 were $64,036.

1934

Oil was discovered near Dickinson.

Hastings oil field was discovered near Friendswood. Meantime, industrial development was beginning in Texas City.

WGH made his first political speech for U.S. Sen. Tom Connally.

CSB deposits on Dec. 31 were $78,186.

1935

CSB was moved from League City to Dickinson on Jan. 1; the bank opened on Jan. 2 at its new address at 2718 Main Street, the building which had been occupied by the closed First National Bank.

CSB deposits on Dec. 31 were $123,283.

1936

Galveston-Houston Electric Co. halts operation of Galveston-Houston interurban line.

1937

CSB deposits on Dec.30 were $257,648.

1938

CSB moved to a new home in Dickinson at 2801 Main Street. The Hitchcock bank liquidated its deposits, paid its depositors in full and closed its doors.

The League City oil field was discovered.

1939

The construction of Camp Wallace, between Dickinson and Hitchcock, was started by the U.S.Army as a troop training center.

WGH initiated the organization and was president of the Water Control and Improvement District in League City.

CSB deposits on Dec. 31 were $276,354.

1941

Camp Wallace was completed and opened as a Coast Artillery training center.

Dec. 7: Japanese aircraft attacked Pearl Harbor, triggering U.S. entry into World War II.

CSB deposits on Dec. 31 were $505,744.

1943

WGH and associates purchased control of the Citizens State Bank from the Hutchings family of Galveston.

WGH was named president of the San Jacinto River Authority.

CSB deposits on Dec. 31 were $1,397,808.

1944

Dave L. Gates added to CSB staff as assistant cashier and director.

CSB deposits on Dec. 30 were $1,746,401.

1945

President Harry Truman ordered the atomic bomb attack on Japanese cities to accelerate the end of World War II.

WGH was named chairman of the Post-War Planning Committee of Galveston County.

CSB staff changes: Dave L. Gates became vice president and cashier; Helen Hall became a director.

CSB deposits on Dec. 31 were $2,416,099.

1946

CSB staff changes: R.L. Vanderpool Jr. added as assistant cashier; Mrs. Lorena Harbison added as assistant cashier.

CSB deposits on Dec. 31 were $2,541,209.

1947

CSB staff change: Grace Lewis added as assistant cashier.

CSB deposits on Dec. 31 were $2,693,095.

1948

WGH was credited with aiding the creation of the Clear Creek Consolidated Independent School District, including the schools at Webster, League City, Seabrook and Kemah.

CSB deposits on Dec. 31 were $3,287,757.

1949

CSB staff changes: Cashier R.L. Vanderpool Jr. named vice president and a director; C.A. Deese added as cashier.

CSB deposits on Dec. 31 were $2,816,723.

1950

CSB was expanded to 2 1/2 times its former size by the addition of a drive-in window, night depository and a community room.

Dickinson's population was 2,704.

CSB deposits on Dec. 30 were $2,849,853.

1951

CSB staff changes: G.J. Hoff added as assistant cashier; Joseph C. Magliolo, M.D., added as a director.

CSB deposits on Dec. 31 were $3,274,591.

1952

CSB deposits on Dec. 31 were $4,217,024.

1953

WGH purchased control of the Alvin State Bank and became president and chairman of the board.

CSB deposits on Dec. 31 were $5,167,853.

1954

WGH resigned as president of the San Jacinto River Authority.

CSB deposits on Dec. 31 were $6,172,847.

1955

CSB staff change: Sam A. Rowe added as agricultural representative.

CSB deposits on Dec. 31 were $6,683,044.

1956

CSB celebrated the "50th anniversary of the Mainland's oldest bank" on Jan. 27 with an open house.

WGH and associates opened the League City State Bank on March 14 (name changed in 1978 to League City Bank & Trust).

CSB staff change: G.J. Hoff promoted to cashier.

CSB deposits on Dec. 31 were $5,564,466.

1957

CSB staff changes: R.D. Holcomb, Wayne Weaver and John Woolsey added as assistant cashiers; Grace Lewis promoted to cashier; G.J. Hoff promoted to vice president.

CSB deposits on Dec. 31 were $6,115,804.

1958

CSB staff change: W.G. Hall Jr. added as assistant vice president.

CSB deposits on Dec. 31 were $6,689,989.

1959

CSB staff change: A. Pat Daniels added as public relations officer.

CSB deposits on Dec. 31 were $7,181,861.

1960

CSB staff changes: R.D. Holcomb promoted to assistant vice president; W.G. Hall Jr. promoted to vice president. New directors added were W.G. Hall Jr. and G.J. Hoff.

Dickinson's population was 4,715.

CSB deposits on Dec. 31 were $6,434,184.

1961

CSB staff changes: Betty Green named assistant cashier; E.W. Platzer added as a director.

CSB deposits on Dec. 31 were $7,406,850.

1962

CSB staff changes: Mrs. Irene Conway added as assistant cashier and public relations representative; R.D. Holcomb promoted to vice president.

CSB deposits on Dec. 31 were $7,945,552.

1963

WGH and associates open Webster State Bank (name later changed to Bay Area Bank & Trust).

President John F. Kennedy assassinated in Dallas on Nov. 22.

CSB staff changes: O.G. Lindquist added as vice president for business development; new directors added were William Hardy Davis, John B. Lee, Amedeo A. Magliolo, M.D., and Darvin M. Winick, Ph.D.

CSB deposits on Dec. 20 were $7,757,297.

1964

CSB granted trust powers by state banking commissioner on Dec. 10.

CSB staff change: Robert B. Sheppard added as vice president.

CSB deposits on Dec. 31 were $7,722,147.

1965

CSB staff changes: John 0. Bailey added as assistant vice president; S. Fred Ramsey added as vice president; R.D. Holcomb promoted to vice president and trust officer.

CSB deposits on Dec. 31 were $9,726,195.

1966

CSB staff changes: John O. Bailey promoted to vice president; R.D. Holcomb promoted to executive vice president and trust officer; directors added were Johnnie Klecka, Robert B. Sheppard and R.D. Holcomb.

CSB executive committee for directors designated, with the following serving: W.G. Hall, chairman; W.G. Hall Jr., vice chairman; and R.D. Holcomb, A.J. Pollastrini and Robert B. Sheppard.

CSB deposits on Dec. 31 were $11,866,152.

1967

WGH bought controlling interest of Bay City Bank & Trust.

CSB staff changes: Mary E. Klotz added as assistant cashier; Betty H. Green promoted to assistant vice president.

CSB deposits on Dec. 31 were $13,639,103.

1968

CSB staff changes: Grace Lewis promoted to vice president; Virginia Weigelt named cashier; Wayne Weaver promoted to assistant vice president; Ara L. Rule named assistant cashier; Alma M. Thompson named assistant cashier.

CSB deposits on Dec. 31 were $15,455,662.

1969

CSB staff changes: H.C. Lewis Jr. added as vice president; P. Katherine Phelps added as assistant cashier; Barbara Bush added as cashier.

CSB deposits on Dec. 31 were $15,397,967.

1970

CSB staff changes: Frank Norris added as assistant vice president; James S. Newcomb, CPA, added as auditor; Frank Renfrow and Patsy Tieken added as assistant cashiers.

Dickinson's population was 10,776 (Dickinson had recorded a 128.5% population increase in the 1960s, and was called by "The Handbook of Texas" the largest unincorporated city in Texas).

CSB deposits on Dec. 31 were $18,071,115.

1971

CSB staff changes: Sterling C. Burke Jr. added as vice president and cashier; Hilton E. Collier added as assistant vice president.

CSB deposits on Dec. 30 were $19,844,462.

1972

Groundbreaking ceremonies held in July for new CSB building at 2401 Termini at Pine Drive.

CSB staff changes: Frank Norris promoted to administrative vice president and cashier; John Bannatyne added as assistant auditor.

WGH acquired major interest in TV station WLBT in Jackson, Miss., an NBC affiliate.

CSB deposits on Dec. 31 were $21,358,561.

1973

WGH received from Rice University the Founders Club Award for 1973-74.

The new CSB building at Termini and Pine Drive was opened Sept. 24.

CSB staff changes: G. Adelle Roberts added as assistant cashier; Ara L. Rule promoted to assistant vice president; P. Katherine Phelps promoted to assistant vice president; Vice President and Cashier Sterling C. Burke Jr. also named assistant trust officer.

CSB deposits on Dec. 31 were $22,217,255.

1974

WGH named Mr. Democrat of Galveston County.

WGH received the Howard D. Payne Award presented by First State Bank of Hitchcock.

WGH sold controlling interest in Bay City Bank & Trust.

CSB staff change: William N. Walterman added as assistant cashier.

CSB deposits on Dec. 31 were $24,388,395.

1975

Walter and Helen Hall bought the 2,400-acre Hill Country Clear Rock Ranch near Johnson City, Texas.

CSB deposits on Dec. 31 were $27,790,269.

1976

CSB staff changes: R.C. Green promoted to senior vice president; William N. Walterman promoted to cashier; Robbye R. Waldron added as vice president and trust officer; Wade Coody added as vice president; Charles E. Yoes added as assistant vice president; Betty Croft added as assistant cashier; Charles F. Hall added as a director.

CSB deposits on Dec. 31 were $29,218,075.

1977

CSB expansion includes installation of data processing equipment.

CSB staff change: William N. Walterman promoted to vice president and cashier.

CSB deposits on Dec. 31 were $33,466,266.

1978

CSB staff change: John R. Taylor added as vice president.

CSB deposits on Dec. 31 were $33,846,167.

1979

WGH received the National Citizenship Award from the Oil, Chemical and Atomic Workers Union at its national convention in Hollywood, Florida.

Dedication ceremonies held Jan. 12 for Walter and Helen Hall Environmental Health Center at La Marque.

"AnyTime Bank" (automatic teller machine, or ATM) introduced at CSB.

CSB staff changes: Barbara A. Young added as assistant vice president; Miranda Sandstrum and Opal Kowis added as assistant cashiers; Novis M. Neal added as assistant trust officer; N. Edward Divers Jr. added as vice president and trust operations officer; Director

Amedeo A. Magliolo, M.D., added to executive committee.

CSB deposits on Dec. 31 were $44,175,719.

1980

Elementary school in Clear Creek Consolidated Independent School District named Walter Hall Elementary School to honor the banker.

WGH named "Banker of the Year" by the Independent Bankers Association of Texas.

Reorganization of top management positions of CSB was completed, with WGH as chairman of the board, R.D. Holcomb as president and R.C. Green as senior vice president.

Other CSB staff changes: Vice President Wade Coody also named assistant trust officer; Harold J. Herman added as vice president; Assistant Vice President Charles E. Yoes also named cashier; Alma M. Thompson added as assistant cashier.

Dickinson's population was 7,505.

CSB deposits on Dec. 31 were $45,885,791.

1981

Death of Helen Hall was mourned throughout a wide area.

WGH sold controlling interest in Alvin State Bank.

CSB drive-in lanes expanded to a total of 10 and the vault was enlarged.

CSB staff changes: Madeleine Rogers and Gwen Neugent added as vice presidents; Robert B. Holley and Charles L. Hutchins added as directors.

CSB deposits on Dec. 31 were $54,261,085.

1982

City of Dickinson is incorporated.

CSB staff changes: Vickie Heckendorn and Lois Jones added as assistant cashiers; G. Adelle Roberts promoted to vice president; John T. Creden added as director, vice chairman of the board and member of the executive committee.

CSB deposits on Dec. 31 were $61,456,883.

1983

WGH and associates sold Mississippi TV station.

CSB staff changes: Senior Vice President R.C. Green named secretary of the board; Robert Lindgren added as vice president and senior trust officer; Vice President Madeleine Rogers and Vice President and Cashier Charles E. Yoes added as advisory directors.

CSB deposits on Dec. 31 were $72,592,375.

1984

CSB staff changes: Vice President Madeleine Rogers also named auditor; Novis Neal promoted to vice president; Patsy Cruse added as assistant trust officer; John M. Crowley added as assistant cashier.

CSB deposits on Dec. 31 were $77,023,603.

1985

Galveston County Park in League City is renamed Walter Hall Park to honor the banker.

CSB staff changes: Betty Croft and William N. Walterman promoted to vice president; Lois Jones, Miranda Sandstrum and Opal Kowis promoted to assistant vice presidents; Richard E. Mohle added as assistant vice president and trust officer; Patricia Stephenson added as assistant trust officer; Frances Carter and Mary M. Crowley added as administrative assistants.

CSB deposits on Dec. 31 were $72,486,568.

1986

CSB staff changes: Harold J. Herman promoted to senior vice president; Barbara Meyer added as trust officer.

CSB deposits on Dec. 31 were $73,478,207.

1987

CSB deposits on Dec. 31 were $70,050,353.

1988

Hall Insurance Agency was incorporated with control held by Charles F. Hall and Walter G. Hall.

CSB staff changes: Charles F. Hall is named to directors' executive committee.

CSB deposits on Dec. 31 were $75,323,635.

1989

West Branch of CSB holds grand opening on March 19 at 215 FM 517 West.

CSB adds trust department, with Stuart Robertson named vice president and senior trust officer and Barbara Liefert as trust officer.

Other CSB staff changes: Charles E. Yoes promoted to senior vice president and cashier and also named an advisory director; Vicki Stumpenhaus added as assistant cashier; John M. Crowley promoted to assistant vice president.

CSB deposits on Dec. 31 were $75,707,543.

1990

CSB purchased Bacliff National Bank, a branch of the Mainland Bank of Texas City; Bacliff Branch of CSB opened at 4021 Highway

146, with T.R. Trail as branch manager and Clint Karm as assistant branch manager.

Other CSB staff changes: Senior Vice President R.C. Green Jr. named as advisory director; Ronald C. Lemon named vice president and director; Vice Chairman and Vice President John T. Creden also designated as trust officer; M.J. Trusty named senior vice president and senior trust officer; Advisory Director Madeleine Rogers named a director.

Dickinson's population was 9,497.

CSB deposits on Dec. 31 were $86,750,047.

1991

CSB staff changes: William R. Taylor added as vice president and senior trust officer; Clint Karm promoted to West Side Branch manager.

CSB deposits on Dec. 31 were $90,541,560.

1992

WGH honored as a Rice University "Distinguished Alumnus."

CSB staff changes: Ronald C. Lemon promoted to president; Michael K. Richardson added as executive vice president and director; Miranda Sandstrum promoted to operations officer; Vicki Stumpenhaus promoted to personnel officer; Director and Senior Vice President and Cashier Charles E. Yoes promoted to executive vice president and cashier.

CSB deposits on Dec. 31 were $90,672,934.

1993

WGH named "Man of Vision" by the Gulf Coast Branch of the Texas Society to Prevent Blindness.

CSB staff changes: Stella Coffman added as assistant auditor.

CSB deposits on Dec. 31 were $84,602,060.

1994

CSB staff changes: Charles F. Hall designated as vice chairman of the board; Charles F. Hall Jr. added as vice president; Madeleine Rogers promoted from vice president & auditor to chief operating officer; Clint Karm named vice president as well as West Side Branch manager; R.L. Trail named vice president as well as Bacliff Branch manager; Stella Coffman promoted to internal auditor.

CSB deposits on Dec. 31 were $84,458,435.

Chapter 10
The Fondren Library's Walter Hall Papers:

A Valuable Resource for Scholars and Writers

When Walter G. Hall contributed his personal papers to Rice University's Fondren Library in the 1970s, he contributed a major source of history—personal history, banking history and political history.

Scholars and writers in the future who want to develop the Walter Hall story deeper or examine more closely much of the political life of the 20th century will find much of it in these papers in the Rice University library.

A total of 25 shelf feet are required to accommodate those papers—and they cover the period only from 1923 to 1979. Undoubtedly more will be added in the future.

The introduction to the "Guide to the Walter Gardner Hall Papers in the Woodson Research Center" of the Fondren Library reflects the wide-ranging subject matter of the papers. It also gives an interesting perspective of the Rice University writers' views of the banker after cataloguing his papers.

The introduction was written by Walter L. Buenger Jr. with Janis S. Richardson. Their "Scope and Content" follows:

"Walter Gardner Hall has been a man of many parts—most of them seemingly incongruous. He has been a successful banker and a champion of the liberal wing of the Texas Democratic Party. He has had important social and business ties with the conservative Houston 'establishment' and at the same time has been a close friend of such 'anti-establishment' figures as John Henry Faulk.* Through the political wars of the 1950s and 1960s, Hall managed to remain on good terms personally and politically with both Lyndon B. Johnson and Ralph W. Yarborough, the oft-feuding leaders of the Texas Democrats on a national level. Within the 25-shelf feet of the Hall Papers there is a record of these diverse associations.

"Contained within these papers as well is much information on the men and women with whom Hall corresponded. Among the most notable politicians are Lyndon Johnson, Ralph Yarborough, Sam Rayburn, Minnie Fisher Cunningham, Jim Wright and Hubert Humphrey.* Hall often served as an access route from the people of the Gulf Coast to these politicians, and his letters to the lesser-known folk of his area are equally interesting. Walter Hall, though, has been more than a political animal; his papers reflect extremely close ties with his sons and with friends such as J.R. Parten, George 'Heap' Alexander, W.A. Cooper, Fagan Dickson and Ralph Yarborough.*

"Besides speaking of politics and Hall's feelings for other human beings, these papers say much about Walter Hall himself. Hall is the piece of the puzzle which makes these incongruous parts fit together into an understandable whole. His ability to accept divergent opinion if honestly held and to work within the practical limits of a situation reveal some of the reasons for his political and economic success. At the same time, his political values and his position in the midrange between political officials and the voting public illustrates why the American system of government has worked as well as it has."

*John Henry Faulk: A Texas entertainment figure who was "blackballed" in New York City and Hollywood during the U.S. Sen. Joseph McCarthy days. Faulk's name was later cleared through court proceedings.

Lyndon Johnson: U.S. president.

Ralph Yarborough: U.S. senator.

Sam Rayburn: U.S. congressman, speaker of the U.S. House of Representatives.

Minnie Fisher Cunningham: Leader in the women's suffrage movement; a founder of the national League of Women Voters; one of the organizers of Women's National Democratic Club; unsuccessful liberal Democratic candidate for U.S. Senate in 1928 and Texas governorship in 1944.

Jim Wright: U.S. representative, speaker of the House.

Hubert Humphrey: Vice president of the United States, candidate for the presidency.

J.R. Parten, Houston oilman, chairman of the board of regents of the University of Texas.

George "Heap" Alexander: Member of the House of Representatives of the Commonwealth of Pennsylvania.

W.A. Cooper: Official with the U.S. Agency for International Development in Sudan; later secretary general of the World Veterans Federation.

Fagan Dickson: Former state legislator, former Texas first assistant attorney general, executive director of the Loyal Democrats of Texas during the 1950s Democratic fights.

Chapter 11
Credits and Thanks!

Credits and thanks for much material in this book, which would not have been as complete without their help, are offered to the following (and please forgive me if I have neglected to mention any person or source; I have tried valiantly not to err!)

Books

"My Name Is Tom Connally," by Sen. Tom Connally as told to Alfred Steinberg, 1954, Thomas Y. Crowell Co., New York.

"Allan Shivers: The Pied Piper of Texas Politics," by Sam Kinch and Stuart Long, 1973, Shoal Creek Publishers, Inc., Austin.

"League City: A History from Its Beginning to 1912," compiled by the League City Historical Committee of the Helen Hall Library, with Judy Warco as chairman; Quality Printing, League City, 1982.

"Recalled Recollections," by I. H. Kempner, 1961, The Egan Company, Dallas.

"The Handbook of Texas," several volumes.

"Texas Almanac," several volumes.

Transcribed Interviews With Walter Hall

By Connie and James P. Simpson in 1976, prepared for the oral history section of the library of the College of the Mainland at Texas City.

By Dr. Anthony Champagne, associate professsor at the University of Texas at Dallas, in 1980, during preparation of two books by Dr. Champagne, "Congressman Sam Rayburn," Rutgers University Press, 1984; and "Sam Rayburn, a Bio-Bibliography," Greenwood Press, 1988.

By Dr. James C. Coomer, senior vice president for academic affairs of Mercer University at Macon, Ga., in 1991. (Dr. Coomer's wife is Jane Coomer, who was the first principal of the Walter Hall Elementary School.)

By historian and author Dr. David G. McComb for the University of Texas at Austin's oral history project in the Lyndon Baines Johnson Library, in 1974.

Magazine Articles

Texas magazine of the Houston Chronicle, March 26, 1989, story by Steven Long.

Bankers Monthly magazine, October, 1989, story by Tim Loughran.

Galveston magazine, July 1950.

High Emprise, date unknown, story by Phyllis Schrader.

Newspaper Articles

Houston Business Journal, Dec. 25, 1989, by Jim Greer.

The Galveston Daily News, Oct. 24, 1974, by Brad Messer.

The Galveston Daily News, date unknown, by Joel Kirkpatrick.

The Houston Post, Dec. 10, 1962, by John Rainey.

League City News, date unknown in 1983, by Kathleen Mayse (also other stories, dates unknown).

The Citizen, date unknown, by Beverly Miller.

Dickinson News, July 17, 1985, by Rebecca LaCroix.

Houston Chronicle, June 10, 1962, by Nancy Fagg.

Galveston County Press, June 8, 1950, by Bill Law.

Texas Observer, Sept. 25, Oct. 9 and 16, 1959, by Ronnie Dugger.

Leon Hale column in The Houston Post, Sept. 25, 1970.

The Galveston Daily News editorial, May 31, 1966.

Miscellaneous

University of Houston football program (vs. University of Texas, Nov. 4, 1993).

Library Staffs

Helen Hall Library, League City; Genevieve Miller Hitchcock Public Library, Hitchcock; Woodson Regional Library, Chicago; Fondren Library, Rice University, Houston; Rosenberg Library, Galveston; Texas Room of Houston Public Library, Houston; Lyndon Baines Johnson Library, Austin.

Great Individuals

Frances Carter, administrative assistant to Walter Hall; Sandra McLenna, a secretary of Walter Hall; R.D. (Bob) Holcomb, retired president of the Citizens State Bank; Ronald C. Lemon, president of the

Citizens State Bank; Gwen Neugent, vice president for marketing of the Citizens State Bank; H. C. Lewis Jr., vice president of the Citizens State Bank; Madeleine Rogers, vice president and auditor of the Citizens State Bank; William Hardy Davis and Charles L. Hutchins, directors of the Citizens State Bank; Charles F. Hall, managing director of Hall's Insurance Agency; Charles F. (Chuck) Hall Jr., assistant secretary of the board of the Citizens State Bank (and of boards of other banks directed by Walter G. Hall); Art Goforth of League City, retired educator; Dr. Robert Sullivan of La Marque, physician; Ike Barrett, surface water operations manager of the San Jacinto River Authority; James P. (Jim) Simpson, Texas City attorney; Ray Holbrook, former county judge of Galveston County; Barbara Englehaft, secretary of Ray Holbrook; Linda Hanson, archivist of the Lyndon Baines Johnson Library at Austin; Casey Greene of the Rosenberg Library in Galveston; Susan Mathews of the Helen Hall Library in League City; Joyce Cummings of the Genevieve Miller Hitchcock Public Library; Dorothy Lyles of the Woodson Regional Library, Chicago; Mark Chery of the DuSable Museum, Chicago; Cathy Nelson, insurance technician with the Texas Department of Insurance, Austin; Martin E. Firestone of Miami, Fla., attorney; Weyman Walker of Houston, businessman; Dr. Chandler Davidson and Dr. William Martin of the Sociology Department of Rice University; John C. White of John White Consulting, Washington, D.C.; Robert K. (Bob) Hutchings of Nations Bank, Galveston; Leslie Knight, secretary of Dr. Frank E. Vandiver of Texas A&M University; Carrie Lemke and Phyllis Teeple of the Texas Department of Banking, Austin; Gale Peterson of the Rice University staff; Betty Tilson, assistant to Mrs. Lyndon B. Johnson at the LBJ Library in Austin; Stanley C. Woods, Houston attorney; Steve Cowan, retired executive of KGBC Radio in Galveston; Clara A. Smith, executive assistant of The Galveston County Daily News; Sherry Adams, librarian of the Houston Chronicle; Mrs. Vicki Gibson, chairman of the League City Historial Committee; Patricia Prather of Houston, author; Mrs. Charles B. d'Etchegoyen of Houston, friend of Walter Hall; V. Lynn Morse, Walter Hall's niece; Wallace Fitzgerald of Houston, retired journalist; Edward B. Cope, Houston playwright; Daniel Carlos Miller, Houston advertising executive; Ben W. Taylor, Houston airlines consultant; Donall Myers, Houston industrialist; Owen O. Young Jr., retired Houston postal executive; David Haworth, Houston businessman; Pat and Don Armstrong, Houston book printers; Frank J. Murphy, retired insurance executive and former Camp Wallace Army officer; Shirley Oakes, my wife, for counsel, support and ferreting out many of my mistakes; the scores of Walter Hall's friends who contributed "nuggets" about this great Texan; and in particular, of course, to Walter G. Hall, whose patience during the process of remembering, helping to compile and counseling during the writing of this history was most unusual and has made my admiration, respect and love of the man even greater.

I thank each of you.

A. Pat Daniels

Index

Not included in the index are the names of Walter G. Hall as an individual and of the Citizens State Bank—both of which appear on numerous pages in the book.

A

B

C

D

I

J

N

O

P

R

S

W

Y